Religion in Britain since 1945

Making Contemporary Britain Series

General Editor: Anthony Seldon
Consultant Editor: Peter Hennessy

Published

Northern Ireland since 1968
Paul Arthur and Keith Jeffrey
The Prime Minister since 1945
James Barber
British General Elections since 1945
David Butler
The British Economy since 1945
Alec Cairncross
Britain and the Suez Crisis
David Carlton
The End of the British Empire
John Darwin
Religion in Britain since 1945
Grace Davie
British Defence since 1945
Michael Dockrill
British Politics since 1945
Peter Dorey
Britain and the Falklands War
Lawrence Freedman
Britain and European Integration
since 1945
Stephen George
British Social Policy since 1945
Howard Glennerster
Judicial Politics since 1920: A
Chronical
John Griffith
Consensus Politics from Atlee
to Major
Dennis Kavanagh and Peter Morris
The Politics of Immigration
Zig Layton-Henry
Women in Britain since 1945
Jane Lewis
Britain and the Korean War
Callum Macdonald
Culture in Britain since 1945
Arthur Marwick

Crime and Criminal Justice since 1945
Terence Morris
The British Press and Broadcasting
since 1945
Colin Seymour-Ure
Third Party Politics since 1945
John Stevenson
The Trade Union Question in British
Politics
Robert Taylor
British Science and Politics since 1945
Thomas Wilkie
British Public Opinion
Robert M. Worcester

Forthcoming

British Industry since 1945
Margaret Ackrill
The Conservative Party since 1945
John Barnes
The British Monarchy
Robert Blackburn
Electoral Change since 1945
Ivor Crewe and Pippa Norris
Sport in Britain since 1945
Richard Holt and Tony Mason
Class and Inequality in Britain
Paul Keating
Parliament since 1945
Philip Norton
British Youth Cultures
William Osgerby
The Labour Party since 1945
Eric Shaw
The Civil Service since 1945
Kevin Theakston
Terrorism since 1945
Paul Wilkinson
Local Government since 1945
Ken Young and Nirmala Rao

Religion in Britain since 1945

Believing without Belonging

Grace Davie

BLACKWELL
Oxford UK & Cambridge USA

Copyright © Grace Davie 1994

The right of Grace Davie to be identified as author of this work has been asserted in accordance with the Copyright, Designs and Patents Act 1988.

First published 1994
Reprinted 1995 (twice), 1996

Blackwell Publishers Ltd
108 Cowley Road
Oxford OX4 1JF, UK

Blackwell Publishers Inc.
238 Main Street
Cambridge, Massachusetts 02142
USA

British Library Cataloguing in Publication Data
A CIP catalogue record for this book is available from the British Library.

Library of Congress Cataloging-in-Publication Data
Davie, Grace.
    Religion in Britain: since 1945 : believing without belonging / Grace Davie.
        p.   cm. — (Making contemporary Britain)
    Includes bibliographical references and index.
    ISBN 0–631–18443–0 (alk. paper). — ISBN 0–631–18444–9 (pbk. : alk. paper)
        1. Great Britain—Religion—20th century. I. Title. II. Series.
    BR759.D38   1994
    306.6'0941'09045—dc20   94–1738
                                                                                 CIP

Typeset in 10 on 12 pt Ehrhardt
by Graphicraft Typesetters Ltd, Hong Kong
Printed in Great Britain by T.J. Press Ltd, Padstow

This book is printed on acid-free paper

In memoriam

H. G. S.

1906–1990

Ordinary God

'Do you believe in a God
who can change the course of events
on earth?'
　　　　　　　'No, just
the ordinary one.'
　　　　　　　　　　A laugh,
but not so stupid: events
He does not, it seems, determine
for the most part. Whether He could
is not to the point; it is not
stupid to believe in
a God who mostly abjures.

The ordinary kind
of God is what one believes in
so implicitly that
it is only with blushes or
bravado one can declare,
'I believe'; caught as one is
in the ambush of personal history, so
harried, so distraught.

The ordinary kind
of undeceived believer
expects no prompt reward
from an ultimately faithful
but meanwhile preoccupied landlord.
　　　　　Donald Davie, *To Scorch or Freeze: poems about the sacred*

Contents

Foreword   *Professor David Martin*   viii

General Editor's Preface   x

Preface   xii

1   Introduction   1
2   A Rapidly Changing Context   10
3   The Sacred and the Secular: Religious Generations in
    Post-war Britain   29
4   Religious Constituencies   45
5   The Ordinary Gods of British Society   74
6   Believing Without Belonging: Variations on the Theme   93
7   Handing on the Tradition: the Significance of Age and
    Gender   117
8   Church and State: a Framework for Discussion   139
9   Religious Professionals: Lay and Ordained   162
10 Religion and Modernity: a Theoretical Postscript   189

Chronology   205

Guide to Further Reading   206

References   210

Index   221

Foreword

For some time a book has been needed on the sociology of religion in Britain and that need has now been met admirably and comprehensibly by Grace Davie. This will be the standard text for at least a decade, if not more. One speaks of a decade because after that time a contemporary account acquires historical value. My own *A Sociology of English Religion* aged rather rapidly, because the latest material it touched on referred to 1964–5, and immediately preceded the watershed of the late 1960s. I did not foresee that watershed or anticipate the shaking of the statistics from California to Trieste. Nor did I imagine the extent to which the churches themselves would collude with the spirit of the age. Grace Davie's book traces the changes since that period, though her retrospective glance is naturally longer than that.

The question as to what happened *within* the churches reminds us that sociologists can sometimes be rather indifferent to the changing inner content of the external indices. It is one of the many virtues of Grace Davie's book that it takes into account the inner life and interior narrative of the life of religious institutions. The icons alter; women become ordained, the Prayer Book is to some extent marginalized, the repertoire of hymns fragments; a generation emerges for which the atmospherics of monarchy or Remembrance Day are nearly meaningless. These are major shifts in culture of central relevance to a sociology of British religion. Grace Davie takes such matters into account, along with such extraordinary outpourings of grief as occurred in the wake of the Hillsborough disaster.

Grace Davie emphasizes the importance of regional climates within Britain, including the four (or five) national cultures mixed together on these islands. And she simultaneously takes account of the European dimension and what it means to be at a junction of the European continent and the English-speaking world, especially the American portion of it. Britain is no longer an island unto itself.

A signal virtue of the book is the ambiguity that it postulates with regard to secularization. When most voluntary associations are under severe pressure one cannot assume that the processes of change relate to the arcane mechanics of rationalization or disenchantment or final freedom from illusion. Indeed it may be that the 'grand narratives' of the enlightenment are themselves collapsing. This book eschews the delusions of sociological grandeur and opts instead for observation, discernment and ambiguity.

David Martin
Emeritus Professor of Sociology
London School of Economics and Political Science

General Editor's Preface

The Institute of Contemporary British History's series *Making Contemporary Britain* is aimed directly at students and at others interested in learning more about topics in post-war British history. In the series, authors are less attempting to break new ground than presenting clear and balanced overviews of the state of knowledge on each of the topics.

The ICBH was founded in October 1986 with the objective of promoting the study of British history since 1945 at every level. To that end, it publishes books and a quarterly journal, *Contemporary Record*; it organizes seminars and conferences for school students, undergraduates, researchers and teachers of post-war history; and it runs a number of research programmes and other activities.

A central theme of the ICBH's work is that post-war history is too often neglected in British schools, institutes of higher education and beyond. The ICBH acknowledges the validity of the arguments against the study of recent history, notably the problems of bias, of overly subjective teaching and writing and the difficulties of perspective. But it believes that the values of studying post-war history outweigh the drawbacks, and that the health and future of a liberal democracy require that its citizens know more about the most recent past of their country than the limited knowledge possessed by British citizens, young and old, today. Indeed, the ICBH believes that the dangers of political indoctrination are higher where the young are *not* informed of the recent past.

Grace Davie's volume reflects the growing interest of the series in sociological issues. Her book fills a major gap in the series, and indeed in the work of the Institute. Religion has been a comparatively neglected topic by the Institute: a reflection, in part, of the interests currently of contemporary historians.

Consideration of the role of religion in Britain since 1945 is, as the author shows, essential to gaining a full understanding of post-war history. The continued attachment to religious belief, if not always religious practice, the continuing political influence of the Church of England, the growth of non-Judaeo-Christian religious practice and the differing religious attachments of region, class, age and gender are all themes explored by Grace Davie. Her book can usefully be read alongside several volumes in the series, particularly Zig Layton-Henry on *The Politics of Immigration*.

Her book will be primarily read by students of the sociology of religion. My hope though would be that it would be read by all, religious professionals or the secular masses, believers, agnostics or atheists, who wish to understand Britain in the fifty years since the end of the Second World War. As with all matters of belief or religion, the issues raised are far profounder and more all-pervasive than many appreciate.

Anthony Seldon

Preface

The aim of this book is straightforward: to describe and to explain (from a sociological point of view) the religious situation in contemporary Britain. I have no doubt that it will evoke diverse responses, not least on the part of those who – for one reason or another – are strongly committed to a vigorous religious presence in British society. Their reactions are likely to be twofold: optimism that contemporary Britain is not as secular as they might, perhaps, have imagined (the proverbial glass is, after all, half-full); pessimism in view of the immensity of the muddle that passes for religious belief in this country (in this sense the glass is not only half-empty, but draining fast). There can, however, be no getting away from the fact that the drifting of belief away from anything that might be termed orthodoxy is a major challenge to the contemporary churches, a far greater one – in my opinion – than the supposedly secular nature of the society in which we are obliged to live.

The following chapters are placed between two rather different evocations of such feelings: the first a poem by Donald Davie entitled 'Ordinary God'; the second (at the beginning of chapter 10) a short, almost poetic piece by David Martin. A word of explanation is required about each. Donald Davie, who is my father-in-law, wrote the poem prompted by an article entitled 'An Ordinary God', which I published in 1990. (The phrase itself emerged from an empirical enquiry into religious belief discussed in chapter 5.) The poem conveys in a few lines the perplexing nature of religious faith, particularly forms of belief which – almost of necessity – are rarely articulated. For this reason, in addition to the more personal connection, I am delighted to 'borrow' the poem back and to place it at the front of this book.

The second piece, David Martin's short description of English religiosity, arose from the first of two Consultations held at St George's House,

Windsor, in the early 1990s. These meetings were co-convened by myself and Canon Paul Avis and gathered a variety of people to discuss the implications of common religion for the churches, utilizing, for the most part, the theme 'Believing without Belonging'. The passage quoted from Martin conveys the mood of these discussions as well as their subject; a mood which can be felt in several places in the following chapters. Once again, however, this particular citation represents a wider 'borrowing'. David Martin taught me as a graduate student at the LSE in the early 1970s and began, almost immediately, to set me on my way in the sociology of religion. He then had the patience to do the whole thing over again, some ten years later, after what is best described as prolonged maternity leave. Among many other things, Professor Martin has encouraged from start to finish the writing of this book, including a close reading of the typescript and the contribution of a foreword.

The two Consultations at St George's provided a forum for debate. So, too, have the meetings of the British Sociological Association's Sociology of Religion Study Group and those of the International Society for the Sociology of Religion. The original version of the 'Believing without Belonging' paper was given at one of the latter in Helsinki in 1989. Both groups of scholars have helped me to refine this particular notion and to consider both this and other ideas within a European as well as British framework. The argument of the concluding chapter was, for example, tried out at the Bristol Conference of the BSA Group (1993) and at the University of Louvain-la-Neuve in Belgium. More immediately Tony Walter (a member of the British group) and the Very Rev. David Edwards, Provost of Southwark, have read the entire typescript and offered me valuable advice. In addition, Philip Mawer, the Secretary-General of the General Synod, looked over a draft of the section in chapter 9 pertaining to the working of the General Synod.

For some of the time that I was writing this book, part of my salary was paid by the Trustees of the St Luke's Foundation in Exeter. I have been very grateful for this support. I would also like to thank Dr David Barker of the European Values Group and the staff of the Christian Research Association for their help in gathering the most up-to-date statistics available.

The dedication of this book is to my mother, from whom I learnt first hand that academic commitment *is* compatible with marriage and parenting despite the pressures of each. Neither activity would prosper, however, without the absolute dependability of my husband, to whom my warmest thanks.

1 Introduction

'Do you believe in God?'
'Yes.'
'Do you believe in a God who can change the course of events on earth?'
'No, just the ordinary one.'[1]

'What's a church?'

Evening Standard, 20 September 1991

We shall come back to these exchanges, whether verbal or cartooned, more than once in the following chapters, for they capture in a phrase or two the sense of paradox that must prevail in any discussion of religion in post-war Britain. It is hard to discover a field of enquiry containing a greater number of apparent contradictions.

These contradictions show up most clearly in a series of questions. Why is it, for example, that the majority of British people – in common with many other Europeans – persist in believing (if only in an ordinary God), but see no need to participate with even minimal regularity in their religious institutions? Indeed most people in this country – whatever their denominational allegiance – express their religious sentiments by staying away from, rather than going to, their places of worship. On the other hand, relatively few British people have opted out of religion altogether: out and out atheists are rare. Secondly, we need to ask why the churches – as supposedly declining institutions – should have achieved in the 1980s and 1990s such a persistently high public profile.[2] Does this signify a change in outlook of the institutional churches themselves or a change in the context in which they are operating; or perhaps in both? A further question arises from this. By what authority and in whose name have the churches intervened in public debate? These issues become, moreover, more rather than less problematic in view of the nature of the churches' membership. Not only do the churches represent a minority of British people, but the members that they do attract remain disproportionately elderly and female, and Conservative in their voting habits. Why, then, has at least a section of the ecclesiastical leadership not only assumed an increasingly active role in public life, but one that has, through the 1980s at least, been critical of a Conservative government?

Exploring the tensions behind these apparent contradictions forms one focus for the following chapters. But they aim in addition to set the discussion within a framework – global as well as domestic – that has changed very considerably in the post-war period and to capture accurately the mood of the early 1990s. One example will suffice for the time being. In 1945 Europe had come close to self-destruction for the second time in a century. The idea of European unity was barely conceivable as individual nations struggled to rebuild the fabric of their devastated societies. Surprisingly quickly, however, the seeds of a European Community began to germinate in the form of Coal and Steel Agreements, which embodied the principle that the weapons of war should themselves be subject to supranational, if not international, control. Since then (the mid 1950s) Europe has moved inexorably, if not very steadily, towards a greater common identity. The religious factor within this identity is of considerable significance, not least in relation to the somewhat ambivalent attitudes within Britain to what is going on; a point all too often ignored by the churches themselves, never mind by those who study them. This should not be the case. This book begins, therefore, quite deliberately, within a comparative perspective, in order to indicate as fully as possible what might be called the nature of British religion as a European, but nonetheless distinct, variant. Or, more accurately, a collection of distinct variants, for Wales, Scotland and Northern Ireland have their own particular qualities of religious life.

If the European dimension provides one aspect of the religious context in post-war Britain, so, too, do the profound economic, social and political changes in British society that have taken place during the same period. Many of these developments form the focus of separate books in this series; they cannot all be discussed in this one. But they include changes of crucial significance for the religious life of this country. The demographic structure of contemporary Britain provides an obvious example. We live in an ageing society in which the nature of family life, including the traditional codes of morality, are altering rapidly. The related revolution in gender roles has, for better or for worse, penetrated the churches and influenced theological thinking. Similarly, the influx of immigrants in the post-war period, not all of them from Christian countries, has introduced significant other-faith communities into this country. The trend towards a greater religious diversity is unlikely to be reversed; it has had, and will continue to have, a lasting effect on many aspects of British religious life. At the same time – indeed as part of the same process of development – the nature of the economy has altered radically, bringing with it changes in the social structure of Britain. Patterns of employment (or unemployment), for example, are now very different from the immediate post-war period. So, too, are patterns of residence; the larger industrial conurbations characteristic of industrial Britain are declining rapidly. One consequence of this combination has been a reduction, relatively speaking, in precisely those areas of society most hostile to religious practice – large cities with high-density working-class populations.[3] A reduction achieved, however, at considerable social cost; a cost borne very often by the most vulnerable in our society, not least by the members of other-faith communities.

Alongside such social and economic changes, some reference must be made to the evolving political context of post-war Britain and its interaction with religious life. This discussion leads in turn towards an important but elusive feature of the following chapters. There have been subtle but nonetheless significant shifts in mood and emphasis since 1945, partly conditioned by the political climate but not necessarily so. These *generational*[4] shifts are difficult to pin down, but their influence pervades a great deal of what is going on both within the churches and outside them. Post-war attempts at ecclesiastical reconstruction, for example, were superseded in the 1960s by far more radical approaches to change. But as the 1960s themselves gave way to a much less confident decade, the mood of the churches altered once again. The emphasis on relevance diminished, replaced by a greater stress on the distinctiveness of the sacred, expressed at times in unconventional ways. Contemporary patterns are harder to grasp, but the emergence of an enormous variety of phenomena, either under the catch-all title of the New Age or as antithetical reactions to this, may turn out to be the dominant mood – or combination of moods – of the 1990s.

Up to a point, therefore, the book embodies a chronological dimension, outlined in more detail in chapter 3. (After all, context should be seen temporally as well as spatially.) The book's principal thrust is, however, thematic; offering an analysis which is vertical rather than horizontal, sociological rather than historical. It should be read alongside two other sources of information: firstly, the considerable variety of publications that describe, in some cases outstandingly, the sequence of religious events in post-war Britain; and secondly, the accounts of British religion that portray each denomination separately, stressing the differences and developments of each religious group rather than the common themes or threads that underlie them. Examples of each will be found in the Guide to Further Reading.

Within this book, one particular theme predominates. It concerns the increasingly evident mismatch between statistics relating to religious practice and those which indicate levels of religious belief. To be more precise, the central chapters in this book explore in some detail the marked difference between two types of variable in the measurement of religiosity. On the one hand, variables concerned with feelings, experience and the more numinous aspects of religious belief demonstrate considerable persistence in contemporary Britain (as they do throughout Western Europe); on the other, those which measure religious orthodoxy, ritual participation and institutional attachment display an undeniable degree of secularization (a word to which we shall return) both before and during the post-war period. These imbalances are, very often, taken for granted, though why relatively high levels of belief and low levels of practice (rather than any other combination) should be considered normal is far from clear. Indeed it seems to me that the combination of believing without belonging (if we may use this shorthand) should be examined in considerable detail – sociologically as well as theologically – for it is this particular imbalance which pervades a great deal of Britain's religious life in the period under review. It should, moreover, be looked at from more than one point of view, across time as well as space.

The relationship between belief and practice was clearly different in the past and may well be so in the future, though not necessarily in predictable ways. But the relationship reflects, in addition, the pressures of particular situations within contemporary Britain. These situations are many and varied. They involve, for a start, important national differences; Scotland, Wales and Northern Ireland display contrasting statistical profiles. So do urban and rural areas. But contexts can also be defined sociologically. There can be no doubt, for example, that there are considerable variations in religious behaviour (in both believing and belonging) between different social classes, between different racial groups and between women and men. Class, race and gender (and the interrelationships between them) are – in addition to nation or region – crucial to our understanding of the religious behaviour of contemporary Britain.

It is for these reasons that the central chapters (4 and 5) of this book are taken up not only with the considerable variety of religious constituencies present in post-war Britain, but with the persistent undercurrents of faith (the ordinary God or gods) that lie beneath these. Chapters 6 and 7 then draw these two dimensions together, exploring from a religious point of view – largely, but not exclusively, through the variations in believing and belonging – some of the very different regional and social contexts of Britain. These four chapters form the core of the book. One further variable needs, however, to be added to the sociological list already mentioned, for time after time the significance of the age factor stands out in the statistical material. In short, a religiously and morally conservative majority among the retired contrasts – across a wide variety of indicators – with a religiously conservative minority among the young, notably among older teenagers and young adults. Clearly the category 'young people' needs careful handling, for there are many variations within this group. Nonetheless, the underlying question remains the same whatever these internal patterns. It is this. Are we, in the late twentieth century, experiencing a profound generational shift in religious behaviour in addition to the normal rejection of conventional religiosity in young adulthood? If this is the case, and it is by no means self-evident, then the future of British religion may be very different indeed. Questions about religious education form an important part of this discussion.

Predictions about the future of religion in this country must, however, remain tentative to say the least. Indeed there are many aspects of the religious present, never mind its future, about which we have hunches rather than clear-cut evidence. An important parenthesis follows from this, the implications of which are considerable for a book such as this. There remains within the subdiscipline of the sociology of religion a serious imbalance of material which cannot be ignored. There is a substantial amount of evidence (some of it excellent) about small pieces of the religious jigsaw in this country, not least about its more exotic edges. In contrast, the picture in the middle remains alarmingly blurred. We discover that there is really very little information indeed about the beliefs of ordinary British people and the significance of these beliefs in everyday life.

Two more substantive areas remain before the theoretical emphases of the book are outlined. These areas are dealt with in chapters 8 and 9, both of which concern questions of authority. Chapter 8, for example, looks at the public interventions of the churches throughout the post-war period, but with a greater emphasis on more recent decades. In so doing, it picks up some of the questions or paradoxes raised at the beginning of this Introduction and asks in particular by what authority and in whose name do the churches intervene in the political process. Chapter 9 introduces material on the religious professionals of contemporary Britain, both lay and ordained. It includes a discussion of synodical government and of ecumenical developments, together with the questions of authority that lie beneath these issues. This leads in turn to the debate about women's ordination, for the Church of England's inability to decide definitively one way or the other about this question reveals deeper inadequacies than the issue itself. These inadequacies need to be probed. Both chapters need, however, to be considered within the context of the broader patterns of religiosity that form the central chapters of this book, for the churches' increasingly prominent role in public life, particularly during the Thatcher period, and the significant changes in the priesthood and the ecumenical process can only be understood with these in mind. Some, if not all, of the apparent paradoxes can be explained.

The approach embodied in this book is sociological. In other words its principal focus lies in the subtle and elusive connections between religion, in all its complexity, and the wider society; in this case an advanced industrial society with a Christian tradition. The following chapters are ordered primarily, though not exclusively, with these connections in mind. They make no attempt to evaluate the relative truth claims of the several religions currently, though less so historically, represented in post-war Britain. The assumptions embodied in a sociological approach need, however, careful clarification. For some, though by no means all, attempts to examine the relationships between religion and advanced industrial societies have been loaded in a particular direction. They have described, often very perceptively, a progressive adaptation on the part of the churches and other religious organizations to a society whose perceived need for a vigorous and effective religious sector is thought to be diminishing. The concept of secularization, a crucial – though problematic – concept in the sociology of religion, has been central to this approach. It has been much used by British sociologists.

Wallis and Bruce (1989), for example, use this theme as a pivot in their recent review of the British contribution to post-war sociology of religion. In so doing they indicate the variety of positions and the range of data that this type of thinking encompasses. The secularization thesis is far from straightforward; it is complex, nuanced and at times contradictory (Martin 1978, Wilson 1982). At its best, the debate is highly illuminating. It has, moreover, provided an effective way forward, a framework for organizing a wide range of ideas and information about religion in contemporary society, particularly in its North European forms. So far, so good. We need to learn as much as possible from this way of thinking. It is, however, becoming clearer almost by the day that an approach based on the concept of secularization is getting harder and harder to sustain. For not all the religious indicators are pointing in the same direction. Indices of religious belief, for example, have not dropped in the way that might have been predicted a generation or so ago. Nor have religious controversies ceased to catch the public's imagination (the Rushdie controversy dominated the media for months on end). And governments, including our own, are increasingly faced with moral, ethical, even religious decisions as they grapple with the consequences of scientific advance. Bioethical and environmental issues remain in the forefront of public controversy, for science, it seems, has become the creator just as much as the solver of society's problems. Indeed just as it seemed possible that secularization might, all other things being equal, begin to assert itself in a big way, all other things ceased, dramatically, to fulfil that condition. Sociologists, including British ones, are left trying to readjust their frameworks.

At the least, they are left trying to come to terms with a great deal of conflicting evidence. Is there a way, for instance, that we can hold together the persistence of religious belief in contemporary Britain alongside the marked decline – though not the disappearance – of religious practice? Can we find satisfactory explanations for the prevalence of Christian nominalism alongside the hardening of religious boundaries associated with the growth of evangelical (even fundamentalist) tendencies within Christianity, and with the increase in other-faith communities? What about the disturbing evidence of fundamentalism worldwide? And what about the increasing tendency for politicians and other public figures to consult the religious sector about matters that they know to be beyond their competence? Diverging and conflicting data make heavy demands on sociological theorists.

But this is begging too many questions, for we must first outline the broad contours of British religiosity. Later chapters will, however, return to this more theoretical theme in two ways. Firstly to re-examine the secularization thesis in light of the evidence concerning contemporary Britain and to offer a possible alternative; but secondly to reconsider the position of Britain with regard to the European context. For the European debate embodies, surely, an excellent example of the complex relationships surrounding the economy (the pressure to extend the market) and questions of national identity, in which the religious factor has, historically at least, played a crucial part. The first question to ask, then, concerns the continued significance of the religious factor in this respect. Can religion have any effective influence at all on this kind of debate in the late twentieth century? But if we conclude that religion does indeed have a continued salience in the making of a New Europe, we need to go further and to grasp exactly how these relationships will work out in practice for the British people; remembering, of course, that Britain encompasses considerable variety in this respect, for the English, the Welsh, the Scottish and the Northern Irish respond to Europe in very different ways. These contrasting responses are, moreover, provoked at least in part by the distinct religious histories of the countries that make up the United Kingdom.

One final point concludes this Introduction. For beneath these relatively empirical questions lies an important theoretical assumption. It can be stated quite simply. Just how far does the religious life of a country (or indeed of a continent) reflect a context rather than create one? In other words, is religion primarily a reactive rather than proactive sociological variable? In my opinion, the potential for proactivity lies at the heart of the matter. This book is written with such a capacity in mind.

Notes

1 The phrase 'an ordinary God' comes from a study carried out in Islington in 1968. It is discussed further in chapter 5. Full details of the original study can be found in Abercrombie et al. 1970.

2 Such a profile was not anticipated in the 1970s. It has grown rather than diminished in the later post-war decades.

3 The inverse relationship between high-density working-class parishes and religious practice is a theme that runs through the relevant literature. Note, for example, Martin (1978). The point is raised again in chapter 10.

4 The significance of *generation* as the most appropriate unit of time to measure religious change will be explained further in chapter 3.

2 A Rapidly Changing Context

This chapter provides a framework within which to consider the subsequent material on British religiosity. It falls into two parts. The first section looks at European patterns of religious life in order to place British religion within its immediate comparative context. It also contains a certain amount of historical material. The second section has a rather different focus: it outlines some of the most salient social and economic changes in post-war Britain, paying particular attention to demographic shifts, including immigration. A short conclusion draws the parts together, pointing out the similarities in demographic developments across a range of West European countries, which share – in consequence – many of the religious implications of such changes.

The European Framework

1. British religion: a European variant

Halsey (1985) summarizes the position of the British *vis-à-vis* the majority of Europeans in the following terms:

> In short, though by no means outlandish from the European culture to which they belong, the British are to be seen and see themselves as a relatively unchurched, nationalistic, optimistic, satisfied, conservative, and moralistic people. (p. 12)

It will be the religious aspects of this positioning that concern us in the following chapters. It can be seen already, however, that the British are more moralistic than one might expect (taking seriously those of the Ten Commandments that have a moral rather than a religious reference); on the other hand, they are less than keen on churchgoing, though the difference between Catholic and Protestant within Europe needs to be taken into account in this respect. But above all they are Europeans. Material for this kind of statement comes from the European Values Study, a cross-cultural analysis of European values covering a wide variety of subjects.[1] The study exemplifies, for better or for worse, sophisticated quantitative social science methodology. Using careful sampling techniques, the EVSSG aims at an accurate mapping of social and moral values across Europe. It has generated very considerable data and will continue to do so. It is important to pay close, but at the same time critical, attention to its findings.

Two underlying themes run through the EVSSG studies. The first concerns the substance of contemporary European values and asks, in particular, to what extent they are homogeneous; the second takes a more dynamic approach, asking to what extent such values are changing. Both themes involve, inevitably, a religious element. The first, for example, leads very quickly to questions about the origins of shared value systems. 'If values in Western Europe are to any extent shared, if people from different countries share similar social perceptions on their world, how had such joint cultural experiences been created?' (Harding and Phillips, with Fogarty 1986: 29). As the European Values Study indicates, the answer lies in deep-rooted cultural experiences which derive from pervasive social influences which have been part of our culture for generations, if not centuries. A shared religious heritage is one such influence:

> Both in historical and geographical terms, religion – or, more specifically, the Christian religion – provides an example of an agency which through the promulgation of a universal and exclusive faith sought to create a commonality of values and beliefs across Europe, and elsewhere. A shared religious heritage based on Christian values, therefore, may be seen as one formative cultural influence at the heart of and giving substance to 'European' civilisation. (Harding and Phillips, with Fogarty 1986: 29)

In historical terms, such a statement is unproblematic. Moreover, it underlines once again the development of Britain as a fundamentally European society.

On the other hand, as soon as the idea of value change is introduced, the situation becomes more contentious. A series of unavoidable questions – some of them already hinted at in the Introduction – immediately present themselves. How far is the primacy given to the role of religion, and more especially Christian religion, in the creation of values still appropriate? Has this role not been undermined by pluralization or secularization? Can we really maintain in the 1990s that the Christian religion remains a central element of our value system? Its influence is becoming, surely, increasingly peripheral within West European – including British – society? Or is it? It will be these questions that occupy us in later chapters. In the meantime it is important to indicate, at least in broad terms, the relative position of Britain (from the point of view of religion) within the general findings of the European Values Study.

There are, generally speaking, five religious indicators within the EVSSG data: denominational allegiance, reported church attendance, attitudes towards the church, indicators of religious belief and some measurement of subjective religious disposition. These variables have considerable potential; they can be correlated with each other and with a wide range of socio-demographic data. In this respect the survey shows commendable awareness of the complexity of religious phenomena and the need to bear in mind more than one dimension in an individual's – and indeed a nation's – religious life. What emerges in practice, however, with respect to these multiple indicators, is the clustering of two types of variable already referred to in chapter 1: on the one hand, those concerned with feelings, experience and the more numinous religious beliefs; on the other, those which measure religious orthodoxy, ritual participation and institutional attachment. It is, moreover, the latter (the more orthodox indicators of religious attachment) which display, most obviously, an undeniable degree of secularization throughout Western Europe. In contrast, the former (the less institutional indicators) reveal a considerable persistence in *some* aspects of religious life. 'In particular, some form of "religious disposition" and acceptance of the moral precepts of Christianity continues to be widespread among large numbers of Europeans, even among a proportion for whom the orthodox institution of the Church has no place' (Harding and Phillips, with Fogarty 1986: 70). Bearing this in mind, it seems to me more accurate to describe late-twentieth-century Britain – together with most of Western Europe – as unchurched rather than simply secular; a paradox that will form an important theme within this book.

If this disjunction between indices of religious belief and those pertaining to religious practice forms a pattern across most of Western Europe,[2] are there variations within this which have particular significance for an analysis of religion in Britain? The first, and most obvious of these lies between the notably more religious, and Catholic, countries of Southern Europe and the less religious countries of the Protestant North. This difference holds across almost every indicator; indeed they are interrelated. Levels of practice, for example, are markedly higher in Italy, Spain, Belgium and Ireland (closer in its religious life to continental Europe than to Britain) than they are elsewhere. Not surprisingly, one effect of regular Mass attendance is a corresponding strength in the traditional orthodoxies through most of Catholic Europe. There can be no doubt that Britain belongs to the Protestant North rather than to the Catholic South in this respect.

A further variation within the overall patterns is, however, important. In France, Belgium and the Netherlands there is a higher than average incidence of no religion, or at least no denominational affiliation. Indeed Stoetzel (1983: 89–91) – in the French version of the 1981 EVSSG analysis – distinguishes not three[3] but four European types in terms of religious affiliation: the Catholic countries (Spain, Italy and Eire); the predominantly Protestant (Denmark, Great Britain and Northern Ireland); the mixed variety (West Germany); and what he calls a *region laique* (that is, France, Belgium, the Netherlands) where those who recognize no religious label form a sizeable section of the population. It is becoming increasingly clear, however, that Britain – and England even more so – barely escapes this category, a conclusion strongly affirmed by the findings of the 1990 study (Barker, Halman and Vloet 1993). Hence the significance of Stoetzel's analysis for British religion; in many ways his categories are more satisfying than groupings suggested elsewhere (see previous note), where countries which have very different religious profiles find themselves thrown together.

2. British religion: a collection of European variants

With respect to the position of Britain – or, more accurately, the United Kingdom – within the European framework, an additional point needs to be underlined. The individual countries that make up the United Kingdom are far from homogeneous, both with regard to their religious histories and to the manner in which their religious sentiments are expressed. Northern Ireland, for example – more like the Irish Republic than mainland Britain – manifests markedly higher levels of religious practice than almost all other European countries; indeed *both* parts of Ireland provide an important exception to the European pattern of high belief and low practice. Scotland and Wales are also distinct in their particular denominational distributions, the denominations themselves becoming carriers of cultural identity. Moreover, in Scotland's case, there can be no doubt that the presence of a Calvinist Kirk enables natural European connections which are rather more problematic for the national Church in England. We shall come back to this point in some detail, but it is important to grasp right from the beginning that in the United Kingdom it is not a question of one European variant, but of four distinct religious – and indeed cultural – variants.

The reasons behind such particularities need some teasing out. They begin to emerge within a discussion of specific religious histories, an approach which tends to emphasize diversity rather than unity both within Europe and within the United Kingdom. Methodologically, moreover, the historical approach provides a necessary balance to the quantitative and at times rather flat analysis which characterizes – inevitably – the European Values Study.

3. Historical explanations

The third chapter of Martin's *General Theory of Secularization* (1978) focuses on the tensions between religion and nationhood within the European situation. It starts from the following premise:

> Europe is a unity by virtue of having possessed one Caesar and one God i.e. by virtue of Rome. It is a diversity by the virtue of the existence of nations. The patterns of European religion derive from the tension and the partnership between Caesar and God, and from the relationship between religion and the search for national integrity and identity. (p. 100)

The following pages will sketch, in the very broadest terms, some of these relationships for the English and Scottish cases. In so doing, the intention is to exemplify the processes at work in each of these countries, not to provide a detailed ecclesiastical history which can be found elsewhere. The approach is necessarily schematic and concerns, for the time being at least, only two of the United Kingdom variants; the others will be included in chapter 6. For more detailed study, a close reading of Martin is essential. This section will also introduce, rather tentatively, an idea that will be taken up again later on. Might it be possible that recent shifts in perspective – shifts that derive both from the implementation of the Single European Act and from the 1989 revolutions in Eastern Europe – need to be taken into account in an up-to-date or ongoing assessment of the tensions or partnerships between Caesar and God in contemporary Europe? Will there, for example, be more room for regional or subcultural identity if national profiles in Western Europe diminish, relatively speaking? Or will the pressure towards greater economic co-operation result in a greater, rather than diminished, awareness of other forms of national identity, a process within which the religious factor might become very significant indeed? Either scenario is possible.

But first, the English case. Patterns of English religion are often taken for granted rather than questioned, an attitude well exemplified in the tendency to regard as normal the fact that there has never been a political split within English society which coincided with a major religious division. Such a situation requires an explanation, however, for other European societies have had rather different experiences. The French – to give the most striking illustration of the opposite tendency – were, for generations, politically divided about religious questions rather than anything else. The animosity of the early years of the French Third Republic culminated in the separation of church and state and the establishment of an emphatically secular school system. The residual bitterness of these quarrels can still be felt; it accounts for the higher profile of anti-religion as well as non-religion in France. In England, it was quite other. A greater degree of pluralism existed at an earlier stage, notably the presence of Dissent in a variety of forms. In addition, the English revolution, the Glorious Revolution of 1688, may well have had religious connotations, but it did not – like the French Revolution a century later (and the timing is important) – split the country into two competing traditions, one Catholic and one Jacobin (Poulat 1987). On this side of the Channel, *de facto* tolerance enabled a certain amount of choice between different flavours of Christianity, a choice quite unlike the obligation in many Catholic countries to accept Catholicism or nothing at all. This is the major reason why the feel of English religious life remains qualitatively quite different from French religious life, despite (on a superficial reading of the EVSSG statistics) a certain resemblance between the two with respect to indices of belief and practice (Davie 1992).

The essential point to grasp is the crucial interactions between religious traditions and a wide variety of other variables in the early modern period; in what Beckford calls the great age of religious activity in England (and he includes Wales at this stage), which opened in the mid sixteenth century and closed in the late eighteenth, a period which saw the emergence of Anglicanism, Quakerism, Congregationalism, Presbyterianism and Methodism (Beckford 1991). Following Martin, Beckford confirms the conclusion outlined above:

> the very plurality and diversity of religious groups prevented British politics from being dominated by a single, major confrontation between church and state, politics and religion, or church and church. The consolidation of the British state did not therefore cast politics into a mold which necessarily polarized or amalgamated religion and politics. (1991: 179)

Out of this situation emerged a limited monopoly; a 'state church partially counterbalanced by a substantial bloc of dissent dispersed in the population at large' (Martin 1978: 20). Both elements are equally significant. It is, however, important to grasp the character of the state church in question, for once again it is unusual in European terms.[4] The Church of England came into being in rather dubious circumstances as the English variant of the Protestant Reformation. Despite setbacks, its position was consolidated under the Elizabethan Settlement, an arrangement which rejected both servility to Rome and subservience to Geneva, giving rise to the celebrated *via media*; a formula which embodied among other things an essentially *English* church designed to meet the spiritual needs of the English people (Moorman 1980: 213), but which developed in ways rather different from those of the Continental reformers. Curiously, and in a rather paradoxical way, the Church of England still does meet the spiritual needs of a substantial proportion of English people, despite their reluctance to attend its services. It has, however, become increasingly disconnected from the European mainland.

In Scotland, things were, and still are, rather different. No *via media* here. For most, if not all, of Scotland has been straightforwardly Protestant for several centuries, and its Protestants remain overwhelmingly Presbyterian (Highet 1972). They are distributed over a variety of denominations, among which the Church of Scotland 'established yet free' is both the largest and most significant. It is 'established' in that it is in historical continuity with the Church of Scotland reformed in 1560 and whose liberties were protected within the Treaty of Union (1707). But the Church is also 'by law made free of the State'; it is very different in nature from the state church south of the border. Brown's *Social History of Religion in Scotland* (1987) describes, but does not oversimplify, the connections between religion and national identity in this part of Britain. Rather more than Highet, Brown stresses the variety within Scotland's religion, a variety protected at least in part by the country's geography. He also points out the possibilities for disagreement about exactly which features of theology or ecclesiastical government have contributed to Scottish distinctiveness; the equations are not entirely self-evident. Nonetheless, Scotland is a region which has lacked its own resident head of state since 1603 and which has had no legislative assembly since 1707, leaving only the legal system, the national church and the educational system as the institutional carriers of national consciousness.

The role of Presbyterianism in general and Scotland's national church in particular have been prominent in these debates, which stress the uniqueness in Scottish religious history (Brown 1987: 6–14). But Brown also counsels caution, for much of Scotland's more recent religious life has been dictated by external pressures, which are much the same for Scotland as they are for the whole of Britain; notably the pressures of industrialization, rural depopulation and, more recently, industrial decline, questions that will be discussed more fully in the following section. He concludes:

The nomenclature may be different in Scottish church life, and theology and doctrines may have differed (though decreasingly as time has passed), but the problems the churches faced, the strategies they adopted, and popular involvement in organized religion were as much characteristic of British experience as they were distinguishing of Scottish society. (1987: 20)

It is clear that balancing unity against diversity is as much a problem within the United Kingdom as it is across Europe as a whole.

Post-war Britain

1. Economic and social transformations

Placing the countries of the United Kingdom within their European context provides one frame within which to locate the religious life of this country, or countries. But alongside the European dimension, we need to consider a second set of variables: that is, the changing nature of British society itself.[5] The two are in fact related, for the economic and social transformations taking place in Britain are, to a considerable extent, mirrored by similar changes taking place across the Channel, a convergence exemplified in the emergence of a growing body of European, alongside national, legislation.

One preliminary point is, however, important. The notion that the immediate context, however looked at, is an unavoidable factor in the lives of religious institutions (or indeed of religious individuals) is not always readily accepted by such institutions, for they regard themselves – not incorrectly – as guardians of the sacred; understanding 'the sacred' as that which is distinct from everyday life. External pressures remain, nonetheless, one of the realities of their existence. Patterns of religiosity are undoubtedly moulded, a word rather different from determined, by what is going on around them. A second point follows from this. A balanced view of the interrelationships between patterns of religiosity and the surrounding society can at times enable a better and more positive understanding of religious life. Trends which seemed, at first, peculiar to the religious sector, may turn out to be common to other areas of society. The marked decline in churchgoing since the war can be looked at in this way. Indeed Beckford (1992) sees this as an underexplored aspect of the secularization debate in Britain. Change in the field of religion, he argues, cannot be understood independently of the wider processes of change in society. Picking up a theme central to this book, he offers the following example:

> the important observation that religious believing seems to have become detached from religious belonging (Davie 1990a, 1990b) should be understood in relation to the parallel observation that virtually all voluntary associations have been finding it difficult in the last few decades to attract and retain members. In other words, 'belonging' has been simultaneously losing its popularity in religion *and* in other fields as well. The split between believing and belonging is therefore part of a broader pattern of change which happens to affect religious organisations amongst others. It is not a problem unique to religion and does not necessarily arise from the inner dynamics of religious organisations alone. (1992: 227, text from the English original)

The corollary leads us to look for the causes of this situation within society as a whole rather than in the field of religion itself. Of course this statement begs many questions, for a redirection in the locus of enquiry does not of itself lead to straightforward answers. In many ways the issues become more rather than less complex. Nor does this kind of approach mitigate the seriousness of the decline in churchgoing for the churches themselves. The fact of the matter remains whatever its cause, *part* of which may still lie within the churches rather than outside them. It does, however, serve as a timely reminder that in assessing the many and diverse aspects of British religiosity in the post-war period, we need to bear in mind a whole series of wider economic, social and political transformations.

British society, like other advanced capitalist systems, is changing in nature as a predominantly industrial model gives way to something rather different; as consumption rather than production becomes the dominant mode of economic organization; as (to use the jargon) modernity gives way to late or post-modernity. A detailed discussion of these rather technical phrases will be delayed until the final chapter, but it is important to grasp the realities of such shifts in so far as they colour the day-to-day existence of the churches and other religious organizations. Patterns of employment and residence, for example, are profoundly affected; so too are the choices that confront individuals as they determine the shape of their working lives, where and with whom they live, and the ways in which they spend the increasing amount of leisure time available to them. What, for example, are the implications of decline in large-scale labour-intensive industries and in the cities which mushroomed around these in the late nineteenth century? Will a considerable level of unemployment simply become a fact of life as such industries continue to shrink and employment patterns change? Is it possible to produce with sufficient speed a flexible and appropriately trained labour force for the high-tech industries that are emerging or for the growing service sector? How will the individuals concerned adapt to being linked by computer screen and fax machine rather than physical proximity? What will be the effect of de-urbanization as the small town or village proves more attractive than the Victorian city? Who will leave such cities and who will be left behind? It is clear that a whole series of complex and interrelated questions present themselves as we try to come to terms with what is going on. And given shifts of such magnitude, is it surprising that traditional political parties (of all persuasions), trades unions and other voluntary associations struggle – like the churches – for members as their natural constituencies evaporate and as the small screen proves considerably more popular than the public meeting as a source of entertainment?[6]

One thing is certain: changes of such magnitude do not occur smoothly. The demand for a highly skilled workforce, for example, places enormous pressures on an already hard-pressed educational system, which struggles to keep up with the demands made upon it. And if education cannot always deliver the required skills to sufficient numbers of people, it is also becoming clear that certain social groups within society are better placed than others to take advantage of the new opportunities – and not only educational ones – on offer. Within such patterns of advantage and disadvantage, moreover, social differentiation has, to some extent at least, become associated with geographical location; a linking most noticeable, in a negative sense, in the centres of those cities once associated with labour-intensive industries. They have become known as areas of multiple disadvantage: characteristically, they house those who have been 'left behind'. How do these changes affect the religious sector? Once again the answers are far from straightforward. Clearly, the churches are part and parcel of such changes and, like all other social institutions, they are subject to external pressures. Some religious groups, for example, are becoming increasingly motivated by the market, tailoring their activities in order to attract a certain kind of religious consumer. But others manifest a distinct unease about current trends. They point out the social costs (rather than benefits) of going too far down the market road, both in society as a whole and within the churches themselves. Not least among these protesters are the defenders of the parochial system within the established Church; an example, surely (to which we shall return), of a production-based rather than a consumption-based provision for spiritual needs.

One particularly pertinent illustration of the complex and subtle inter-actions of the churches with wider social changes can be found in the demographic shifts of post-war Britain. In more ways than one these shifts have profoundly altered the context within which religious organ-izations are obliged to operate. But the relationship works both ways, for changes in the climate of cultural values – including religious values – can themselves (both directly and indirectly) alter demographic beha-viour; affecting attitudes towards the family, for example, but at times influencing the reproductive process itself.

2. Demographic changes

Birth and death, marriage and divorce are crucial events in individual lives. Moreover, the effects of these events on the formation, attrition and dissolution of households 'are of great cultural, social, economic and biological salience' (Hobcraft and Joshi 1989: 1). All of us would agree with such a statement, but what is its significance for contemporary British religion?

There are three ways of responding to this question. The first is to stress the very immediate links between the crucial events of life and the religious sector, for religious personnel are frequently asked – and for the most part they co-operate – to mark births, marriages and, most of all, deaths with an appropriate symbolism. The beginning and end of life remain for the great majority of people an important focus for questions about the sacred. From a second and rather broader perspective, the complex and elusive links between religion and morality frequently prompt religious individuals – often in the name of particular creeds – to pro-nounce on changes in reproductive behaviour and, more particularly on 'the formation, attrition and dissolution of households', for decisions con-cerning this area of life are seen as moral acts. Lastly shifts in demographic (including migratory) behaviour interact with a whole range of social and economic variables to produce a constantly evolving environment in which the churches are called to minister; they are closely linked to the changes considered in the previous section of this chapter.

Currently, the total population of Britain, in common with most West European countries, is relatively stable. In consequence, changes concern the population structure rather than its size; that is, its age composition, its grouping into households, its geographical distribution and its ethnic composition. Earlier on in the post-war period, size was the more important factor: a brief but substantial post-war surge was followed by the baby boom of the late 1950s and early 1960s. The equally dramatic baby 'bust' of the late 1960s and 1970s led to more or less stable fertility levels since 1977, though *patterns* of fertility continue to alter, including later child-bearing and single parenting. Exactly what causes these shifts in fertility rates remains a constant source of speculation. Why do people decide to have more or fewer children? Any number of factors interact in this process, not all of which are economic. In this connection, Simons (1986) argues from a Durkheimian perspective to stress the significance of the relationship between the individual and society in such decisions, a relationship which he describes, following Durkheim, as religious.[7] Whether or not we accept this kind of categorization, the links between fertility, attitudes towards the family, feelings towards nationality and indices of religiosity clearly merit further investigation, for we simply do not know what makes people tick in this respect.

Within the complex process of decision making about fertility, the widespread availability of contraceptives remains a significant, if not always predictable, factor;[8] an availability, moreover, which has undoubtedly had a dramatic effect both on sexual mores and on family life. Almost all women are now able to control their fertility. They are, in consequence, likely to be sexually active at an earlier age, but to delay child-bearing until their mid or late twenties. Whatever goes on in these very personal decisions, one fact remains increasingly clear: for most people for most of the time, sexual activity has become divorced from reproduction. The former need not, and – many would argue – should not, in the vast majority of cases, lead to the latter. And if this has been the case since the mid 1960s when contraceptives became freely available to married women (a decade or so later for the unmarried), a second revolution is now in process. It is now technically possible, though not widespread, for reproduction to take place apart from the sexual act. Welcomed as a means of helping the childless, the moral questions raised by the technology involved are immense. Theological thinking is only just beginning to respond; indeed the older question of contraceptive use remains problematic for an important religious minority in Britain. In both cases the churches are attempting to come to terms with technical developments over which they have very little control. Who does or should have control of such events remains, not surprisingly, a question of considerable significance for contemporary society. The more so in that such technology is intimately connected to the traditions of family life, a crucial area for the nurture of values, including religious values. Hence the delicacy of the whole debate.

Be that as it may, we find ourselves in Britain in the early 1990s in a situation where both birth and death rates are relatively low. The population is ageing (a significant fact for statistics concerning religiosity) and the majority of women spend a relatively short period of their lives in bearing and rearing children. They may, conversely, find themselves disproportionately responsible for other forms of caring, notably for the growing number of elderly; a situation undoubtedly exacerbated by recent changes in government policy, for community care very often means, in practice, care by women (with little or no payment) in a not very evident community.

The changing role of women in contemporary society is undeniable. Shifting gender roles remain, however, a complex and difficult area of study within which description and prescription are frequently confused. Certain facts are, nonetheless, beyond dispute. Most women will expect to enter the labour force at some point in their lives in addition to assuming the greater part of responsibility for the nurture of their relatively small families. On the other hand, their careers are very differently shaped from their male counterparts. It is also evident that increasing numbers of women – rather than men – may be single parents, not infrequently assuming the responsibility of breadwinner as well as carer. The churches respond variously to these changes in role, but it is clear that decisions about church policy become particularly problematic when pastoral care demands one set of reactions, ecclesiastical traditions another. The debate about the ministry of women (both lay and ordained) should be seen in this context. It is but a small part of a much wider issue: the fundamental – so unavoidable – reappraisal of the role of women in contemporary Western society, a debate developed more fully in chapter 9.

A particularly sharp encounter between traditional teaching and pastoral care occurs over the 'dissolution of households', the more so when the dissolution arises as a result of marital breakdown. For divorce, even separation, questions very directly the lifelong commitment embodied in the Christian view of marriage. It is certainly true that divorce has increased dramatically in the post-war period, notably since the 1967 Divorce Act. But whether or not this represents a corresponding increase in the breakdown of marriage is, of course, very hard to say; cause and effect are notoriously difficult to disentangle in a debate where judgemental attitudes abound. Despite a sharply increased divorce rate, marriage remains a popular institution, the family even more so, though not necessarily in its conventional forms. It is also the case that longevity demands a quality of endurance within the marriage relationship rather different from expectations a century ago. Marriages which ended in the death of one partner in the late nineteenth century may be brought to an end by divorce in the 1990s. Change does not necessarily mean things are getting worse.

The churches are, however, required to exist within a constantly evolving situation. There was no need, for example, to debate the eligibility of the divorced for priesthood until there were sufficient numbers of individuals in that category to create the problem, if such it is. Nor did the Mothers' Union need to change the rules about divorcees becoming members of an organization primarily concerned with family life until there were noticeable numbers of potential members in this situation. As ever, circumstances alter cases. But how far can the churches – the guardians of the sacred – go in their efforts to redefine the boundaries? This crucial question pervades every area of church life; it is developed more fully in chapter 3.

3. Immigration

As befits a sea-faring nation, Britain has always been a multi-ethnic society. Immigrants have been motivated by pull factors such as demand for labour and push factors such as the need to escape religious persecution. (Diamond and Clarke 1989: 177)

The second part of this statement implies a certain degree of religious tolerance within the host country, the implications of which need careful examination, for 'tolerance' and 'pluralism' are problematic terms, whose meaning should never be taken for granted. Such concepts are, however, of crucial significance given the increasing interdependence of the global economy; an interdependence which demands, among other things, considerable mobility of labour.

Some international movement has, of course, always existed. Immigration into Britain in the nineteenth century, for example, was characterized first by a large Irish component and subsequently by significant numbers of Russians, particularly Jews fleeing from an anti-Semitic policy. Both, whether Christian or non-Christian, influenced the religious make-up of this country. The first half of the twentieth century saw a further influx of Jews, together with the emergence of small ethnic communities (Chinese and African) in the major ports. Britain's multi-ethnicity was slowly but surely increasing. Post-war immigrations, however, the focus of this section, have been much larger. They have introduced into Britain considerable numbers from the New Commonwealth and Pakistan, but also some smaller groups escaping persecution (notably Chileans, Ugandan Asians and Iranians). Three factors have influenced the post-war influx: the demand for labour in the 1960s, government policy in the form of Immigration Acts and events elsewhere in the world. Bearing these in mind it is not surprising that patterns of post-war immigration vary over time, both in country of origin and in gender. With reference to the latter, early arrivals tended to be men looking for work; more recent immigrants have been women joining their husbands. Precise destinations within Britain also differ, influenced by a variety of factors. In some cases, employers have recruited directly from particular parts of the world; in others new migrants have been persuaded to join those already established in this country. The geographical distribution of each religious minority depends upon these factors. But a further more fundamental point should be emphasized. The presence of pluralism in Britain should not be exaggerated; it is an urban phenomenon and differs from region to region. Large tracts of the country (notably, but not only, the more rural areas) remain uncompromisingly mono-cultural.[9]

The arrival of significant numbers of black Christians, Muslims, Sikhs and Hindus has, nonetheless, brought a new dimension to post-war British religion. The Christian churches were offered an unexpected opportunity for growth – never mind renewal – as black (usually Afro-Caribbean) Christians arrived in the major cities. That they failed to take this opportunity is one of the saddest indictments of mainline Christianity in this period. Inter-faith dialogue, on the other hand, acquired a greater immediacy, for it began to concern neighbours in this country rather than hypothetical conversations with communities overseas. The concept of pluralism, however, was not as self-evident as many people had thought. Indeed early notions of assimilation have given way to a rather different emphasis where, in theory at least, distinctiveness (whether ethnic, cultural or religious) is celebrated rather than denied; though how such differences cohabit on a practical level within one society is not entirely clear. The Rushdie controversy brought many of these issues to the fore. They remain, for the most part, unresolved.

Conclusion

Drawing the threads of this chapter together, it is important to remember that other European countries also house significant immigrant communities, though the precise make-up of the minorities in question varies from country to country. Britain is unusual in having considerable numbers of Hindus and Sikhs as well as Muslims. Such variations are determined by the particular colonial or economic connections of each European nation.[10] There is, once again, both unity and diversity across Europe. The implications remain the same in each case, however: how do we accommodate the religious aspirations of diverse communities within a continent dominated for centuries by one religious tradition rather than another? The answers are not immediately apparent. The situation has, moreover, been exacerbated – particularly from an economic point of view – by the opening of the East European border since 1989 and the unanticipated arrival of large numbers of newcomers (mostly Christian, including a substantial representation of Orthodoxy) from a rather different quarter. Britain will experience this latest influx less directly than other West European countries, though an open-border policy within the European Union will render this, in the long run, as much our concern as anybody else's.

It is, moreover, clear that wherever they come from, ethnic minorities are just as much subject to the shifting social and economic conditions of post-war development as the rest of the population; indeed in many cases, more so. In the British case, an expanding economy in the 1960s required alternative sources of labour, supplied from overseas. A decade or so later, a declining economy led to rising levels of unemployment and fewer resources, a situation in which the ethnic groups find themselves handicapped. Internal migratory patterns reflect this handicap as the ethnic population becomes disproportionately present in precisely those areas most beset by economic difficulties; they are, very often, part of the left-behind population of the inner city, losers rather than gainers in the enterprise culture. Paradoxically, the religious life of the inner city has undoubtedly been enriched. Finally, the demographic behaviour of ethnic minorities is, not surprisingly, different from the host community or communities. Once again religious mores interact with a whole range of other variables to produce particular, though constantly evolving, demographic profiles. Careful monitoring of these profiles is a more sensible policy than jumping to conclusions about the future size of ethnic or religious communities. In the meantime the other-faith categories represent a growth area in post-war European religiosity, the implications of which will form an important part of the chapters that follow.

Notes

1 The European Values Study is a major cross-national survey of human values, first carried out in Europe in 1981 and then extended to other countries worldwide. It was designed by the European Values Systems Study Group (EVSSG). Analyses of the 1981 European material can be found in Harding and Phillips, with Fogarty (1986) and in Stoetzel (1983). The British material is written up in Abrams, Gerard and Timms (1985). Other national studies are listed in Harding and Phillips, with Fogarty (1986: xv).

   A restudy took place in 1990. Published material from this study is beginning to emerge (Timms 1992, Ashford and Timms 1992, Barker, Halman and Vloet 1993), though the detailed analyses are still awaited. A further restudy is planned for the turn of the century. The longitudinal aspects of the study enhance the data considerably.

2 Two comparisons are interesting in this respect. First the situation in parts of Central and Eastern Europe where, prior to 1989, religious practice became one form of protest against a corrupt regime, even among non-believers, for whom the 'conventional' relationship between the variables believing and belonging was reversed (Michel

1991: 5). Secondly the situation in the United States where religious practice has remained, by European standards, extremely high, though still lower than indices of religious belief, which in comparison with Europe are astronomical.

3   Halsey (1985), for example, places British attitudes in a European perspective offering three categories: Scandinavia (Denmark, Sweden, Finland and Norway); Northern Europe (Britain, Northern Ireland, Eire, West Germany, Holland, Belgium and France); and Latin Europe (Italy and Spain). The Northern Europe category contains some very divergent religious contexts.

4   Sociologically, its closest parallels can be found in the state churches of Scandinavia.

5   Raising, in other words, precisely those issues mentioned by Brown with reference to the *parallel* developments of England and Scotland.

6   Data for this kind of statement can be found in the annual publication *Social Trends*. The European Values Study provides useful European comparisons in this respect.

7   Adopting, in other words, a very broad understanding of the term 'religious'; very nearly coterminous with the idea of society itself.

8   For it is quite clear that the availability of contraceptives does not lead automatically to their use. The causal connections in this respect are infinitely complicated.

9   Depending, of course, on the definition of ethnicity, for many parts of rural England contain populations of, for example, Celtic origin.

10 As a rule of thumb, British immigrants have come from the countries of the New Commonwealth and French immigrants from North Africa. German migrants are, however, rather different, coming from the countries of Southern Europe (notably the former Yugoslavia) and from Turkey. Not surprisingly, the nature of European Islam – to take but one example – varies in its aspirations depending upon the particular provenance of each Islamic minority.

3 The Sacred and the Secular: Religious Generations in Post-war Britain

Any attempt to suggest particular periods of time within post-war religious development must to some extent be arbitrary, for it is always possible to offer alternative and equally plausible sets of dates. Nor are such periods – however decided upon – tidy or self-contained units; the thread of events will be continuous whatever the shifts in mood and emphasis. This chapter attempts, nonetheless, to outline four such generations, chosen primarily because they reflect significant changes in the way that the religious dimension of society relates to the wider environment. Or to put this another way, the chapter tries to put some sort of time-scale on the subtle but important developments in the relationship between the sacred and the secular in post-war British society.

In many respects, the sections within this chapter – especially the earlier ones – follow the divisions adopted by most of the chroniclers of post-war religious life, for example Welsby (1984) and especially Hastings (1986), to whose masterly narrative the debt will be obvious. They also fit rather conveniently with archiepiscopal periods of office. But the notion of a *generational* shift will have wider implications in this book, for it conveys two things: a period of time as well as the notion of handing on a religious culture from one generation to the next. After all, religion – like language – is largely acquired rather than learnt, with much of this acquisition taking place within the family at a very early age. Religious notions are, therefore, strongly related to a particular cultural inheritance;

they are absorbed as a whole package of wisdom, some worldly and some other-worldly (Ahern and Davie 1987: 53). Significant changes tend, therefore, to occur as a new generation is – or is not – offered the necessary wisdom.

As a period of time, a generation has, of course, its advantages and disadvantages, for sometimes it corresponds with a convenient marker in other aspects of social or political development and sometimes it doesn't. Longley, for example (1991), points out that the relatively slow rhythms of a nation's religious life are bound to sit uneasily alongside the faster tempo of daily journalism, developing the contrast into a persuasive climatic analogy:

> There is an impatience about journalism which attracts a certain sort. Religion is often a waiting game: the only view which makes sense is the long view. Newspapers are bound to be concerned with the ripples on the surface of life; religion is about the deep ocean currents which are often completely hidden and which move enormous masses of water over long distances very slowly. But we know, particularly in Britain astride the Gulf Stream, that deep ocean currents are crucial to the overall climate while making little difference to today's weather. (p. x)

Bearing this and the necessarily hazardous nature of the task in mind, four post-war shifts are suggested in this chapter, though one section could easily be subdivided further, when alternative – and equally important – time-scales are taken into account. Further dimensions of generational change will be explored later on.

1945–1960: Post-war Reconstruction

Six years of war left Europe, never mind Britain, in ruins. Not only was the need for material reconstruction obvious, there was, in addition, the task of reconstituting the whole fabric of political, economic and social life. In the diocese of London only 70 out of 700 churches remained unscathed after the bombing and many had been completely destroyed. At the same time the need to provide new church buildings and personnel to keep pace with post-war housing programmes was all too obvious. And if London was to some extent a special case, similarly daunting figures could be quoted for a number of other dioceses, particularly those containing the larger cities. Faced with the enormity of the challenge, the churches managed pretty well. For there was, in the 1950s at least, a distinct feeling of well-being, of revival even, within church circles. Hastings describes this as follows:

> The general feeling of religious revival or, perhaps better, of restoration, continued for about a dozen years. It fitted well with the dominant mood of the fifties, its politicians, its literary figures, its art. 'The church', declares a character in Pamela Hansford Johnson's novel, *The Humbler Creation*, 'is respectable again. People have to say they believe in God.' (Hastings 1986: 444)

More particularly, the 1950s were an Anglican decade, in which the social role of the church was confirmatory rather than confrontational. The sacred (at least in its Anglican forms) synchronized nicely with the secular in this predominantly Conservative period.

The moment which caught this sense of restoration – symbolic as well as material – most vividly was the Coronation of Elizabeth II in June 1953, described by Jenkins as 'the most universally impressive ceremonial event in history' (1975: 74). Whatever the case, it undoubtedly brought together the Church of England, the monarchy and the nation in an act of sacralization, witnessed for the first time by a television audience numbered in millions. For many (myself included), the Coronation became a crucially remembered event for precisely this reason; it was their first experience of television. Not surprisingly it also caught the attention of contemporary sociologists who, equally predictably, were divided in their interpretations. Did the Coronation merely reflect the values of British society current at the time (assuming, in other words, a unitary view of British society); or was the ceremonial a conscious effort to *construct* a consensus whose existence should not be assumed at the outset? Bocock and Thompson (1985: 214–18) outline the contours of this particular controversy. But whatever the sociologists conclude, the Coronation undoubtedly embodied in high-profile form what might be termed the establishment spirit of the 1950s.

But – and this is the crucial point – the emphasis lay essentially on what the words 'restoration' or 'reconstruction' imply: that is, an attempt to put back what had been destroyed and to rebuild the institutions of the past. The assumption that this might be possible conveys better than anything else the mood of this decade and a half. Once again, Hastings sums up such feelings – perilously close to complacency – in the following:

> By the middle of the 1950s it may well have seemed that the Church was right after all to dodge any more radical measure of post-war reform. It had not been needed. The leadership had re-established confidence quite effectively without it. The Captain of England's cricket team in 1954 was ordained in the Church of England in 1955 – David Sheppard, a bright young product of the old Cambridge Evangelical stable. It was a most satisfying moment, symbol of what the fifties seemed all about. (1986: 447)

It was not to last. The gradual realization that the old order could not be rebuilt and that a majority in the nation remained very largely indifferent to what was going on in the churches required a very different type of response.

Such indifference was, of course, unevenly spread, but there was a growing awareness that the urbanized and industrialized parts of the country were increasingly slipping away from the churches' influence. Wickham's important study of church life in Sheffield was published in 1957. Its message about the effectiveness – or rather ineffectiveness – of the churches in many working-class areas was hardly reassuring (Wickham 1957). Exactly what form this 'slipping away from the churches' influence' took, however, is more problematic. Hoggart's celebrated *The Uses of Literacy*, for example, also published for the first time in 1957 but written from a very different perspective, offers a more nuanced view of working-class religion. Practice was unusual except in pockets. On the other hand Hoggart affirms very strongly the working-class hold on what G. K. Chesterton called 'the dumb certainties of existence' or Reinhold Niebuhr's 'primary religion'. Nor should such beliefs be taken lightly, Hoggart maintains, for in coming to their religious institutions at the important moments of life or in times of personal crisis 'they [the working class] are not simply taking out a saving policy; they still believe underneath, in certain ways. At least, middle-aged people do, and here I am thinking chiefly of them' (1984: 113). Two themes crucial to this book are already evident: the mismatch in belief and practice in this country and the generational factor. They are, of course, interrelated.

The 1960s: a Desire for Relevance

The churches were, inevitably, in for a bumpy ride in the 1960s. The world into which they appeared to fit so well was being challenged on every front. Not everything happened at once, but by the end of the decade a profound and probably irreversible revolution in social and, above all, sexual attitudes had taken place. Significant immigration had occurred and expectations of and about the role of women were evolving fast. Traditional, often Christian-based, values (many of them associated with family life) were no longer taken for granted; questioned by many, they were abandoned by increasing numbers. Given changes of such magnitude, a loss of confidence on the part of those in the churches was hardly surprising; a collapse which provoked in the first instance considerable confusion. Bit by bit, however, the emphasis changed and confusion gave way to calls for radical reaction. Such reaction took a variety of forms: intellectual, organizational and liturgical (categories to which we shall return). But the underlying motive was very similar in each of these cases. The churches – all too aware of the changes taking place around them – were looking for ways to adapt to and to penetrate this shifting world. All might still be well if the Church could shake off its image of belonging essentially to the past; it must, instead, present itself and its message as modern, up to date and, above all, relevant. In terms of the structure of this chapter, the emphasis lay, precisely, in 'breaking down the walls of partition between the sacred and the secular', or more directly still, in removing 'the dead hand of traditionalism' (Welsby 1984: 104).

David Sheppard's career illustrates this metamorphosis nicely. By this stage that 'bright young product of the Cambridge evangelical stable', with all its emphasis on the importance of individual conversion, was hard at it in Canning Town, coming to terms with some radical shifts in perspective (Sheppard and Worlock 1988). Clearly there was no room for complacency, for church life in its conventional forms had very largely collapsed. (The Mayflower Centre had six regular communicants, mustering no more than twenty or so for a special service.) Any effective penetration of the local community had, inevitably, to take place in new and different ways and in a society that was itself subject to previously unknown pressures. The immediate neighbourhood of Canning Town might remain solidly white and working class, but increasing numbers within the East End were by this stage members of racial minorities, a factor which had to be taken into account, alongside the increasing demands for collective rather than individual action in the search for social justice.

By any standards, the Mayflower Centre was an impressive undertaking. It – and a number of similar ventures – should not be underestimated; they represented a real effort to make contact with working-class people. But membership figures, together with almost any other indicator of religiosity in the 1960s reveal all too clearly the churches' continuing inability to stem the growth of religious indifference in Britain. Relevance *per se* was not going to solve the problem. But relevance was the order of the day. The churches looked to the secular world for a lead and borrowed, in some cases rather uncritically, both its ideas and forms of expression. The desire to be modern, to be in rather than out of step with the world, lay behind a whole series of 'reforms' within the Anglican and the free churches: intellectually, in the theological and moral debates of the period (notably the *Honest to God* controversy); organizationally in the rearrangement of parishes, priests and people (in which the commissioning of the explicitly sociological *Paul Report* should not be overlooked); liturgically, in the 'modernizing' of scripture and worship (numerous new translations of the Bible and the steady – some would say relentless – revision of the Prayer Book); and ecumenically in a variety of endeavours towards greater ecclesiastical collaboration (notably the Anglican–Methodist Unity Scheme). No church involved in this process was going to be quite the same again, for important and lasting shifts were undoubtedly taking place.

It could be argued, however, that such changes pale almost into insignificance compared with the transformation in Roman Catholicism brought about in this decade by the Second Vatican Council, for Vatican II altered the framework of ecclesiastical life on a global scale for Protestants and Catholics alike, in an enormous variety of ways and in a remarkably short time. It was, Hastings argues, the most important ecclesiastical event of the century, never mind the 1960s. 'It so greatly changed the character of by far the largest communion of Christendom (and by and large, in a direction which we may describe not too unfairly as one of "Protestantization"), that no one has been left unaffected' (1986: 525). For not only did the Council alter very tangibly the ordinary practice of parochial life, it set in motion a whole process of discussion and change which very quickly assumed a momentum of its own. Hornsby-Smith (1987, 1989a, 1989b, 1991) has documented in considerable detail the evolution of the Roman Catholic community in Britain in the post-war period, sources to which we shall return in chapter 4. The important point to grasp at this stage, however, is the steady dissolving of the walls surrounding the English Catholic community; a process which has come about as the result of two factors. First the rapid social change in the post-war decades, permitting, among other things, social as well as geographical mobility for large numbers of Catholics, and second the internal religious *aggiornamento* brought about in the 1960s by Pope John XXIII (Hornsby-Smith 1989b: 89–90). This *aggiornamento* (literally the bringing up to date) of the Catholic Church – the more dramatic because it had been longer delayed than in other churches – sums up better than anything else the mood of religious life in the 1960s.

Not everyone, however, was sure that this was the right way to go. Douglas, for example, in her celebrated essay on the 'Bog Irish' captures a distinct sense of loss rather than gain. More precisely, she describes the move in educated Catholic circles in England from symbolic to ethical action, epitomized in the rationalization of Friday abstinence. She continues:

> Now there is no cause for others to 'regard us as odd'. Friday no longer rings the great cosmic symbols of expiation and atonement: it is not symbolic at all, but a practical day for the organization of charity. Now the English Catholics are like everyone else. (1973: 67)

And what, she implies, is the point of that? Taken to extremes, policies which break down too many barriers between the sacred and the secular can be dangerous, for they leave the sacred in a vulnerable position. The process of secularization, many would argue, has penetrated the churches themselves. Never more so than in the 1960s.

1970–1990: the Re-emergence of the Sacred

1. The oil crisis: a change in mood

The 1960s were, above everything, a confident decade. Conditional sentences (if they were conditional at all) began with the conjunction 'when' rather than 'if'. Standards of living had risen fast and continuously; it was assumed that they would go on rising. Confidence bred excitement and enthusiasm – sometimes over-enthusiasm – but chiefly optimism, which was not always ill-founded. For man had landed on the moon in 1969; 'when' had been the right word to use in this case. But, like all good things (or at least things that were good for some), it came to an end. Domestic economic indicators took a downturn at the same time as the oil crisis dominated the world scene; oil prices quadrupled in 1973. British industry was in decline (Britain doing far less well than its competitors), the currency was in difficulties, while both inflation and unemployment were rising. Public spending cuts became increasingly inevitable. Politically the troubles in Northern Ireland – within which the religious factor has an undoubted significance – were becoming depressingly prominent as news items. Above all, the political will to do anything about these things was lacking; none of the relatively short-lived governments of the 1970s seemed able to tackle the problems.

The religious constituency was not immune to what was going on. While changes set in motion in the 1960s were continuing to run their course – for there was no going back in many respects – at least some within the churches were beginning to think again about the nature of religious life. If a new image for the churches, free from the shackles of the past, expressing its relevance (not to mention its worship) in the language of the people, was one reaction to the complacency of the immediate post-war period, a second formulation was now beginning to suggest itself; a formulation that was far more mistrustful of secular life. As the 1960s gave way to a far less confident decade, it was hardly surprising that borrowing from the secular became less and less attractive. So much so that the pendulum began to swing once again towards a greater emphasis on the distinctiveness of the sacred.

But it did not always swing evenly, or in the way that many within the churches might have wished. Firstly, because the distinctiveness of the sacred began to show in unusual places. New religious movements, for example, already apparent in the 1960s, became a focus of public as well as religious attention as at least some (though never all that many) people looked outside the mainline churches for spiritual satisfaction. Such movements are infinitely variable in type but, following Wilson, they are in the main exclusivistic, that is, standing 'in some degree of protest against the dominant traditions of society and rejecting prevailing patterns of belief and conduct' (Wilson 1990: 1). At the same time house churches, sociologically if not theologically similar to at least some new religious movements, began to multiply in response to a somewhat similar demand among Christians (usually evangelicals) for a greater distinctiveness in church life (Walker 1985). The house church movement is, once again, enormously diverse – or, to put it another way, notoriously fissiparous – but in all its manifestations, it clearly embodies one thing: a desire for something special or distinctive about religious activity. Once again there is a stepping away from the majority, whether from the assumptions of secular society or from the inclusiveness of mainline religion. Lastly, and in a rather different section of British society, it was becoming increasingly clear by the mid 1970s that the immigrant communities – by this stage a significant feature of many British cities – were anxious to retain their own forms and styles of religious life, resisting pressures to adapt to British ways of thought, not least its markedly understated religiosity. Such resistance marked a wider trend: assimilation – the minimizing of differences, however conceived – was no longer the principal assumption of the thinking about minorities, religious or other. Differences should be celebrated rather than denied.

Each of these phenomena will be documented in more detail in the next chapter, but taken together they evoke an important shift in emphasis. For they represent not only an increasing awareness of the distinctiveness of the sacred, but the growing value placed on such a category by markedly different groups of people. An important point follows from this. The sacred should be approached with great sensitivity. Part of such sensitivity lies in taking care not to lump together widely diverse religious organizations and belief systems; a tendency all too often found in discussions of new religious movements and of other faiths. Admittedly, there are important sociological arguments for looking at the shared characteristics of a range of minority religious movements, but always with an appropriate respect for distinctive systems of belief, each with its own sense of the sacred. Such respect is, of course, much more readily accorded to some groups than others; what Barker (1989b) terms a 'tolerant discrimination' pervades a good deal of British thinking about our diverse religious minorities.

By this stage in the post-war period, the evidence about religious life begins to become, therefore, curiously contradictory. Certain characteristics of the 1960s persist, particularly those which had acquired a momentum of their own. Widespread indifference, however, remains the norm, though it is important to remember that such indifference usually takes the form of Christian nominalism rather than anything else; relatively few people adopt alternatives to Christianity, religious or otherwise. But overlaying such nominalism, significant minorities (Christian and non-Christian) are undoubtedly beginning to develop. And for such minorities there is an important shift in emphasis: church membership becomes something sought after and chosen; no longer can it merely be assumed or taken for granted. And for these groups, there can be no doubt that the line between the sacred and the secular is beginning to harden rather than to dissolve.[1]

Interestingly, such a tendency is also beginning to penetrate the mainline churches, not least the Church of England. If the house church phenomena provided one alternative for evangelical Christians, another was found in the increasing number of evangelical 'parishes' within the established Church. Once again more detailed documentation will be found in the following chapter, but one manifestation of this tendency has been a greater awareness of – indeed insistence upon – proper criteria for membership. Contracting in begins to replace contracting out. The tension between the assumptions embodied in such phrases can be exemplified in the heated debates about who does or does not have the right to bring their children (a new generation) for baptism in the parish church. Is the rite of / right to baptism open to every parishioner? Or should it be restricted to the children of those who attend the church with reasonable regularity? The former are working on a contracting out model; the latter on contracting in. Taken to extremes the two attitudes are very hard indeed to reconcile.

2. The Thatcher decade: a curious reversal of roles

Looking back at the 1970s, it is important to remember that spending cuts were already part of the scene well before 1979, the date which marks Margaret Thatcher's arrival as Prime Minister. Economically, the change in mood had already occurred. But in other ways the 1980s – the Thatcher decade – have to be seen as a separate entity in the evolution of post-war religion, outside the longer-term shifts between the sacred and secular. The Thatcher years were so distinct, so unlike anything which has gone before, that they cut across other time-scales. They and the agenda that they set will be the focus of a separate discussion in chapter 8. One point is, however, important at this stage, for in some ways it counters the emphasis on the separateness of the sacred. For there occurs in the 1980s a curious reversal of roles. There can be no doubt that the pace was set by the government as the so-called Conservative administration set about an unprecedented programme of radical reform. The churches could do little but react; but their reaction, more often than not, took the form of inclusiveness. Claiming – with a certain justification[2] – to be more representative than any political party, the churches found themselves defending their ground against an increasingly separate or sectarian government. The guardians of the sacred become the defenders of the whole nation, paying particular attention to those least able to defend themselves; in many cases those, paradoxically, least likely to attend their churches. This episode serves once again to illustrate just how very atypical the Thatcher decade has been in the evolution of post-war Britain, considered from whatever point of view – economic, political, social or religious. It simply doesn't fit into other time-scales.

The 1990s: New Formulations of the Sacred

1. Religion in a consumer society

Contemporary British society is often described as consumerist, an adjective which has a certain ambivalence with respect to the sacred. For there are two possible reactions to this kind of language, reactions already hinted at in the previous chapter. The first is to extend the notion of consumption into the sacred. Not only do we purchase our material requirements; we then shop around for our spiritual needs. Religious organizations (conventional and otherwise) respond to such requests by 'marketing' particular products, of an enormously varied nature, some with greater success than others. But a second reaction can also be found: one that rejects the notion of consumerism altogether, alongside the materialism that this is seen to represent, and perceives the sacred as an alternative and different – with the strong implication of better – way. *De facto* many religious organizations pursue a both/and rather than an either/or policy in this respect, for it is only by marketing an alternative, less materialistic lifestyle that such an option can be brought to public attention in the first place.

Whatever the motivation, alternative lifestyles undoubtedly abound in this last decade of the twentieth century, within which there are, very often, religious dimensions. Two examples can be taken to illustrate this process, both very much part of the 1990s agenda. The first concerns alternative medicine, which takes a wide variety of forms, some more, some less compatible with conventional medical practice. But many alternative approaches have one feature in common: they attempt to treat the whole person rather than the presenting medical symptoms, whatever these may be. And it is increasingly recognized that the whole person includes some sort of spirit, together with mind and body. 'Holy' and 'whole' have reacquired their common root; the set-apart or the sacred becomes once more integral to the well-being of the individual in question, for no healing can take place while mind, body and soul remain fragmented.

If this is the case at the level of individuals, a rather similar process is taking place with reference to ecological issues, in a debate which evokes profound and difficult questions about the relationship of humanity to the environment. It is, moreover, closely related to the process of globalization, since both the immensity of the risks involved and the first steps towards some sort of answers relate increasingly to the planet as a whole rather than to separate nations or continents. Yet despite the vast difference in scale, the underlying issues are curiously similar to those relating to individual health.[3] For the well-being of the planet plainly depends on a right relationship between its various parts, the crucial relationship being the place of humanity in the creative process. Is humanity master of the planet, controller of the evolutionary process, at liberty to extract from the earth's resources whatever is economically useful? Or are we part – rather than master – of creation, part of the process of evolution, by implication intimately related not only to the earth itself but to all other living things? And once the relationship between the parts is disturbed, the health of the whole is, inevitably, impaired.

There is, clearly, no necessary connection between ecological issues and religion, particularly if the latter term is restricted to its traditional forms. On the other hand, there can be little doubt that preoccupations with the environment have led to profound and probing questions about the origins of the planet and of the human race. Within this debate, moreover, the conventional divisions between science and religion become less and less salient. As Robertson (1991) indicates with reference to the globalization process, there is no longer any point in dividing our experience into 'this-worldly' and 'other-worldly' categories. For if everything is related to everything else, the separation of the sacred and the profane begins to lose its plausibility. The sacred starts to spill over into everyday thinking. Indeed, in many respects, things seem to be turning full circle. If, in the 1960s the sacred borrowed somewhat indiscriminately from the secular, the reverse may – perhaps – be true in the last decade of the twentieth century as the sacred is plundered by the secular.[4] At the very least, the lines between the two categories are undoubtedly becoming increasingly blurred.

2. The New Age

It is in this context that we should, in my opinion, approach the multifarious phenomenon of the New Age; a phenomenon that affirms the continuing significance of the sacred in contemporary society but in far from conventional forms. The New Age embodies an enormous range of ideas and practice, from alternative medicine and green issues to business management and the publishing world.[5] It is a rich amalgam of philosophies and practices (from both Eastern and Western traditions), involving contrasting groups of people in a wide variety of places. A glance at the range of titles concerning spirituality in any general bookshop provides one indicator not only of the range of ideas involved, but also of their popularity; far greater in many cases than that of traditional religious publications. It is hardly surprising, therefore, that the issues embodied in the New Age have a very ambivalent relationship to Christianity. On the one hand, the emphasis on the wholeness of an individual or of creation has many echoes in Christian teaching; there is a shared preoccupation with the spiritual dimension of life. But the answers offered by New Age philosophies are a long way from orthodox (in the Christian sense) and the phenomenon emerges, inevitably, as an alternative to, even a rival of, conventional religiosity. Christians respond to this dilemma in a variety of ways. Some react very positively, looking again, for example, at their teaching on creation to accommodate contemporary thinking about the environment. Others are far more negative and respond to this and other issues by retreating yet further into their own particular certainties, defining these ever more closely. The tendency towards fundamentalism, though less marked in this country than elsewhere, cannot be ignored in this respect, for retreating into certainty (the artificial maintenance of boundary) is one way to ensure survival in an increasingly fragmented world. Hence its significance in a theoretical analysis of contemporary religion, a significance discussed further in chapter 10.

Interestingly, the New Age also embodies the dilemma posed at the beginning of this section: it both feeds on a consumer society (marketing its own particular and infinitely varied products), but at the same time rejects many of the assumptions that underpin contemporary materialism. Like so many other manifestations of religion, it both extends and critiques the motivations of late-twentieth-century Western society.

Conclusion

This chapter has examined various stages in post-war religiosity from the point of view of the relationship between the sacred and the wider context. Complacency in the 1950s gave way to a radicalism dominated by the values of the secular world. But this in turn led, eventually, to a renewed emphasis on the sacred, sometimes in unconventional forms, from whose preoccupations the secular world begins increasingly to borrow. In some respects the wheel has indeed turned full circle, but it would be foolish to imagine that it is possible to recapture the past. For one underlying trend remains throughout the post-war period: that is, the failure of the mainline (that is, most Christian) religious organizations to maintain *regular* contact with the majority of people in this country (irregular contact is still relatively widespread), a loss of influence which will form one theme of the following chapter. On the other hand, less conventional forms of religiosity have increased in the same period and even within the mainline churches new ways of affirming the sacred have been discovered.

The crucial point to grasp is that some sort of religiosity persists despite the obvious drop in practice. The sacred does not disappear – indeed in many ways it is becoming more rather than less prevalent in contemporary society.[6] The disjunction between practice and what I have labelled 'belief' (as a convenient shorthand) characterizes a great deal of Britain's religious life in the post-war period, a disjunction accentuated in each generation. If the institutional link has been weakened at every stage in the handing-on process, the sacred has, undoubtedly, found other outlets. Beckford explains this process as one of the hidden ironies of secularization (1992). The decrease in institutional religion has not destroyed religious belief (not so far anyway) but it has rendered such belief vulnerable to all kinds of external pressures. Nominal (as opposed to organized) Christianity, for example, provides a rich seedbed for alternative versions of the sacred. Hence for certain kinds of people, though by no means the population as a whole, the undoubted attractiveness of New Age ideas. Their prevalence should not, however, be exaggerated, for they remain as yet a minority rather than majority interest. The following discussion will permit a more accurate appreciation of this particular phenomenon.

Notes

1   Taken to extremes, of course, this hardening becomes a feature of fundamentalism, or, to be more precise, of fundamentalisms. See chapter 10 for a fuller discussion of this point.

2   Ecclesiastical maps are more inclusive than electoral ones, the more so given the increasingly sharp regional differences in the political divisions of the 1980s.

3   A point well recognized in the sociology of Giddens who frequently relates the themes of globalization to the intimacies of personal life, demonstrating – among other things – the essential interconnectedness of social phenomena.

4   An interesting example in this respect is the use of the term 'mission statement', now common parlance in business administration. A second illustration can be found in the human potential movement and

its adoption by those responsible for management training (Heelas 1991 and 1992).
5   Each of these areas poses, moreover, the related question of who, precisely, is providing the necessary finance. A second point follows from this. Will the New Age continue to thrive as the relatively prosperous late 1980s give way to a much more diffident decade? Or will the recession return the British to a rather more materialistic outlook on life, unable to afford the spiritual extras that characterize some, if not all, aspects of the New Age.
6   A point also noted by American authors, despite the very different patterns of religiosity in the United States (Hammond 1985).

4 Religious Constituencies

A Statistical Overview

Sociologists are always suspicious of statistics, often with good reason. They are even more suspicious of religious statistics, which are, undoubtedly, among the most difficult sources of social data to handle.[1] Take, for example, the question of church membership, which is the focus of this chapter and is often considered a relatively unambiguous, if rather limited, measurement of religiosity. But church membership means different things for different people; the range is considerable even within the Christian churches. Membership should, moreover, be distinguished from attendance. Sometimes the two coincide, but not necessarily (Brierley 1991a: 56–7). Nor are comparisons over time as straightforward as they first appear – even within denominations – in that churches may, for a variety of reasons, become more or less enthusiastic about emphasizing the number of members that they have. A decision in the mid 1980s to assess financial contributions at least in part on the basis of numbers, for instance, wonderfully concentrated the minds of Anglicans with respect to their electoral roll figures.

Bearing these, and other, pitfalls in mind, we can, nonetheless, begin to mark up the principal features of church membership in Britain in the post-war period. Much of the material that follows is taken from figures published by Marc Europe,[2] notably the latest editions of the *UK Christian Handbook* (Brierley with Longley 1988, Brierley and Longley 1991, Brierley and Hiscock 1993) and the variety of church censuses produced by this organization through the 1980s and 1990s (see Guide to Further Reading). This material, though by no means perfect as a tool of analysis, has the considerable advantage of consistency over time. Used

Table 4.1   Church summary

Church members

	1975	1980	1985	1990	1992
Anglican	2,297,571	2,180,108	2,016,593	1,870,429	1,808,174
Baptist[a]	236,212	240,211	243,736	232,118	230,772
Roman Catholic	2,518,955	2,337,853	2,204,165	2,167,994	2,044,911
Independent[a]	252,172	252,991	308,258	342,319	356,921
Methodist[a]	596,406	540,348	500,702	475,440	458,773
Orthodox	196,850	203,140	223,686	265,918	275,805
Other churches[a]	155,835	138,948	127,632	129,823	130,703
Pentecostal[a]	104,648	126,743	138,316	158,695	169,782
Presbyterian	1,641,520	1,505,290	1,384,997	1,288,505	1,242,406
TOTAL	8,000,169	7,525,632	7,148,085	6,931,241	6,718,247
of which					
Free churches	1,345,273	1,299,241	1,318,644	1,338,395	1,346,951
Percentage total is of adult population	18.5	16.8	15.6	14.9	14.4

[a] The five components of the free churches

Ministers

	1975	1980	1985	1990	1992 Total	1992 Female
Anglican	15,911	14,654	14,064	14,137	13,920	820
Baptist[a]	2,418	2,469	2,648	2,803	2,936	85
Roman Catholic	8,892	8,854	8,408	7,980	7,798	0
Independent[a]	1,575	1,483	2,022	2,786	2,903	67
Methodist[a]	2,726	2,632	2,617	2,668	2.657	246
Orthodox	126	160	187	241	249	0
Other churches[a]	1,884	1,850	1,922	2,324	2,321	1,054
Pentecostal[a]	1,605	2,243	2,580	3,359	3,462	532
Presbyterian	3,776	3,632	3,412	3,159	3,060	324
TOTAL	38,913	37,977	37,860	39,457	39,306	3,120[b]
of which						
Free churches	10,208	10,677	11,789	13,940	14,279	1,984[c]

[a] The five components of the free churches
[b] 8.0% of the total
[c] 13.9% of the total

Table 4.1 (Continued)

Churches/congregations

	Number of denominations 1992	1975	1980	1985	1990	1992
Anglican	7	19,783	19,366	18,892	18,340	18,236
Baptist[a]	9	3,619	3,344	3,375	3,627	3,614
Roman Catholic	15	4,104	4,132	4,222	4,297	4,290
Independent[a]	27	4,536	4,611	5,331	5,932	5,898
Methodist[a]	6	9,066	8,492	7,954	7,591	7,401
Orthodox	19	135	150	179	207	218
Other churches[a]	43	1,992	2,004	1,988	2,064	2,148
Pentecostal[a]	69	1,655	1,935	2,041	2,143	2,215
Presbyterian	13	6,177	5,897	5,650	5,489	5,450
TOTAL	208	51,067	49,931	49,632	49,690	49,470
of which						
Free churches	154	20,868	20,386	20,689	21,357	21,276

[a] The five components of the free churches
Source: Tables adapted from Brierley and Hiscock 1993: 246

critically it provides a useful framework within which to work. For the earlier post-war decades, the Marc Europe statistics have been supplemented with data selected from Currie, Gilbert and Horsley, *Churches and Churchgoers* (1977), from which a useful longer-term perspective can also be gleaned.

To start with a contemporary snapshot, only 14.4 per cent of the population in these supposedly Christian islands now claims membership (in an active sense) of a Christian church, though the national variations masked by this overall percentage are considerable (table 4.1 and figure 4.1). Church membership in Northern Ireland, for example, is more than six times as high as it is in England. In Scotland and Wales, the differences are less dramatic but they continue to mark the greater religiosity of the Celtic lands as a whole, a distinction reinforced by variations in denominational allegiance. Within the overall percentages, however, it is worth noting two things about the relative strength of the various Christian groups in contemporary Britain: firstly that Roman Catholics have for some time outnumbered the active Anglicans (in 1991 these two groups accounted for 56 per cent of active church members); secondly that the

Table 4.2   Community size: total religious community in millions

	1975	1980	1985	1990	1992	1995[a]
Anglicans[b]	27.2[c]	27.1[c]	27.0	26.9	26.8	26.7
Baptist[e]	0.6	0.6	0.6	0.6	0.6	0.6
Roman Catholic[b]	5.5[c]	5.5[c]	5.6[c]	5.6[c]	5.6	5.6
Independent[e]	0.5	0.5	0.6	0.8	0.7	0.7
Methodist	1.6	1.5	1.3	1.3	1.3	1.3
Orthodox	0.4	0.4	0.4	0.5	0.5	0.5
Other churches[e]	0.3	0.3	0.3	0.3	0.3	0.3
Pentecostal[e]	0.2	0.3	0.3	0.3	0.3	0.4
Presbyterian	1.9	1.7	1.7	1.6	1.5	1.5
TOTAL Trinitarian churches	38.2	37.9	37.8	37.9	37.6	37.6
Church of Scientology	0.1[c]	0.2[c]	0.3[c]	0.3[c]	0.3	0.4
Other non-Trinitarian churches[e]	0.5[c]	0.5[c]	0.5[c]	0.6[c]	0.6	0.6
Hindus	0.3[c]	0.4[c]	0.4[c]	0.4	0.4	0.4
Jews	0.4	0.3[c]	0.3	0.3	0.3	0.3
Muslims	0.4[c]	0.6[c]	0.9[d]	1.0[c]	1.1	1.1
Sikhs[e]	0.2	0.3[c]	0.3[c]	0.5	0.5	0.6
Other religions	0.1	0.2	0.3	0.3	0.3	0.3
TOTAL non-Trinitarian and other religions	2.0	2.5	3.0	3.4	3.5	3.7
TOTAL all religions	40.2	40.4	40.8	41.3	41.1	41.3
Percentage of population:						
Trinitarian churches	68%[c]	67%[c]	67%[c]	66%	65%	64%
Non-Trinitarian churches and other religions	4%	5%	5%	6%	6%	7%
Total all religions	72%[c]	72%[c]	72%[c]	72%[c]	71%	71%

[a] Estimate
[b] Baptized membership
[c] Revised figure
[d] 852.900 more exactly
[e] Taken as approximately double membership
Source: Table adapted from Brierley and Hiscock 1993: 282

'other Protestants' category (that is, the free churches together with the Presbyterians) have membership figures higher than either the Roman Catholics or the Anglicans. It is, on the other hand, equally important to grasp the very different picture that emerges from the table for community size (table 4.2) rather than that for active membership, for it is at this

Table 4.3   Rates of change 1975–1995

	Percentage rate of change per annum of members		Percentage rate of change per annum of ministers		Percentage rate of change per annum of churches	
	1975–85	1985–95	1975–85	1985–95	1975–85	1985–95
Anglican	−2.6	−3.1	−2.4	−1.3	−0.9	−0.8
Baptist[a]	+0.6	−0.9	+1.8	+2.4	−1.4	+1.8
Roman Catholic	−2.6	−2.4	−1.1	−1.9	+0.6	+0.5
Independent[a]	+4.1	+3.0	+5.1	+7.6	+3.3	+2.3
Methodist[a]	−3.4	−2.6	−0.8	0.0	−2.6	−2.0
Orthodox	+2.6	+5.1	+8.2	+7.8	+5.8	+5.3
Other churches[a]	−3.9	+0.6	+0.4	+4.3	0.0	+2.0
Pentecostal[a]	+5.7	+5.9	+10.0	+7.9	+4.3	+2.8
Presbyterian	−3.3	−2.9	−2.0	−3.1	−1.8	−1.2
TOTAL of which	−2.2	−1.9	−0.5	+0.4	−0.6	−0.1
Free churches	−0.4	+0.4	+2.9	+4.5	−0.2	+0.7

[a] The five components of the free churches
Source: Table adapted from Brierley and Hiscock 1993: 251

point that the latent power of the Church of England begins to show. Nominal allegiance, moreover, is by no means the same as no allegiance at all.[3] These categories have quite different implications, not only for the sociologist but also for those responsible for pastoral care. And in Britain, nominal allegiance is by far the most prevalent form of religious attachment; no allegiance is moderately rare, though less so than in many countries of Europe (figure 4.2).[4] The description of the Church of England as the church from which the English choose to stay away still – though for how much longer is difficult to say – catches the religious mood of a significant proportion of the population.

Looking at trends over time, it is undeniable that the membership of the principal Christian denominations in this country is declining (table 4.3). The rate of this decline is, however, uneven and some denominations have managed – temporarily at least – to arrest this trend altogether. In addition, some of the fall in membership has been offset by the rapid growth in the independent churches[5] and among pentecostals, and by a steady increase in the Orthodox population. These fast-growing

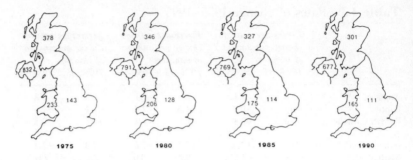

Figure 4.1   National variations in church membership, 1975–90. The figures show total church members per 1,000 of the adult population (reproduced from Brierley and Hiscock 1993: 251)

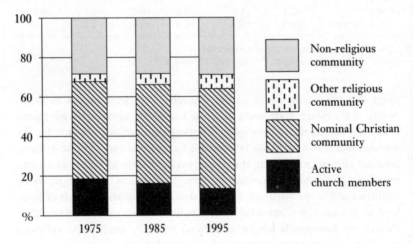

Figure 4.2   Religious components of the population (adapted from Brierley and Hiscock 1993: 282)

congregations are, however, small; in consequence any changes in their numbers – though noticeable (sometimes extremely so) in terms of pro-portional increase – make little impression on the membership statistics of the Christian churches taken as a whole. Up to a point the same could be said of the non-Christian presence in Britain (table 4.2): the proportional growth is considerable but the overall figures remain relatively small. There is, however, significant diversity within this category which needs constant recognition, for not all of the groups in question have expanded in the post-war period. The Jewish community, for example, used to be larger than it is. For this, as well as for other reasons, it is important that each non-Christian minority is looked at separately, for here, as much as with the Christian groups, merged categories mask individual differences. Bearing this in mind, a *limited* pluralism is probably the best way to describe the religious life of Britain, though underlining the geographical concentrations of particular minorities, the significance of which will be discussed further in later chapters.

In the meantime, it is necessary to flesh out the bare bones of these statistics with a brief portrait of each of the major religious groups in this country in the post-war period: that is, the Anglicans, the Roman Catho-lics, the Orthodox, the free churches (including Black African churches and house churches), other-faith communities and new religious move-ments. The portraits will in fact be little more than outline sketches, which can be filled in with reference to a wide variety of complementary sources (see Guide to Further Reading). Here, they should be read as much in terms of their commonalities as their differences; in other words with a particular eye to the cross-cutting themes which will be drawn together in a short conclusion. An important area of debate emerges from this discussion: are the principal lines of demarcation between different Christian persuasions in this country beginning to lie across rather than between the various denominations? This question will recur more than once in the following chapters, not least in the sections which relate to post-war ecumenical development.

The Anglicans

The term 'Anglican' includes not only the main state Church of England but the Church in Wales, the Episcopal Church of Scotland and the Church of Ireland. Technically speaking the tiny Free Church of England, the Protestant Episcopal Reformed Church of England and one or two other similar bodies should also be mentioned if only in passing. Within these bodies, the Church of England accounts for more than 80 per cent of the Anglican membership. The following section will look primarily at this Church; the non-English Anglican communities in the United Kingdom will be covered in chapter 6.

Statistically there can be little doubt about the trends; they go downward. Whichever indicator is selected – electoral roll figures, communicant numbers, baptisms per live births, the proportion of marriages taking place in church, confirmations or ordinations – a similar picture emerges; though care is needed if the figures are to be properly interpreted, for the decline occurs at varying rates with respect to both time and place. The detailed profiles that emerge from this kind of analysis, moreover, *do* depend upon the indicators selected, for they measure rather different things. Figures for infant baptism, for example, an indicator which gives at least some measurement of Anglican penetration into society at large, reveal a pretty constant downward curve from 1950 on. More precisely, baptisms per thousand births were 672 in 1950 (up a little since 1940), 554 in 1960 and 466 (that is, under 50 per cent for the first time) in 1970. By the early 1980s they were well under 40 per cent; and in 1990, they had fallen to 27.5 per cent. Anglican confirmations of young people, in contrast, demonstrate a rather different pattern. They rose fairly steadily until 1960 (251 per thousand in 1940, 279 in 1950, 315 in 1960), but fell sharply thereafter. Between 1960 and 1982 the actual number of confirmations taking place each year fell from 191,000 to 84,500, a fall of more than 50 per cent. A rather similar shape of post-war rise and subsequent decline can be found for the number of ordinations. Up to a point, the latter can be measured with reference to the provision of theological college places: in 1961, for example, there were 26 Anglican colleges able to accommodate 1,663 people; by 1977, the number had fallen to 15 with 769 places and is still falling. But an immediate caveat is necessary in this respect, for increasing numbers of Church of England clergy are now prepared for ministry (both full and part time) by means of ministerial training courses, themselves indications of changing – not necessarily declining – patterns of ministry. And with regard to the colleges themselves, overall figures mask the fact that some of these (the evangelical ones) are bursting at the seams while others have considerable difficulty finding recruits.

Nothing is ever very straightforward with regard to such data. Nonetheless the contrast between the following two statements – selected once again from Hastings and borne out by the longer-term figures in Currie, Gilbert and Horsley – is devastating in its starkness. The first sets the religious practice of England in the immediate post-war period into a broader context:

> It should, first of all, be repeated that – all in all – there had been no very sharp statistical alteration in the religious practice of England between 1890 and 1960: Free Church figures fell fairly considerably, Roman Catholic figures rose, the Anglican decline was pretty steady but seldom appeared calamitous. (Hastings 1986: 551)

Post-1960, the Anglican decline could hardly be described as anything else. 'It is not exaggerated to conclude that between 1960 and 1985 the Church of England as a going concern was effectively reduced to not much more than half its previous size' (1986: 603). The situation in the Roman Catholic community and most of the free churches will be dealt with later, for they present rather different issues, but for a supposedly national church, the Anglican figures were – and still are – a pretty catastrophic situation to come to terms with. More recently the situation has stabilized at least to some extent. Brierley's analysis for the 1980s (Brierley and Longley 1991, Brierley 1991a) reveals a certain – though far from total – steadying in the statistics, increasingly so as the decade wore on. But most of all, the data indicate the need for considerable sensitivity in interpreting what is going on, for religious activity is not the only sign of Anglican significance. Some statistical trends, moreover, are the result of church policy rather than, or at least in addition to, changes in societal practice.

The question of infant baptism illustrates this point nicely. In many ways this is a crucial indicator of Anglican penetration, for it permits some measurement – if not always an entirely accurate one – of the value placed by the population at large on a ceremony associated with Christian initiation. To be baptized in the Church of England provides at least one criterion used in the self-ascription of membership. On the other hand, the Church itself is thoroughly inconsistent in its application of this particular rite. Such inconsistency, moreover, varies locally depending on the policies of individual clergy and their parochial church councils; infant baptism can be encouraged and discouraged in neighbouring parishes. Paradoxically, it tends to be the large, flourishing eclectic (often evangelical) parishes which restrict baptism to the children of active churchgoers rather than the parishioners in the strict sense of the term. Precisely those congregations which undoubtedly produce disproportionate amounts of money and manpower for the Church may – at one and the same time – depress the figures for infant baptism in that particular area.

This is not the only example of diversity in Anglican practice. The following extract is taken from a bishop's letter in a diocesan news-sheet in 1992. It describes – from the point of view of a visiting bishop – the liturgical unpredictability characteristic of much of contemporary Anglicanism. It is, quite clearly, no longer possible to enter a parish church almost anywhere in England at 11.00 a.m. or 6.30 p.m. and know – fairly precisely – what is going to happen next.[6]

> We come across every rite authorised for use in the Church of England, and occasionally liturgies which seem to have been borrowed from other sources or simply originated in the mind of the incumbent; we move from places wreathed in incense to those in which the unwary production of a stole causes a sharp intake of breath; we lead services in which the congregational response barely amounts to a background murmur, and those in which there are so many participants it is difficult to find something to do; we change musical key from decorous Anglican chant to deafening enthusiastic chorus; we bellow to a handful of 20 scattered throughout a mini-cathedral, and we whisper through technological devices concealed in our garments to sardine-packed hundreds; we find ourselves in totally impracticable medieval buildings of great beauty, and in modern liturgically-efficient warehouses; we sing from more hymn books and hear the Bible read from more translations than Wesley or Wycliffe ever dreamed of; at the Peace we may give the congregation the most imperceptible half-smile before moving swiftly to the safety of the sanctuary, or we may be expected to greet every member of the congregation like a long-lost relative.

No wonder there is a need for a publication entitled *The Good Church Guide* which uses Michelin-type symbols to convey for the benefit of outsiders, even bishops, what might be termed the 'house style' of individual churches.

The diocesan news-sheet quotation also reveals the unevenness of Anglican attendance. The overall trends may be downwards but certain parishes are undoubtedly flourishing; notably – in terms of numbers (and there are plenty of alternative criteria) – the eclectic parishes of suburbia, which gather the like-minded, usually middle-class evangelicals, from a moderately large and well-populated geographical area. The increasing strength of the evangelical group within the Church of England can be seen in a variety of ways.[7] It is all the more important in that it is part of a wider trend and not only in this country; it reflects changes towards a greater conservatism in religiosity that can be seen on a global scale and go well beyond Christianity. Within the Church of England, however, a second and rather different section is also beginning to flourish. In the late 1980s and 1990s the cathedrals – not so long ago considered the dinosaurs of the established Church – are attracting increasing numbers both of visitors and worshippers. Explanations for this increase in cathedral popularity vary, but a number of them reflect the growing sense of the sacred already referred to. The cathedral provides a focus for tourism (not so very far, sometimes, from pilgrimage), for liturgy, for music and for architecture, which inevitably relates to – indeed in many cases encapsulates – the sacred space or place. It is hardly surprising that the proper management of its cathedrals has become in the early 1990s an urgent priority for the Church of England, for the pressures on both buildings and staff are considerable.[8]

These are the exceptions, which may or may not be signs of a different future. But the dominant impression of Anglicanism remains a rather depressing, though regionally varied, statistical profile, alongside an increasing fragmentation in liturgy and worship. Are there, in contrast, compensating factors which retain, despite everything, the wholeness of the Church of England including its historic relationship to the state? The parochial structure is, surely, crucial in this respect, in that it continues to give the Church of England a unique foothold in English society; providing manpower as well as plant in every part of the country, North as well as South, urban or rural, thriving or striving. There are, it must be said, places where the network is stretched to the limit. This is mostly the case, paradoxically, where churchgoing remains proportionately strong; that is, in rural areas where population is sparse and villages are grouped, increasingly, though not always very sensitively, under one incumbent. Nonetheless the obligations of the parochial structure have held the Church of England, both geographically and socially, in every section of English society (not least in the inner cities), which is more than can be said for many other social institutions. A second, and related, point is also important. The provision of tied housing – though problematic in some places – has enabled a degree of occupational mobility among clergy, long since lost by anyone dependent on the housing market.

There is, finally, the question of establishment itself, which cannot be ignored in even the shortest discussion of membership in the Church of England. There can be little doubt that the nature of establishment has altered considerably in the post-war period, but the essential link between church and state remains intact. It is, however, a connection very much less taken for granted in the 1990s than it was in the immediate post-war period and one reason for questioning its continued viability undoubtedly lies in the marked decline in active Anglican membership (now a little under 2 million). But an equally plausible reason for maintaining the constitutional connection can be found in the relatively large latent membership of the state Church (estimated by Brierley at 25.5 million in 1990). And both elements (that is, latent as well as active) should be taken into account in an adequate assessment of the contemporary Church of England. The Anglican penumbra remains a large one; it is, I would argue, the distinguishing feature of the Church of England compared with other Christian denominations in this country. Latent or nominal Anglicanism persists as the most common form of English religiosity. Common or folk religion normally takes Anglican forms and the occasional offices of the state Church continue to play an important part in the lives of individuals and communities. And if baptism is to a considerable extent declining in popularity, it is still relatively rare for an English person to die without some form of religious ceremony. At the end of their lives if not before, the Church of England will take responsibility for those who are not looked after by anyone else, a demanding, difficult and time-consuming ministry. 'Contracting in' may well be edging into the organization of baptisms; the same phenomenon has not occurred up to now in the administration of funerals.[9]

The Roman Catholics

Sociologically we know more about the Roman Catholics in Britain (or at least in parts of Britain) than we do about almost any other religious denomination. This is largely due to the work of Hornsby-Smith who has established an impressive body of empirical evidence concerning, in particular, the Roman Catholics in England and Wales. This material can be found in a growing series of publications listed in the References, which should be consulted for a detailed picture of this particular constituency. The data reproduced here are selective.

The essence of Hornsby-Smith's thesis concerning post-war Catholicism in England and Wales is contained in the following extract:

> In sum, the evidence reviewed in this book points clearly to the conclusion that the transformations which have taken place in English Catholicism over the past three to four decades can best be interpreted as a process of dissolution of the boundaries which once defended a distinctive Catholic sub-culture from contamination in a basically secular society. It is too simplistic to regard such a process as one of decline. Rather it indicates that far-reaching changes have taken place in the relationships between the Church and British society since the Second World War. These have necessarily entailed radical changes in the nature of Catholic identity in England and Wales today. (Hornsby-Smith 1987: 214)

In that it looks primarily at the relationship between the Catholic community and the wider society, and attempts to assess the impact of changes in each of these upon the other, the thesis fits well within the structure of this book. A similar study could, of course, be conducted for the Catholics in Scotland and in Northern Ireland. In some respects the results would be similar; in others the context would determine very different outcomes indeed. Some of these outcomes will be covered in chapter 6.

Hornsby-Smith's data was obtained from a series of enquiries which took place in the middle and late 1970s and the early 1980s. The 'social portrait' that he offers dates, then, from the third post-war decade. It is important to remember, however, that statistics accumulated by Hastings (1986: 602–5) and elsewhere indicate that the peak for Roman Catholic activity occurred in the 1960s; in the next ten to fifteen years, the figures start to turn downwards. Mass attendance, for example, for the estimated Catholic population fell from 49 per cent in 1968 to 32 per cent in 1978. Brierley's figures (Brierley with Longley 1988) indicate a similar drop but rather differently dated (47 per cent in 1970 to 34 per cent in 1986). Subsequent *UK Handbooks* (Brierley and Longley 1991, Brierley and

Hiscock 1993) point to a continuing decline in Mass practice through the 1980s, though this is unevenly spread through the United Kingdom. Such changes should be borne in mind in assessing the detailed data presented by Hornsby-Smith. The following figures are nonetheless striking. They suggest that around 11 per cent of the adult population of England and Wales is Roman Catholic. As a community, Catholics tend to be relatively young and working class; tendencies which are also reflected in the lower home-ownership levels and higher than average Labour voting. Of the Catholics sampled, 25 per cent were first-generation immigrants, six times the proportion of the rest of the population. Around 40 per cent of the sample attended church weekly compared to 8 per cent of non-Catholics. Among the attenders there were more women than men and the age factor was also significant. Social class differences were discernible, with professional and managerial Catholics attending church more often than manual workers. In the post-war period, there has been considerable geographic and social mobility, persistent migration away from the North and West towards the South and East; away, that is, from the old, traditional, working-class and largely Irish parishes into the new suburban estates of all the major conurbations.

The portrait indicates that in many respects Catholics continue to display the characteristics expected of a largely immigrant group. Not least they retain norms of churchgoing which distinguish them sharply from the rest of the population. So, too, do the sizes of their congregations; far larger than any other denomination. The emphasis in Hornsby-Smith's work, however, lies elsewhere. His purpose is to examine – with the aid of carefully collected empirical data – the extent to which Catholics 'can continue to be regarded as a distinctive sub-culture with a vital community life and identifiable religious belief and moral value-systems' (1987: 46). Hence the emphasis on the increasing heterogeneity of English Roman Catholics rather than the common characteristics of the community. What emerges from the data is considerable internal diversity; a diversity discernible with respect to origins, beliefs and practice and increasingly noticeable with each post-war decade that passes. This evolution in post-war Catholicism has been dominated by two interacting factors: first, the shifts in the English Catholic community occurring through increasing contact with the surrounding – and rapidly changing – society and, second, the internal metamorphosis within the Roman Catholic Church brought about by the Second Vatican Council. The overwhelming importance of the Vatican Council in the post-war period has already been underlined. It is hardly surprising that the outworking of its deliberations has dominated the Catholic agenda in this country in the second half of the post-war period. More than that, it has altered the framework in which the relationships between all the British churches take place. Two very contrasting incidents, among others, illustrate the changing climate of opinion in post-war Britain in this respect. The first was an enormously public event attracting exceptional media attention; the second was perceptible chiefly to ecclesiastical *aficionados* but nonetheless significant for all that.

In 1982 the Pope visited Britain for the first time in history, an event which caught the attention of most British people, Catholic and non-Catholic alike. Britain, on the other hand, was by no means the first innovatory destination for the Polish Pope. By this stage in his career, John Paul II had already travelled widely, attracting plane-loads of the world's media wherever he went. The reaction to his visit to Britain was coloured by such attention. Although the visit was in many respects highly significant – particularly the visits to Anglican as well as Catholic sacred places – it was difficult to persuade young people that there was anything all that unusual about what was going on. They had experienced papal travels on television, perceiving them as the norm rather than the exception. If the Pope went everywhere else, why should he not visit Britain? Television images outweighed several centuries of Protestant history. Reservations do, nonetheless, remain when it comes to any mention of papal authority in this country. The response to such a suggestion (or supposed suggestion) was unexpectedly vehement after a rather loosely worded press release was taken up in the tabloid press in the autumn of 1989, when Dr Runcie, as Archbishop of Canterbury, visited Rome.[10] For old habits, it seems, die hard. The situation can, perhaps, be summarized as follows. There can be little doubt that the Catholic community is now a valued and permanent feature of British society and no one has any desire to reverse this process of acceptance. But the old animosities remain, and are discovered at times surprisingly close to the surface. They have, moreover, a curious resonance with respect to the issue of Europe, a point to which we shall return.

But more immediately, 1990 saw the inauguration of a new ecumenical body, or series of bodies, in this country, a much less publicized event than the papal visit. Nonetheless the attitude of the Roman Catholic community to these revised 'ecumenical instruments'[11] provides the second example of a shift in the climate of inter-church relationships in the post-war period. Its significance lies in the explicit Roman Catholic *commitment* to these bodies, a word Catholics use considerably less lightly than some (*The Tablet*, 1 September 1990) and an attitude always withheld from the British Council of Churches, in which the Catholic Church took no formal part. There has, quite clearly, been a very significant evolution in Roman Catholic opinion in recent decades, a change that has enabled previously impossible, if not always very steady, ecumenical advances.

The Orthodox

Small but growing is probably the best way to describe the Orthodox community in Britain. It is, in addition, very largely an English phenomenon with only minimal representation in the other United Kingdom countries. The majority within the British Orthodox community have, up to now, come from the Greek tradition (mostly Greek Cypriots), but the dramatic events in East Europe in 1989 may well alter the religious map of West Europe in this respect. Increasing numbers are likely to arrive in the West – including Britain – from a variety of Orthodox traditions, a trend that cannot but enrich the religious life of this country.

The Free Churches

In many ways, the free churches are the most difficult category to deal with in this kind of overview, for the conclusions that emerge about such churches depend very largely on exactly which denominations are included and which are not. For the category 'free churches' encompasses, on some readings at least, groups which are struggling quite badly but also those which are growing exceptionally fast. To make matters more difficult, those which are flourishing are doing so for different reasons: the Afro-Caribbean churches serve a particular immigrant community; the independent or house churches attract a very different section of the population. Indeed a crucial question lies beneath the popularity of the latter, for it is necessary to ask what kinds of people are attracted to these fast-growing congregations and why. Are they, in other words, picking up the disaffected members of the declining churches, and, if so, which ones in particular? Or are they making inroads into sections of the population previously unconnected with any church? Whatever the case, the house churches have undoubtedly emerged as a significant part of contemporary British religion, deserving of serious consideration.

First, though, Old Dissent and the Methodists, remembering that the latter should, strictly speaking, be distinguished from the earlier Nonconformist traditions in this country. For the Methodists are, in many ways, a unique denomination within Protestantism, a situation that becomes all the more significant with reference to Europe. Whereas the Presbyterians (the United Reformed Church) or the Baptists can make very obvious connections with the European mainland, the Methodists cannot. Their tradition – derivative of Anglicanism – looks in a different direction.[12] Methodism shares, nonetheless, in the indisputable decline in membership that has afflicted the major Nonconformist churches in this country in the greater part of the twentieth century; a decline that has accelerated in the post-war period.

> The main Free Churches in England and Wales – Methodists, Congregationalists, Baptists and Presbyterians – reached their maximum membership in the years just before the First World War: the actual year is different for each denomination. Between 1914 and 1970 their total membership dropped by one third. . . . This decline has been much sharper since the Second World War than it was before it: in the period between 1914 and 1939 the average decline in England and Wales was 6 per cent (in England alone it was slightly higher), but between 1939 and 1970 the average decline in England and Wales was 30 per cent (in England alone it was slightly less). (Thompson 1989: 100, quoting figures from Currie, Gilbert and Horsley 1977)

Post-1970, Brierley's figures (see table 4.3) indicate that this decline for the most part continues, though rather more so for some denominations than others. To be more precise, the Baptists – the partial exception – have through most of the 1980s arrested this trend. The Methodists and Presbyterians have been unable to follow suit, though it is important to remember the regional variations in these denominations. Quite apart from the presence of Presbyterianism in Scotland (see chapter 6), Methodism retains even at the end of the twentieth century a surprising degree of influence in some localities. In parts of the Southwest, for example, it was still possible in the mid 1980s to find a statistical correlation between the presence of Methodism and the Liberal vote.[13]

In many ways it is not surprising that the Baptists provide the exception in terms of statistical trends, for they form something of a bridge between Old Dissent and newer forms of church life, notably those groups which have become known as house churches. For the Baptists are, to a certain extent at least, similar in outlook to the kind of congregation included within this rather problematic category. Indeed Walker (1985) has misgivings about using the term 'house church' at all. He looks instead at the common features of 'restorationism' within the house church movement. Restorationism rejects the idea of another denomination. Rather it aims to return church life of whatever kind to the New Testament pattern; that is, to restore a charismatically ordained church, 'one in which Christians are seen as living in a kingdom run according to God's order and rules' (1985: 22–3). Following Walker, the movement encompasses two strands: firstly, a relatively organized movement which has, despite everything, taken denominational form and, secondly, a rather more extended and amorphous collection of independent churches sharing similar doctrines and lifestyles but having little organizational unity. But however categorized, and however distinguished from older models of evangelicalism and pentecostalism (and the boundaries are not easy to define), it is the house churches which demonstrate the most striking growth among British churches in the last two decades. Brierley and Hiscock's figures indicate that the membership of 'independent churches' (within which the house churches form the largest section) grew in the 1980s by nearly 40 per cent, from 250,000 to 350,000 plus.

One or two further remarks are, however, important. First, that the impressive percentage increases operate from a relatively small base; the overall numbers are not, in consequence, all that large. Nor is it possible to say very much about the future. Persistently high levels of growth may or may not be sustained as the house churches move into their second generation, a crucial stage in the development of denominational life. A final point follows from this and reflects the character of free churches more generally. They (including the house churches) are, essentially, gathered churches around which the penumbra is by definition limited. There are, of course, partial exceptions to this rule in those parts of the country where one or another form of Dissent has become, almost, the 'established' church. But for the most part, gathered congregations rely on the active commitment of their members for their very existence. This is one reason why the older Nonconformist denominations have not survived in the inner city. Quite simply, the populations that sustained them are no longer present in that part of society and there is no compensating structure through which to maintain a presence. The same phenomenon may be true of some house churches in the not too distant future.

In a number of cities, or, more precisely, in particular parts of particular cities, the place of the traditional free churches has been taken by the Afro-Caribbean churches; that is, black-led churches catering on the one hand for African, often Nigerian, populations in this country, and on the other for the West Indian immigrants. (Different histories account for the distinct character not only of each of these populations, but of their churches as well.) Both groups, however, came into existence for essentially negative reasons. There were exceptions, but for the most part the black population – whatever its provenance – was not made welcome by the mainline denominations of this country, a situation regrettable from many points of view. Out of this rejection were born the Afro-Caribbean congregations, which have become – in more ways than one – the free churches of urban Britain in the last quarter of the twentieth century. Membership in 1990 was almost 70,000, grouped into 965 congregations, which have in difficult circumstances become an important hub of effective community life. They represent an impressive undertaking.

Other-faith Communities

Knott (1988a) provides an excellent introduction to the other-faith traditions of contemporary Britain, including a detailed bibliography for each group. She offers, in addition, a valuable framework in which to evaluate the religious situation in post-war Britain from this point of view. This framework relates not only to the past experience of Britain, where intra-pluralism (pluralism within Christianity) preceded inter-pluralism (pluralism between faiths), but also to a changing international situation, the phenomenon which has become known as globalization. The *existence* of religious pluralism, for example, is by no means an unusual phenomenon in an increasingly interconnected and mobile world. It is probably the norm rather than the exception. The *nature* of religious pluralism, however, varies markedly from country to country; a fact already stressed in relation to religious variations in Western Europe. Within the British situation, moreover, each religious group or community is likely to develop in a different way, bearing in mind the diversity of origins and the particularities – ethnic, religious, social and economic – both of the groups in question and of the host community. Broad generalizations are unlikely to be helpful; indeed they almost always do more harm than good.

In this connection it is interesting to note that the Jews – unlike most other religious minorities in this country – have experienced relatively little in-migration since the war (Waterman and Kosmin 1986). And in this respect, the British situation differs very markedly from the French, where Jews from North Africa have in the post-war period almost doubled the size of the French community taken as a whole. In Britain, the Jewish population peaked in the 1950s at just over 400,000. Subsequently it declined – for a variety of reasons (among them migration to Israel, assimilation, marriage outside the community and reduced family size) – to around 330,000. It is an ageing population concentrated in particular cities, notably London, Manchester, Leeds and Glasgow. It remains, nonetheless, the fifth largest Jewish community in the world, after the United States, Israel, the former Soviet Union and France (Lerman 1989). Its significance should not be underestimated.

The Muslims form the largest non-Christian minority in this country. Exact figures are difficult to estimate, but in 1990 Brierley suggested a figure of 1.1 million for the Islamic community (less for the actively religious population). British Muslims come from a variety of countries but the largest group undoubtedly originates from the Indian subcontinent, notably Pakistan and Bangladesh. Pakistani Muslims tend to live in Bradford and the West Midlands, Bangladeshis in London's East End.[14] Considerable – perhaps belated – attention has been paid to the British Muslims in response to recent events: the Salman Rushdie controversy and the episode which became known as the Gulf War. Regarding the former, the sequence of events in the spring of 1989 has been recorded in *The Rushdie File* (Appignanesi and Maitland 1989) which also gathers together a useful range of contemporary press comment. More disturbing, however, were the subsequent analyses of Modood, which probe beneath the events of the affair itself to pose the following hard-hitting, indeed almost shocking, statement:

'the Rushdie affair' is not about the life of Salman Rushdie nor freedom of expression, let alone Islamic fundamentalism or book-burning or Iranian interference in British affairs. The issue is of the rights of non-European religious and cultural minorities in the context of a secular hegemony. Is the Enlightenment big enough to legitimise the existence of pre-Enlightenment religious enthusiasm or can it only exist by suffocating all who fail to be overawed by its intellectual brilliance and vision of man? (Modood 1990: 160)

Leaman (1989) puts the same point in a different way: how do we accommodate 'that unusual phenomenon in our society, the person who takes religion seriously', and who is, in consequence, deeply offended by blasphemy? We shall come back to this point which lies at the heart of what it means to live in a pluralist society. It raises complex, difficult and controversial issues.

In the meantime, the evidence about the Pakistani and Bangladeshi minorities in this country is not all that easy to assess. Modood, for example, maintains that these are some of the most deprived communities in contemporary Britain, suffering high rates of unemployment, disadvantage in the educational system and a disproportionate number of attacks on both property and persons. The explosions of anger surrounding the publication of *The Satanic Verses* should, in consequence, be understood in terms of social and economic disadvantage as much as anything else. Other commentators (Pilkington 1984, Reid 1989) offer a more nuanced view, indicating – to give one illustration – that Asian children, particularly boys, have done moderately well in the British educational system. But Asian is not coterminous with Muslim, nor is the Muslim community necessarily homogeneous, a state of affairs reflected in outlooks as well as in background. Muslim attitudes towards specifically Muslim schools are, for example, divided, though the lack of such schools in British society must remain, surely, an anomaly when they are permitted (indeed encouraged) for Anglicans, for Roman Catholics and for Jews, a situation discussed further in chapter 7.

There are two other religious minorities with appreciable numbers in this country. Approximately 400,000 Hindus live in Greater London and the cities of the Midlands, and rather more Sikhs can be found principally in Southall and Gravesend (figures from Brierley and Longley 1991). Most of the Hindus and some Sikhs came to this country from East Africa; they are, therefore, a twice displaced community. And bearing in mind (following Knott 1988a) that migration is always a disruptive experience and that religion, like all other aspects of personal and social life, is changed by it, a very wide range of factors need to be taken into account in our understanding of the nature of immigrant communities. Each minority within this country deserves sensitive and careful attention, as much from sociologists of religion as from anyone else.

As a conclusion to this section, it is perhaps worth repeating a point made earlier. We do indeed live in a multicultural society, but not in one where the various minorities so far described are evenly spread throughout the population. There remain large tracts of Britain – even England – where ethnic or religious pluralism (in the most obvious understanding of the term) is virtually unknown. No wonder the politics of religion (and race) in this country turn to a considerable extent on social geography (Martin 1989: 333), for both within Christianity and between faiths, the regional variations within our not all that large country remain very marked indeed.

New Religious Movements

The Introduction to this book pointed out a persistent paradox in the sociological work done on British religiosity. There exists a marked imbalance in the material in this field, an imbalance which is even more striking bearing in mind the membership statistics discussed in this chapter, and – in anticipation – the wider patterns of belief discussed in the next. For we know, sociologically at least, considerably more about what have come to be known as new religious movements than we do about the religious beliefs and practices of most British people. There is, to put the same point in a rather more positive way, an important and growing body of sociological material on both sects and new religious movements carried out by some of the most distinguished scholars working in this field. The broad outline of this work is referred to in the Guide to Further

Reading, but much of what follows is drawn from Barker's *New Religious Movements: a practical introduction*, which – as the title suggests – provides in a readily accessible form a large amount of practical as well as sociological knowledge in this area. Equivalent studies relating to widespread but rather less visible patterns of religiosity are very much more difficult to come by.

Exactly how many people are involved in new religious movements is, of course, almost impossible to say. Following Barker (1989a: 145–55), some hundreds of thousands may have had passing contact with such movements in the past twenty-five years or so (a far from negligible figure); very few of these, however, will have developed any sustained commitment to the groups in question. A further problem arises with respect to definition: which groups should and which should not be included in this inevitably problematic category? At one edge lie the well-established sects (Jehovah's Witnesses, Mormons), difficult to distinguish, sociologically if not theologically, from the smaller Protestant denominations. At the other extreme what Heelas has termed 'self-religions' (or the human potential movement) exist in abundance, themselves difficult to distinguish from the New Age, at least in its 'psycho-spiritual' forms. In between can be found a huge variety of groups, distinct in many ways from the surrounding society, but also from each other. A useful glossary of these movements can be found in appendix IV of Barker (1989a).

What can a sociologist learn from this multifaceted phenomenon? Beckford (1985) develops two themes in this respect which are particularly relevant to this book. The first (1985: chapters 7 and 8) looks at new religious movements from a comparative perspective. More specifically Beckford compares the situation of new religious movements in Britain, in France and in what was West Germany. He demonstrates that 'the cult problem', if such it is, clearly varies with the social, political and cultural characteristics that prevail in each of these countries. He concludes:

> In order to understand the distinctive animus against certain NRMs it is essential to examine not only their individual structures and teachings but also each country's religious communities in the case of European societies. Thus, in the absence of an all-encompassing constitutional separation of Church and state the nexus of inter-religious relationships is more important in the FRG and France than, for example, in the USA. (p. 271)

In other words, new religious movements – like all religious phenomena – have to be seen in context. Debates concerning such movements will have different outcomes depending upon the particularities of the national situation in which the discussion occurs. In Britain, for example, the Charities Law is a key piece of legislation in this area; this will not be the case elsewhere.

The second point can be seen as a corollary of the first, for it suggests that new religious movements, though numerically of limited significance, can provide us with a moderately powerful lens through which to view the wider society (see also Barker 1982b). By looking at the way that society reacts to new religious movements and the controversies that they generate, we can discover more about that society itself. What, for example, is regarded as normal or abnormal; as acceptable or unacceptable in the name of religion; or, to use another word, as tolerable or intolerable. Similarly, a whole series of legal definitions concerning the rights or otherwise of individuals and/or religious groups follow from judgements in the courts concerning new religious movements. Controversies surrounding new religious movements become, therefore, 'the barometers of changes taking place in a number of different societies' (Beckford 1985: 11). And to pursue the analogy a little further, they may well offer signs of stormy weather ahead. Nowhere more so than in questions of religious toleration. For what we discover in practice is that the British are not altogether unfriendly towards religious diversity but some religions appear easier to accept than others (Barker's 'tolerant discrimination'). But is this what we mean by living in a pluralist society or should we be doing better? And what in this connection do we mean by 'better'? In this instance, the debate emerges from the literature on new religious movements. It has, however, considerably wider implications, not least those indicated by Modood and others in connection with the Salman Rushdie controversy. Some of these implications will be pursued further in the following section.

Conclusion: the Emergence of Cross-cutting Themes

The bare bones of this summary of church membership are easily conveyed. Relatively few British people either belong to a church or attend religious services with any regularity, and those among the indigenous population that do either of these things divide their attentions pretty evenly between the Anglican, Catholic and free church categories, with the latter, relatively speaking, gaining in popularity (assuming that the house churches and Afro-Caribbean groups are included). And given this state of affairs, it could be argued, surely, that the religiously active – of whatever Christian denomination – have more in common with each other than with the majority of the population. Indeed such a statement could, in some respects at least, be extended to include the members of other religions as well, in that they, like the actively Christian, take faith – of whatever kind – seriously.

But taking faith or religion seriously is becoming, increasingly, the exception rather than the norm in British society, a situation exemplified not only by the data reviewed here but by the genuine incomprehension at the heart of contemporary debates about religious pluralism. To start with the most obvious illustration, many – indeed most – British people had great difficulty in understanding the hurt of the Muslim community after the publication of *The Satanic Verses*. Their religious sensibilities were, quite simply, of a different order. Why was it necessary to prevent the publication of a book hostile to Islam? No one was obliged to read this against their will, so why not leave it at that? Part of being British, it seems, is to accept a low-key approach to religiosity, with the strong implication that those who come to live in these islands – for whatever reason – should conform, in public at least, to this or a very similar point of view. But does this essentially conditional statement provide an adequate basis for a truly tolerant and pluralist society? The unexpected vehemence of the Rushdie controversy would seem to indicate otherwise.

It is equally true, however, that the majority of the population are seldom hostile to religion *per se*, even if they are bewildered by its more extreme supporters. For most, if not all, of the British retain some sort of religious belief even if they do not see the need to attend their churches on a regular basis. The phenomenon of unattached belief will form the focus of the following chapter, but it is important to grasp that the considerable diversity both within Christianity and between faiths in this country overlays a more or less Christian nominalism, which (in England at least) tends to take Anglican form. In contrast, secularism – at least in any developed sense – remains the creed of a relatively small minority. The situation can, perhaps, be summarized as follows. In terms of belief, nominalism rather than secularism is the residual category; in terms of institutions, an established Church remains an integral part of a far from secular state. Interestingly, more than one spokesman for the religious minorities has argued that an established Church may well be better equipped to 'hold the ring' in a pluralist society than a rigorously secular state, a point that will be examined further in chapter 8.

A second aspect of the actively religious constituency in this country concerns the steady advancement of those who have become known as 'evangelicals'. Both within and without the established Church, the evangelical movement is making striking gains, relatively speaking, a tendency that reflects the growth in religious conservatism, both Christian and other, worldwide. This is, in fact, a global phenomenon which needs to be carefully monitored, not least in its British manifestations. In some respects, the third area of debate follows from this, but it also picks up the theme of chapter 3, in that it focuses on the attitude of churches or churchgoers to the 'world', that is, to the particular situation in which they are working. One focus of this debate concerns the role of the churches in secular affairs: should they or should they not intervene in the political process and in whose name should such interventions be made? Once again, the answers to such questions tend to divide churchgoers across rather than between the denominations. The views of the evangelical constituency are particularly interesting in this respect, the more so in view of their growing predominance and their traditional emphasis on the conversion of the individual believer. Any change in society will come about as the result of cumulative decisions on the part of individuals rather than by changes in social structures. A significant body of evangelicals are, however, beginning to shift their ground. While most of them remain conservative (or moderately so anyway) on moral issues – both individual and collective – increasing numbers are beginning to look more critically at the social and economic agenda. A prominent leader in this respect is the Bishop of Liverpool; from conventional evangelical roots to the chair of the Church of England's Board of Social Responsibility, his career exemplifies an important evolution in evangelical thinking (Sheppard and Worlock 1988).

Morally conservative but increasingly critical of the social and economic agenda. The combination flags up immediately the fallacy of dividing church members, whatever their denominations, into traditionalists and liberals; but life, more especially ecclesiastical life, is never that simple.

There are, quite clearly, differences of opinion that attract this kind of labelling, but they are seldom clear cut. Such differences as do exist, moreover, become more rather than less complex once liturgical predilections or attitudes to ecumenism are taken into account. More recently, the changing role of women – both lay and ordained – has provided a further dimension in the discussion. These are questions that will be considered in greater detail in due course, but their significance in assessing the continuing salience or otherwise of denominations in the later post-war decades should not be ignored. It may well be that other lines of division are becoming increasingly significant. But over-simplification into neat packages of traditionalists or liberals is not the answer. Pragmatic alliances of like-minded people, from a variety of denominational backgrounds, over relatively specific issues, are a much more likely outcome.

A concluding point puts the question of religious constituencies into a broader and necessary perspective. Religious membership and/or attendance has declined throughout in the post-war period, markedly so between 1960 and 1990. There can be no doubt about that. It remains, however – taking figures from the 1990 European Values survey – a very popular form of 'belonging' (in the sense of membership of a voluntary organization) in contemporary Britain. More people – and especially women – find outlets for such activity in religious groups than in any other type of voluntary organization; far more than in political or ecological associations to give but two examples (Timms 1992: 28–32). Timms points out that religious organizations should not be confused with denominations, but the figures remain, nonetheless, striking. Religious organizations of whatever kind, despite their minority status, continue to be a significant feature of contemporary British society. Their influence should never be taken for granted.

Notes

1 The introductory sections to the volume on *Religion* in the series Reviews of United Kingdom Statistical Sources (Maunder 1987) offers a good summary of pitfalls in this difficult area. So, too, does Barker's introductory article in the 1982 edition of the *UK Christian Handbook* (Barker 1982a).

2 In 1993 Marc Europe ceased to exist. Its activities have been taken over by the Christian Research Association, still under the directorship of Peter Brierley. The Articles of Association for the two organizations are virtually identical.

3 The precise use of terms can cause difficulties in this area. Brierley (1991a: chapter 10), for example, differentiates between nominal and notional Christians; the European Values Study between core and marginal members (Barker, Halman and Vloet 1993: 42–4). I have used nominal to mean non-active but self-ascribed church members.

4 The number of British expressing no allegiance grew dramatically between the 1981 and 1990 European Values Studies. The 1990 figure of 42 per cent surprised everyone, but should probably be treated with caution.

5 Once again there is a problem with definition. See the *UK Christian Handbooks* for a full discussion of the terminology used in these surveys.

6 It is interesting that C. S. Lewis resisted liturgical change for precisely this reason.

7 In, for example, the number of candidates coming forward for ordination from such churches and the corresponding growth in evangelical colleges.

8 Hence, in 1992, the establishment of an Archbishops' Commission under the chairmanship of Lady Elspeth Howe. Its terms of reference were 'to examine the future role in the Church and nation of the cathedrals of the Church of England and to make recommendations as to how best that role could be fulfilled, including proposals for their government and support'.

9 Considerable changes in funeral practice and administration have, however, occurred; they will be discussed further in chapter 5.

10 The Archbishop left for Rome on 29 September 1989. On 1 October, he spoke of recognizing the Pope as the central and leading figure of a united Church.

11 See chapter 9 for details of these instruments.

12 Martin (1990), for example, discusses the significance of Methodism for emigrants to the New World. See chapter 6 for a fuller discussion of this 'stepping westward'.

13 For a full discussion of this point, see chapter 6, pp. 101–3.

14 In terms of countries of origin, the contrast with other European

countries is, once again, striking. In France, for example, the words 'Muslim' and 'Arab' are almost interchangeable in popular parlance, indicating the North African origins of the great majority of the French Muslim community. In Germany Muslims have come as migrant workers from Southern Europe (what was Yugoslavia) and Turkey.

5 The Ordinary Gods of British Society

Believing Without Belonging: a Persistent Theme

Studies of religious belief immediately come up against a problem of definition. What should or should not be included in this rather imprecise area of discussion? In fact the problem concerns the definition of religion itself, for if sociologists are agreed that the study of religion in contemporary society should include more than observations about its conventional or institutional practice, they are certainly not agreed about an alternative frame of reference. Hence, in part, the ever-increasing number of terms that have emerged to describe the non-institutional dimensions of religiosity: privatized religion, invisible religion, implicit religion, popular religion, common religion, customary religion, folk religion, civic or civil religion to give but the most obvious examples. Each of these has a slightly different focus, reflecting the shifting nature of the social reality they are trying to describe. Taken together they are probably getting somewhere close to the truth.[1]

One thing is certain: the evident need to find some sort of focus for such studies, for even a casual glance at the data concerning religiosity in contemporary Britain indicates an important area of investigation. Regarding practice or active membership of religious organizations, the findings of the last chapter were unequivocal. Such activities involve a relatively small proportion of the population (just under 15 per cent on average). But it is equally evident that between two-thirds and three-quarters of British people indicate fairly consistently that they believe in some sort of God, though exactly what they mean by this phrase is not at all easy to say. Bearing this disparity between belief and practice in mind, a whole range of questions – of pastoral as well as sociological significance – begin to suggest themselves. What, for instance, is going to be the relationship between the active religious minority and the less active believing majority? How far is one dependent on the other? Does a believing majority make the work of the minority harder or easier? Do the former constitute a pool from which the latter can fish, or do they become, in part at least, a rival set-up, an alternative religious focus for society? If so, what is the nature of this alternative belief? Is there – on a rather different tack – a minimum size beyond which the active minority is no longer effective in a society? What factors, apart from size, might determine this effectiveness? Is one of them, the wider religious culture, indicated by the relative prevalence of religious belief? Or is this simply a distraction?

But questions, it seems, suggest themselves far more readily than answers. In the majority of cases, we simply do not know what the relationship between religious practice and belief might be, or whether it is likely to vary between different sections of society or between different groups of people, and what form such variations might take. The possibility that such differences do exist will be explored further in chapter 6. In the meantime, the present discussion will look at the nature of belief in postwar Britain from two perspectives: firstly the individual or personal point of view (common religion), and secondly the social or public (civil religion). The final section takes the form of a case study which describes the experience of one particular British city during the aftermath of a major disaster. The mourning after Hillsborough captures a curiously rich combination of conventional and less conventional religiosity experienced in heightened form. It illustrates, among other things, the importance of taking situational variables into account for a proper understanding of what was going on, thus providing a link to the further exploration of contexts in the chapter that follows.

Common Religion

The phrase 'privatized religion' is frequently used to describe the most prevalent form of religiosity in Western Europe in the late twentieth century, including contemporary Britain. In certain respects, the phrase gives an accurate impression of the current state of affairs, for it is true that religion has very largely become a matter of personal or private choice. So long as the expression of your views does not offend anyone else, you can believe whatever you like. On the other hand, the phrase 'privatized religion' is misleading to the extent that it over-looks the origins of our beliefs and the context in which they are held. Belief is not self-generated, nor does it exist in a vacuum; it has both form and content – albeit unorthodox form and content – which are shaped as much by the surrounding culture as by the individual believer. Hence my preference for the term 'common' rather than 'privatized' religion to describe the less orthodox dimensions of individual believing.

There is, in fact, no real gap between orthodox theologies and wider patterns of believing. The relationship between the two is a complex one, but it is better described as a continuum than as a dichotomy, in that very few individuals escape the influence of common religion altogether, even if they are moderately regular churchgoers. Having said this, it is equally true that those who attend church less frequently are bound to have less contact not only with religious teaching but with the associated sanctions as well. It is hardly surprising, therefore, that belief begins to drift further and further away from Christian orthodoxies as regular practice diminishes; a drifting of belief that is, probably, a greater challenge to the churches of the late twentieth century than the supposedly secular nature of the society in which we are obliged to live (Ahern and Davie 1987: 59). In short, Christian nominalism remains a more prevalent phenomenon than secularism. Nor should the fact that belief in this country derives primarily from a Christian and largely Protestant culture be taken for granted. Christian assumptions and Christian vocabulary remain important even if the content has altered quite significantly. This is one reason why most British people have such difficulty understanding Muslim reactions. Muslim teaching embodies ways of thought and of action that are not easily understood in Western society. To a lesser extent, a residual Protestantism in most of Britain also explains a certain degree of caution, suspicion even, with respect to some aspects of Roman Catholicism,[2] not least the question of papal authority. And what is passive and residual on the mainland, becomes active and articulate in Northern Ireland.

1. The sociological evidence for common religion

The evidence for the existence of common religion is persuasive; it can be found in a variety of studies. A clutch of these took place in the early post-war decades, an important reminder that confusion in the area of belief has existed throughout the post-war period. The confusion may be increasing as the century draws to an end, but it is certainly nothing new.[3] These earlier studies are gathered together in Martin's *Sociology of English Religion* (1967: chapter 3), though reference to the originals, especially Gorer's studies and Mass Observation's *Puzzled People* will flesh out the bare bones of Martin's summary. On one point they all agree: in the early post-war decades, the British were by a considerable majority a believing people. Mass Observation (1948), for example, found that four out of five women and two out of three men 'give at least verbal assent to the possibility of there being a God, and most of the rest express doubt rather than disbelief. Uncompromising disbelievers in a Deity amount to one in twenty' (p. 156). The enquiries continued through a varied range of questions, revealing a high incidence of private prayer (though again not by any means always related to churchgoing), much sympathy for religious education, a fair amount of antipathy towards organized religion and a truly wonderful confusion of doctrine. It is not difficult to see how elements of common religion antithetical to Christianity became incorporated in such beliefs, for it seems that orthodox Christian theology played a relatively small part in the everyday thinking of most British people.

How far do these results hold some thirty to forty years later? Several enquiries came together in the 1980s. One very detailed study took place in Leeds and involved some 1,600 people, each of whom answered a lengthy questionnaire covering a wide variety of common religion themes. (For a full discussion of the project, including the terminology employed and the outline results, see Ahern and Davie 1987, especially appendix A.) A second was the European Values Study, to which reference has already been made, first carried out in 1981 and repeated in 1990. The results of the 1981 and 1990 studies for a variety of religious indicators are given in table 5.1; broadly speaking the Leeds investigation confirms these findings. Underlining a few of these, we see that 76 per cent of the sample reported a belief in God (71 per cent in 1990); 58 per cent (54 per

Table 5.1 Indicators of religious commitment, Great Britain compared with the European average/percentages

Indicators of religious disposition	Great Britain		European average	
	1981	1990	1981	1990
Often think about meaning and purposes of life	34	36	30	33
Often think about death	15	19	18	20
Need moments of prayer, etc.	50	53	57	60
Define self as a religious person	58	54	62	63
Draw comfort/strength from religion	46	44	48	48
God is important in my life	50	44	51	52

Indicators of orthodox belief	Great Britain		European average	
	1981	1990	1981	1990
Believe in personal God	31	32	32	39
(Believe in a spirit or life force)	39	41	36	30
Believe in:				
God	76	71	73	72
Sin	69	68	57	54
Soul	59	64	57	61
Heaven	57	53	40	42
Life after death	45	44	43	44
The devil	30	30	25	26
Hell	27	25	23	23

Source: Table adapted from Abrams, Gerard and Timms 1985: 60. 1990 figures for equivalent countries provided by Dr D. Barker, European Values Group

cent in 1990) define themselves as 'religious persons'; 50 per cent (53 per cent) regularly feel the need for prayer, meditation or contemplation; and 46 per cent (44 per cent) draw comfort or strength from religion. Conversely only 4 per cent (4.4 per cent in 1990) of the population emerge from the EVS data as convinced atheists. The 1981 correlations with socio-demographic factors such as age, gender and occupational status can be found in table 5.2; it is worth noting the particular significance of the age variable.

An additional study took place in Islington in the late 1960s (Abercrombie et al. 1970). Though limited in scope and by now a little dated, the rigour with which this study was carried out has earned for it a high reputation. It also includes the best quote of the literature; the one used at the beginning of chapter 1. When respondents were probed about their belief in God, they were asked 'Do you believe in a God who can change the course of events on earth?' To which one respondent replied, 'No, just the ordinary one.' Answers such as these point up the paradox at the heart of this whole question. What is the significance, sociological or otherwise, of an *ordinary God*? Is this, or is it not, evidence of religious belief? If it is not belief, what kind of categories are necessary to understand this persistent dimension of British life and how would these relate to more orthodox dimensions of religiosity? It is at this point that the sociological evidence becomes distinctly thin. Indeed the discussion comes, almost, to a complete standstill. The conclusions to the Islington study are, however, worth quoting in some detail in that they begin to provide clues towards understanding at least some of the issues involved:

> The analysis in the section above suggests the tentative conclusion that religious belief, when not associated with active membership of a church, tends to be associated with superstitious belief while church attendance tends to be antithetical to superstition. Moreover, we have some evidence that for those people who do not go to church yet say they are religious and pray often, religious belief has moved quite far from the orthodox church position and is really much closer to what would normally be called superstition. (Abercrombie et al. 1970: 124)

These and other patterns that emerge from the study of common religion will form the focus of the following section.

Table 5.2   Socio-demographic profile

Variable	Overall religious commitment: combined scale					Total sample N = 100%
	Low %	Low–medium %	Medium %	Medium–high %	High %	
Age:						
18–24	39	27	15	11	9	193
25–44	24	31	16	16	14	446
45–64	14	21	19	20	27	335
65 & over	14	11	18	28	28	202
Significance 0.000						
Gamma 0.29						
Sex/Employment status of women:						
Male	27	25	18	14	15	576
Working female	18	23	17	23	20	311
Non-working F	15	23	14	22	26	314
Significance 0.000						
Gamma 0.21						
Terminal education age:						
14 yrs or under	15	15	18	25	28	361
15–17 yrs	24	29	17	16	14	628
18 yrs or over	26	23	14	15	22	208
Significance 0.0000						
Gamma 0.14						
Locality:						
Village	17	22	19	21	21	322
Small town	24	23	17	19	17	547
Large town	22	27	14	16	21	330
Significance 0.13						
Gamma 0.05						
Socio-economic group:						
AB	22	23	17	18	20	192
C1	25	24	16	14	21	263
C2	23	24	19	18	17	387
DE	17	24	15	23	21	353
Significance 0.21						
Gamma 0.05						
Income level: (327 missing cases)						
Under £3840	15	20	15	25	26	250
£3840–£7199	19	26	16	17	21	307
£7200 and over	28	27	18	13	15	322
Significance 0.0001						
Gamma 0.15						
Missing cases 32						
Total	22	24	17	19	19	1201 (max)

Source: Table reproduced from Abrams, Gerard and Timms 1985: 70–1

2. Variations in religious belief

At one end of the spectrum are the 'Christian' aspects of common religion, expressed very often in the widespread tendency of British people to approach the churches at the turning-points in human life. These are individual *rites de passage* which may or may not become community celebrations. (A village wedding may still involve a substantial section of the village community; its urban equivalent will gather a rather different group of people.) The Church of England has a larger constituency than the other English churches in this respect (the Anglican penumbra already referred to); in Scotland the uptake will normally be in the Church of Scotland. But whatever the particular church involved, the pastoral implications of these individual demands are considerable. It is at this point, for example, that the controversy surrounding baptism policies within the Church of England begins to bite, a debate which reveals among other things the very ambivalent nature of the relationship between common religion and orthodox Christianity. Inextricably linked, the two are not necessarily in harmony, a tension revealed in the different – indeed conflicting – understandings of Christian initiation. Such confusion is, moreover, one (but only one) reason why the number of – though not necessarily the demand for – baptisms has decreased markedly within the post-war period, from, roughly, two-thirds of all births in this country to one-third. One-third remains, nonetheless, a substantial amount. It represents a significant number of encounters between individuals, families and their churches; encounters which are absorbed for the most part by the parish clergy of the state church either north or south of the border.

It is, however, a characteristic of the last quarter of the twentieth century that a far higher percentage of the population experiences this kind of contact through the arrangement of funerals rather than baptisms, for it remains rare to exclude, or to be excluded by, the churches' personnel at the moment of death. It is hardly surprising, therefore, that the taking of funerals is a less controversial aspect of pastoral policy than baptism, though here too, important changes have taken place both in practice and administration. Regarding the latter, contact with the clergy will usually occur indirectly, through funeral directors, in whose hands the organization of funerals increasingly lies.[4] But more significantly – and moving across the line from administration to practice – a growing number of funerals now take place in crematoria rather than the parish church, reflecting a crucial shift in post-war religious practice. This shift, amounting in fact to a revolution in religious mores, is summarized in the following:

> Of all changes in the English way of death, cremation seems the one most likely to abide. Its adoption is a fascinating story. Legalised only in 1884, cremation accounted for only a tiny minority for half a century (4 per cent in 1939). After 1945, cremation took off: 50 per cent of deaths in 1966 and 70 per cent today. Last year the Audit Commission discussed the trend. It is involved in the matter because local authorities run most of the 223 crematoria where 400,000 funerals are performed each year. (Jupp 1990a)

There has clearly been a very significant change in religious practice in the last forty to fifty years, a change, moreover, that appears to be more developed in Britain than almost everywhere else.[5] But whether or not such shifts in practice have had a corresponding effect on religious belief (in, for example, the existence of an afterlife) is much more difficult to say. Davies (1990) argues for a close interrelationship between the two; a change in one must lead – at the very least – to a serious consideration of the other. But once again questions are easier to come by than answers in this, as yet, under-researched area. In the meantime, according to Davies, the clergy are, perhaps, rather too ready to assume that the burial service can be transferred with minimal change to a rite that appears to have very different pastoral and theological implications.

Interestingly, the Roman Catholic version of common religion provokes a rather different line of discussion. Like many other aspects of post-war Catholicism, it has been researched more thoroughly than its Anglican counterpart, once again by Hornsby-Smith (1991), who argues – prompted by his empirical findings – for an additional sociological category. The term 'customary religion' is suggested to cover the sort of beliefs that have at least some relation to the official teaching of the church as opposed to the much more inclusive common religion, which, Hornsby-Smith maintains, blurs distinctions between belief and what is little more than magic or superstition. How far such customary beliefs are distinguishable in practice from the wider area of superstition or even the remnants of pre-Christian religion would seem to be the crucial question in deciding between these two approaches. But it is interesting that the argument for greater distinction comes from those particularly interested in Catholic beliefs and teaching. These may well stand out rather better from the surrounding culture than a residual Anglicanism, thus requiring a rather different terminology. A second point emerges from the debate concerning concepts. Whatever distinctions may be made by the analyst in observing different types of religiosity, these distinctions are not, for the most part, shared by the participant. For what arises in practice derives from the cumulative effect of a large number of individual choices, most of which incorporate blurred distinctions and a somewhat approximate grasp of Christian doctrine. The content of common religion may well, at one end of the spectrum, have some link to Christian teaching. At the other it is enormously diverse, ranging through a wide range of distinctly heterodox ideas: for example – using the Leeds Study questionnaire as a guide – healing, the paranormal, fortune telling, fate and destiny, life after death, ghosts, spiritual experiences, prayer and meditation, luck and superstition.

Two areas may be selected to exemplify this diversity. The first concerns the phenomenon known as religious or spiritual experience. The patiently collected evidence of those working in this field (in particular, associates of the Alister Hardy Research Centre in Oxford) points to an appreciable number of people in this country who, if prompted, will claim to have had a religious experience of one kind or another. But by no means all of these people are churchgoers and a significant proportion of those interviewed admitted to hiding such experiences for fear of appearing foolish. The research interview was very often the first place where this kind of experience could be openly acknowledged; normally it was kept secret in what was perceived as a hostile environment. The growing body of data in this important area of research provides convincing evidence of a persistent – if partially hidden – phenomenon in contemporary society.[6]

Some of these spiritual experiences merge into the second example of religious diversity, one which has already been discussed in chapter 3. For it is in this context, surely, that the New Age should be categorized. Once again, it spans an enormously wide range of ideas, many of which embody an ambivalent relationship to more orthodox Christian teaching. For a variety of reasons, moreover, New Age ideas have become increasingly prevalent as the twentieth century draws to a close; they have become almost a *fin de siècle* or millennial version of common religion.[7] Bearing this in mind, it will be interesting to see how far the phenomenon persists into the new millennium. Whatever the case, the New Age provides yet further evidence that the British are far from being – or becoming – a secular society in any strict sense of the term, 'particularly if by that omnibus adjective we mean an increasing approximation of average thinking to the norms of natural and social science' (Martin 1969: 107). Despite a marked decline in religious practice in the post-war period, this process simply has not happened. But nor are we a Christian society if this expression is used at all precisely. So how can we proceed? In many ways the conceptual framework within which to describe the nature of belief in contemporary Britain still seems to be lacking.

Public or Corporate Beliefs: a Durkheimian Frame of Reference

It is hardly surprising that the problem of social order has provoked sociologists since the earliest days of the discipline, for it is central to the understanding of society. It is, moreover, a problem that can be approached in an infinite variety of ways, many of which have little to do with religion. But one aspect of this many-sided question is central to the argument of this chapter: it concerns the role or *function* of religion in society rather than – or at least alongside – more substantive issues, for functionalists are preoccupied by what religion does, not by what it is. A variety of questions follow from this. If religion does something significant in or for society, what is going to happen if that role is no longer properly fulfilled? Or to turn this a slightly different way round, if that role has to be fulfilled, what – in contemporary society – has replaced conventional religiosity? These are the questions of Durkheimian sociologists; equally pertinent in the late twentieth century as they were in the early days of sociology, despite the changing nature of society.[8] A second issue runs parallel. This concerns the complex relationship between religion and morality (both personal and social), a relationship suggested surprisingly often in contemporary British society.

A recent and without any doubt one of the most direct of such suggestions came in 1992 from the newly appointed Secretary of State for Education, John Patten, whose widely publicized essay on public morality (The *Spectator*, 18 April 1992) evoked the connection with religion quite explicitly:

The now derided Victorian 'values' of godfearingness and hope of redemption developed towards the end of the 19th century. They rose, with church attendance, to their apogee in Edwardian times. Despite unemployment at its highest levels, crime fell to its lowest precisely in that near-mythical age when no one bothered to lock his door and the world was a village.

Since the second world war, crime has risen. So has secularisation. What is to be done?

Not surprisingly, the essay provoked a torrent of correspondence, for it challenged many assumptions of contemporary thinking, not least the expectations of the chattering classes. It also confuses correlation with causality. It is true that churchgoing has diminished. (Is this to be equated with secularization?) It is also true that crime rates have risen, but this does not mean that the two are necessarily connected in any direct sense. Might it not be the case that increasingly rapid social change affects both phenomena adversely? Similarly, the premise that belief in the fundamentals of redemption and damnation used to provide the bedrock of civil behaviour is not one that everyone would share. It is much more likely that the Victorians and Edwardians accepted or rejected the moral values of society for the same mixture of motives that characterize later generations. But given Mr Patten's premise, the corollary follows naturally enough: belief in these fundamentals is no longer widespread, so what will replace it as the basis of social order? And most people are concerned about social order even if they express their concerns in ways rather different from the Secretary of State for Education.

In some ways a similar problem – if we may use such a term – arises in an area that has already been mentioned: that is, the attempt to find an acceptable basis for decision making in areas where technological changes run ahead of moral frameworks. The problematic worlds of medical ethics and nuclear power provide the most obvious examples. The traditional (often religious) basis for such decision making is questioned, and rightly so in many cases, for relatively few people subscribe to the religious orthodoxies involved; but finding appropriate alternatives to replace the traditional basis is proving more difficult. The search for such a replacement – that is, an acceptable and shared framework within which difficult moral decisions can be made (decisions which are seldom clear cut) – remains, however, an urgent task for contemporary society. The more so in that scientific advance throws up issue after issue in precisely this area of thinking.

The suggestion that there are continuing, if unspecified, links between religion and morality re-emerges in chapter 7 with reference to the debate about religious education. In the meantime we need to turn to a rather different formulation of the religious in public life and one which is rather more concerned with questions of identity than with morality. The Durkheimian frame of reference remains, however, central. For a second dimension of Durkheimian sociology can be found in the concept of civil religion, a term which embodies, once again, a distinctly ambivalent relationship to Christian orthodoxy. To be more precise, civil religion is not identical to Christianity but, in both its American and British forms, it borrows legitimacy from that world religion in particular (Bocock and Thompson 1985: 205; see also Thompson 1988 and 1992). In Britain, the rituals surrounding the royal family exemplify the essence of the relationship in question. Constructed primarily to represent the nation, to convey a sense of Britishness, such rituals embody national feeling rather than Christian doctrine. But the British monarch is not only the Head of State; he or she stands in a particular relationship to the Church of England and, in a rather different sense, to the Church of Scotland as well. These ecclesiastical relationships, far from being ignored, are consciously reinforced through highly publicized events. The role of the media, and particularly of television in the post-war period, is crucial in this reinforcement. The monarchy appears therefore as something sacred as well as something national.[9] Sociologically, perhaps, the two dimensions of civil religion can and should be kept distinct – that is, the civic from the more specifically religious – in order to understand the particular processes at work. Such a distinction is not, however, generally shared by those who participate in royal or indeed other civic rituals; there is, rather, a deliberate confusing of the nation and the sacred. A confusion which can, but does not always, slip towards an uncritical sense of national feeling. For it is important to remember that religion may challenge – as well as legitimate – national or civil authority. The relationship between religion and nationhood is both complex and unpredictable. What happens in each particular case is a question for empirical research, not for a priori assumptions.

Two examples from the British case illustrate this point. One has already been referred to: the Coronation of Elizabeth II. Such controversy as there was in 1953 lay between the sociologists rather than between politicians and church leaders. For whether or not the Coronation was designed to reflect or to construct an underlying unity in British society (the heart of the sociological dispute), there could be no doubt that the creators of this particular example of civil religion were all 'on the same side'. They succeeded, furthermore, in producing a powerful act of sacralization, endorsing a pattern for British society that re-emerges, usually in more modest forms, on a regular basis. The Jubilee celebrations, for example, or the yearly repetition of Remembrance Sunday, include a significant church presence in order to provide a sacred dimension at a civil or civic ritual. Such presence is rarely controversial; indeed – and this is the crucial point – the lack of it would be more so.

In 1982, however, a notable exception occurred in this pattern of mutual reinforcement, an exception articulated by Bocock:

> This was over a service of thanksgiving for victory. The service was meant to express thanks to God for Britain's victory over Argentina at the end of the Falklands/Malvinas fighting in 1982. The church authorities at St Paul's did not want, and did not allow, a nationalistic victory celebration because they thought that the loss of life on both sides was not something to give thanks for. . . . This led to a sense of tension and conflict of view between the Church and the government. It illustrated that the state authorities could not always assume that they had a 'tame' church in the Church of England or the other denominations involved. (1985: 213)

This was a powerful example of the Church challenging the state rather than legitimating its activities. The media reported the occasion in precisely these terms. All sorts of questions follow. In what circumstances are the churches likely to react in a critical rather than supportive manner? Are these circumstances becoming more or less common? Are the ceremonies of civil religion becoming less and less appropriate in a society where churchgoing is no longer the norm? Or are they, conversely, more than ever necessary for precisely the same reason? Given the latter scenario, how are such ceremonies to be constructed in a society which contains not only a great diversity of Christian beliefs but a certain representation of other faiths as well? Will civil religion in this country become less Anglican, less Christian even, or will it disappear altogether?

Will a European civil religion begin to emerge? Does the concept of civil religion hold up at all in an increasingly diverse society? Did it ever?

The latter point is important. For the notion of civil religion conveys some aspects of religiosity better than others. Religion is not necessarily an agent of cohesion; it may, and often does, operate equally well as an agent of division. Northern Ireland is the most obvious example of religious divisiveness in the United Kingdom, but Scotland and Wales also possess religious identities which are distinct from, if not always hostile to, Englishness. In many respects the United Kingdom displays a whole series of civil religions, not all of which are immediately compatible with each other. A collective identity is, nonetheless, significant. Religion is not entirely privatized. Indeed in many ways religion operates far more effectively at a public level, for it remains, despite everything, a sign or a symbol, a marker of history, a reminder of the past, a powerful source of identity; *functions* of religion that can be seen even more clearly in other parts of Europe but which continue to exist, albeit in understated form, in Britain. In contrast, personal codes of morality – very much privatized – owe less and less to the churches' teaching, which to a large extent is seen as irrelevant. Paradoxically those who reject the churches' interference (for it is seen as such) at an individual level still seem to welcome a certain degree of public activity in which the state churches inevitably play an important role. Chapters 7 and 8 will develop this discussion further.

The Mourning After Hillsborough: a Liverpool Case Study

Sociological material about religious belief can be found in a variety of sources, ethnographic as well as statistical. The pros and cons of these sources, examples of each and the ways in which they can be used can be found in Ahern and Davie (1987). In addition to these, a relatively new possibility is – sadly – beginning to present itself, in the kind of evidence that emerges from what have become known as 'disasters'. Just as there are particular moments in the life cycle when the sacred becomes an acceptable topic of conversation (at or after a death, for example), so too do these moments occur from time to time in public life. Disasters exemplify this process. Not only do they provoke out of the ordinary behaviour; they also permit, encourage even, a certain level of debate, both public and private, about the sacred. The questions are predictable enough. Why should such disasters occur? Why to me or to my family? What has happened to my loved ones? Will I ever see them again? The answers to such questions, or indeed the lack of them, provide valuable material, highlighted by public discussion, about the nature of contemporary religious belief. One such disaster was the Hillsborough football tragedy in April 1989. But an immediate caveat is necessary in this and probably other instances, for – like many crises – they reveal the distinctiveness just as much as the typicality of a locality's reactions at a time of heightened emotional tension. Nowhere more so than in Liverpool, where both conventional and common religion derive at least some of their characteristics from an exceptionally rich popular culture. Having said this, what happened in Liverpool following the tragedy undoubtedly illustrates a number of points from the previous sections, not least the inseparability of conventional and common religion and the significance of collective as well as individual responses in this area. (For a fuller description of the Hillsborough disaster and its sociological implications, see Walter 1991, and Davie 1993a and 1993c. The following is a shortened account.)

On 15 April 1989, Liverpool played Nottingham Forest in the semi-final of the FA Cup at the Hillsborough stadium in Sheffield. Play was abandoned after six minutes. That afternoon ninety-four people – most of them young and all of them Liverpool supporters – died, watched not only by a capacity crowd but by a television audience numbered in millions.[10] Too many had been let into one end of the ground and those at the front were crushed against the perimeter fence as play was about to begin. The aftermath of this tragedy provides rich sociological data, for if the semi-final match itself was part of a well-established sequence of events in the English football calendar, what followed in the next few days was totally without precedent.

Walter (1991) has given us an invaluable account of the mourning rituals that emerged in Liverpool in the days following Hillsborough. He divides these into categories – formal and informal, civic and political, sporting and religious – but adds an immediate and vital caveat. 'The categories will mislead if the reader is not aware how religious, civic and footballing rituals were intertwined' (p. 608). Not only was it impossible to disentangle common from conventional religiosity, it was equally difficult to separate either from other dimensions of Liverpool life. Informal merged into formal and boundaries – those dividing religious from sport for

example – were crossed and recrossed all the time. It was entirely acceptable to bring football regalia to the cathedrals; conversely religious representatives were welcomed at Anfield. One aspect of Liverpool's mourning
rituals illustrates what happened with particular clarity, the Anfield Pilgrimage. It is worth looking in some detail at what occurred at the Anfield
stadium, for it was this, above everything, that astonished the world.

Nothing was, or could have been, organized at the outset. But people,
still in shock, found comfort in coming together on the day after the
tragedy. They came primarily to their churches, to the Roman Catholic
Cathedral or to Anfield, the home of Liverpool Football Club. So much
so that at noon, the Club opened its gates officially and began the daunting
task of shepherding the endless stream of mourners who came to the
ground. Sunday was just the starting point. By the end of the week, an
estimated 1 million people had filed through the ground, twice the
population of the city. The pilgrims, as they were called, queued for
hours to get into the stadium, where they were gently marshalled, and –
if they so wished – were counselled with great sensitivity. The 'counsellors'
included the expected (religious personnel and trained social workers),
but also the less expected (professional football players and their wives).
Here, as elsewhere, there were some remarkable reversals of role. The
following description of the Anfield Pilgrimage is taken from an article by
the Liverpool Bishops, Archbishop Derek Worlock and Bishop David
Sheppard. The article describes part of the scene in the stadium, but also
the difficulty that many people, particularly outsiders, had in understanding
what was going on:

> Over the goalpost and crush barriers hung red and blue scarves,
> with flags and banners portraying the Liver Bird emblem and the
> inevitable assurance that 'you'll never walk alone'. On the turf
> below lay a field of flowers, more scarves and caps, mascots and
> souvenirs, and incredibly, kneeling amidst wreaths and rattles, a
> plaster madonna straight from a Christmas crib.
>
> Blasphemy, unhealthy superstition, tawdry sentimentality. Or a
> rich blend of personal mourning, prayerful respect and genuine
> faith? (Sheppard and Worlock 1989)

Which was it? Blasphemy, superstition, sentimentality; or personal mourning and genuine faith? The Bishops go on to describe the atmosphere at
Anfield as being like the days before a funeral when visits are paid to the

home of the bereaved; when the family recall together the person they have loved and exchange stories about the bereaved, based on shared memories. The sense of family, of mutual support, of the need to be together is the most important aspect of such activity; it is, moreover, a notoriously difficult thing to experience vicariously. It is hardly surprising, therefore, that many non-Liverpudlian visitors left Anfield not only bewildered, but, at times, critical of what seemed – from the outside – like 'tawdry sentimentality'. In contrast, the people of Liverpool, together with Liverpudlians returning to the city from elsewhere, found the Anfield experience enormously reassuring.

A certain amount of local knowledge, including an appreciation of the Celtic and Irish dimensions of Liverpool life, enable a better understanding of this and other episodes in the mourning after Hillsborough. But even the most sympathetic observer would have difficulty in squaring everything that they saw or experienced with Christian orthodoxy; it simply is not possible. But the common religion aspects of what happened (the ordinary gods) cannot be separated from the more conventional; they are part and parcel of each other. Both, moreover, are experienced at a corporate as well as at an individual level. What started as a series of spontaneous actions by individual mourners (the laying of flowers on the pitch, for example) became within twenty-four hours a shared or communal activity. The Anfield Pilgrimage expressed, indeed enacted, the mood of an entire city, a city united in grief, an example surely of effective civic religion. To what extent might this episode become typical of British behaviour or will Liverpool – in this as in other ways – remain the exception rather than the norm? I have argued elsewhere (Davie 1993a) that what happened at Anfield depended very considerably on the prior existence of Liverpool's exceptionally strong communal identity. For this reason, such an explicit, conscious and collective acknowledgement of death is, I think, unlikely to be repeated. It is a special case. We can, nonetheless, learn from this episode something more about the curious mixture of common and conventional religiosity that continues to pervade contemporary British society.

Notes

1 For a full discussion of this point and the pros and cons of different terminologies, see Ahern and Davie 1987.

2   The British are, of course, the only people to employ the adjective Roman, thus accentuating the foreignness of Catholicism.

3   It is in fact a phenomenon observable in almost any historical context. See, for example, the classic work of Thomas on *Religion and the Decline of Magic* (1971) and Obelkevich's study of nineteenth-century religion in rural Lincolnshire (Obelkevich 1976).

4   The study of death and funeral practice in modern society has become a burgeoning field of sociological discussion. Walter (1990a) provides an admirable introduction to this literature and to the sociological questions raised by changes in this area.

5   This is partly explained by a Protestant rather than Catholic culture, but not entirely. The Protestant countries of Scandinavia, for example, are rather similar to Britain in this respect. In the United States, in contrast, the practice of cremation has not developed to any great extent.

6   For fuller information concerning this work, see the publications list available from the Alister Hardy Research Centre, Westminster College, Oxford.

7   It is worth noting in this respect that the term 'New Age' does not appear once in the 1982 Leeds questionnaire, the most thorough of research instruments in this field.

8   It is important to remember that the founding fathers of sociology were preoccupied with incipient industrialism; their concepts do not automatically translate to advanced industrial society. This point is discussed in some detail by Beckford 1989. The central argument of his book turns on the need to appreciate the particularities of *advanced* industrial society in so far as these affect religiosity.

9   Attitudes to the monarchy are, however, changing. This question will be discussed further in chapter 9, including the related question of establishment.

10 Two more people died subsequently as a result of their injuries; one in the following week, one almost four years later.

6 Believing Without Belonging: Variations on the Theme

The two previous chapters have sketched the broad contours of religious life in this country. Chapter 4 provided information about the major religious constituencies in contemporary Britain. Chapter 5 indicated the backdrop against which active religious participation takes place; that is, the pervasive current or currents of latent religiosity which persist despite everything in our advanced industrial society. We need now to bring these themes together, exploring their connections in a wide variety of situations. These variations will be approached in two ways. Firstly geographically, looking initially at the different countries that make up the United Kingdom, but also at some regional patterns within these countries and especially within England. The particular regions selected as examples in the English case – one urban and one rural – act as bridge to the second approach to the subject in that urban and rural are more often than not related to important social and economic differences. The latter will then be underlined more firmly in a suggested typology of belief. A final section will consider the extreme case: asking whether the relative popularity of religious broadcasting in contemporary Britain might not exemplify believing without belonging *par excellence*?

But first one word of caution. The terms 'believing' and 'belonging' are not to be considered too rigidly. The disjunction between the variables is intended to capture a mood, to suggest an area of enquiry, a way of looking at the problem, not to describe a detailed set of characteristics.

Operationalizing either or both of the variables too severely is bound to distort the picture. Hornsby-Smith (1992) and Short and Winter (1993) both do this to some extent.[1] But the question very quickly becomes semantic, for it is clear that we need some way, if not this one, of describing the persistence of the sacred in contemporary society despite the undeniable decline in churchgoing. 'Believing without belonging' seems to me as good a way as any of doing this. Hence the use of this theme as an important but by no means exclusive framework for the major arguments of this book.

Celtic Variations

1. Wales and Scotland

A text on Latin America may seem an unusual place to start for information on Scotland, Wales and Northern Ireland. But Martin illustrates in *Tongues of Fire* (1990) the essential 'stepping westward' of Northern European religion; from, that is, the overwhelmingly dominant state churches of Scandinavia, through the limited pluralism of Britain to the competing denominations of the United States. With reference to the Celtic fringe of Britain, the essential point to grasp is the following:

> England itself retains some elements of aristocratic hierarchy, and
> of the relationship of church to state, whilst its Protestant peripher-
> ies in Wales, Scotland and Ulster, as well as its overseas extensions
> in Canada, Australia and New Zealand, variously evolved towards
> something closer to the American pattern. (Martin 1990: 19)

Wales, Scotland and Northern Ireland are one step out (or westward) in this process, noticeably more Protestant and more egalitarian than England. But the detail of this Protestantism takes different forms in each of the Celtic countries; as Martin suggests, each country has evolved and continues to evolve variously.

In Wales, for example, dissenting or Protestant culture persists in splitting itself – both denominationally and linguistically – into a number of smallish groupings, each of which is numerically inferior to either the (disestablished) Church in Wales, with its English connotations, or to

Roman Catholicism. Taken together, however, the chapels add up to something rather more significant. They amount to what Martin calls 'established dissidence', becoming thereby important carriers of Welsh cultural identity. More specifically they have provided the cultural background from which emerged a whole stream of political leaders, mostly of Liberal and Labour persuasion, destined for Westminster (1990: 34–5). Up to a point the same could be said of Dissent in Scotland; it too has encouraged a political culture rather different from that south of the border. But there is a crucial difference between the two countries with respect to their ecclesiastical arrangements, for there is no equivalent in Wales to the national Church of Scotland. It is not, therefore, surprising that the Welsh chapels tend to function as identity carriers at local or community level rather better than they do as national representatives, a point to which we shall return.

In Scotland, on the other hand, the national Church (the Kirk) remains – alongside the independent educational and legal systems north of the border – a continuing and obvious focus of Scottish nationhood. Care should be taken, however, to avoid over-simplification of this issue, for in Scotland as well as in Wales an undeniable degree of fragmentation within the Protestant tradition is apparent; a situation which argues against a totally self-evident relationship between Presbyterianism and Scottishness (Brown 1987). Denominational differences, moreover, are compounded by regional variations, a factor reinforced not only by Scotland's geography but by the proximity of its west coast to Ireland. Irish immigration in the nineteenth century was a significant factor, a movement that brought appreciable, though never huge, numbers of Catholics to Scotland; communities which remain concentrated in a relatively small part of the southwest (Wallis and Bruce 1986: 230–2). The implications of regionalism for religious practice – for belonging – in Scotland are considerable. Northcott (1993), for example, argues that the noticeably higher membership figures for Scotland as opposed to England (almost three times greater according to Brierley) are skewed both by the high rates of attachment in the Highlands and Islands (traditional rural areas) and by the considerable Catholic presence on the west coast. Religious practice in southeast Scotland, in contrast, is not so very different from the patterns prevailing south of the border. Patterns of religious behaviour, as opposed to denominational affiliation, do not necessarily coincide with national boundaries. Be that as it may, religious membership (institutional attachment) remains markedly stronger north of the border. The difference is much less marked in the case of Wales, where membership figures are about one and a half those in England.[2]

The national dimension of Scottish Protestantism has a further significance with reference to a second theme of this book. The Scottish Presbyterians have been among the most enterprising religious bodies in their capacity to establish effective links with their European counterparts. That they have such counterparts is the first point to make, for Scottish Calvinism has a Continental home in Geneva, a home denied to the state church south of the border. The Scots have, for a variety of reasons, made the most of these opportunities. Motives, however, may well be mixed in these undertakings, for it is undoubtedly true that Scotland's aspirations towards a greater European identity – whether these be economic, political or cultural – are related to its somewhat negative feelings towards England. And it so happens that the religious factor can, and does, operate to reinforce this Europeanness. In Wales the situation is a little different. It may well be that Welsh culture (including dissenting culture) can find encouragement in the regionalism associated with greater European identity (Bowie 1992). On the other hand the direct linking of Welsh Dissent – more local and more fragmented than its Scottish equivalent – with its European counterparts (themselves rather more difficult to discern, particularly in the case of Methodism) is harder to foresee.

The somewhat problematic relationship between the English churches and Europe will be discussed later – following the discussion of church and state – but it is important at this stage to note the Anglican presence in the Celtic countries: in, that is, the relatively small, but significant Episcopal Church in Scotland and in the proportionally larger disestablished Church in Wales. The latter is considerably bigger, for example, than the Welsh Roman Catholic community, the reverse being the case in Scotland. In terms of growth and decline, the Anglican churches of the Celtic lands suffer statistical trends rather similar to the Church of England. This is hardly surprising, for the societal pressures are similar in each case.[3]

With respect to statistics, the quantum leap, the really significant difference, lies in the Northern Irish case. Why should this be so? Examining this question Wallis and Bruce (1986) offer a useful comparative analysis of conservative Protestantism and its impact on politics. The comparison goes well beyond the Scottish and Irish cases, but the importance of considering external variables – the detailed relationships between Caesar and God – to account for the differences stands out. The following section focuses on these comparisons. But however explained, the statistical profile of Northern Ireland, like that of the Irish Republic, must be considered an exception both within the United Kingdom and in Western Europe; both religious membership in some form or other and religious practice remain conspicuously high for both communities. The high levels of Protestant membership and practice – though lower than those of the Catholics – are particularly noteworthy, given the prevailing patterns of Northern European Protestantism.

2. *The Northern Irish case*

> Ulster is a clear case of a society in which conservative Protestant values have occupied a pre-eminent place in the political arena. Formed as a result of the refusal of the Protestant population of Northern Ireland to be assimilated into the Irish Free State on its formation in 1921, the identification of the interests of the Northern Ireland state with those of its Protestant majority has been assured by their constant fear of the nationalist aspirations of the Republic in the south, and of the large Catholic minority in the north. (Wallis and Bruce 1986: 229)

The situation seems, moreover, to be self-perpetuating, for each time a more ecumenical, more liberal or more secular set of assumptions suggests itself, the reaction sets in. The lines are hardened and the support for Unionism – embodied in the fundamentalism of a Paisley – strengthens.

What is it that has brought about this state of affairs? Working comparatively, Wallis and Bruce indicate low-impact, intermediate-impact and high-impact cases with respect to the role of conservative Protestantism on politics.Within this framework Ulster (together with South Africa) comes into the high-impact category, whereas Scotland and England are low-impact cases. The explanation for these differences lies in the detailed analysis of a number of crucial factors: the circumstances in which the socio-religious culture was formed; the changes that might subsequently have affected this culture (one way or the other), especially patterns of migration, secularization and church accommodation; and the structures of politics and communications in the surrounding society. Thus in the case of Ulster we need to take note of the situation which brought about the partition of Ireland in the first place and the emergence of Calvinism as the dominant politico-religious culture in the North; to examine what changes have occurred since that time to diminish or reinforce this frame of reference; and, finally, to study the ongoing interactions between Ulster and the United Kingdom on the one hand, and the Irish Republic on the other. It is an approach entirely consonant with the framework suggested by Martin in chapter 2.

The detail of Northern Irish developments since 1921 (and indeed the centuries of Anglo-Irish mismanagement that lie behind the partition) are beyond the scope of this chapter. They are the subject of a separate monograph in this series. But one point emerges all too clearly: there can be no doubt that the Northern Irish conflict is a religious one. Other factors are, of course, crucial to a full understanding of the tragedy that continues to unfold both in the Province and increasingly on the British mainland, but 'the fact that the competing populations in Ireland adhered and still adhere to competing religious traditions' gives the conflict 'its enduring and intractable quality' (Bruce 1986: 249). 'Still adhere to' is the significant phrase, but it is one full of irony. For the actively religious Protestants of Northern Ireland aspire to a Union with a Britain that has long since lost the religious disciplines that continue, sometimes very positively, to motivate Ulster. Precisely that which underpins Northern Irish aspirations is missing in the goal of their political undertakings.

The particularities of the Northern Irish case stand out best in a comparison. In Scotland, for example, religious affiliation, ethnic identity and political action – though persuasive as a combination in the inter-war period – no longer call the tune of Scottish political life. Once again the explanation for this rather different trajectory can be found in the combination of factors that surrounded the original contact between indigenous Protestantism and Catholic immigration. One variable is crucial: the degree of secularization already evident in the host society at the time of this encounter (Wallis and Bruce 1986: 352). For even at this stage, religious affiliation was no longer the central element of Scottish identity, enabling a degree of toleration to exist, at first between different brands of Presbyterianism, but which in the course of time was extended to Roman Catholics as well. The arrival of Catholics in Scotland gave contemporaries considerable cause for concern (it *was* indeed a bumpy ride), but religious identity failed to develop as an all-consuming passion, which was the case in Northern Ireland. A second contrast underlines this point. Whereas the Calvinism of Scotland has reinforced a certain independence from England with respect to European connections, this is manifestly not so in Northern Ireland. For the Unionists, Europe – like so much else – is perceived through sectarian spectacles, and the image that emerges through such lenses has more to do with Catholic majorities centred on Rome than with a Genevan base for Calvinist theology. Catholic majorities, moreover, are already too close for comfort south of the border for the Unionists to advance with any confidence down the European road. Their agenda is caught in an earlier historical period. But the Unionists are not entirely alone in this attitude towards Europe. For what is explicit in the Northern Irish context (articulated vehemently in the speeches of Paisley) can surely still be seen – though less often than it used to be and in muted form – on the British mainland as well. The language will be political rather than religious, but a loss of identity (a Protestant identity) remains central to such arguments.[4]

The Northern Irish situation must, like everything else, evolve over time, however reluctantly. One relatively new pressure in this respect may come from recent demographic developments in the Province. From this point of view the outline returns for the 1991 census are far from reassuring for the Unionists, for they indicate a distinct shift in the two-thirds to one-third ratio between Protestants and Catholics; a ratio which underpinned the establishment of the Province in the first place and which has remained stable over a long period. But following the 1991 returns, Catholics now make up 43 per cent of the population, a figure which indicates a noticeable percentage rise over ten years.[5] More specifically, Catholics form a majority in eleven of the twenty-six council areas and completely dominate the west of the Province, figures which also indicate a greater geographical separation between the two communities. Demographic patterns reflect elusive combinations of variables, in this case changes in the birth-rate alongside shifting patterns of emigration.[6] These may or may not be continued. In the meantime the manner in which the Unionists are likely to react isn't easy to predict. One approach might be to become more hardline than ever, closing ranks and denying accusations of discrimination. The other – rather more realistic – might involve a degree of power sharing between the Unionists and the nationalist Social Democratic and Labour Party. Which of the two approaches prevails in the long run could well determine much of the Province's future. But optimism isn't easy in this problematic corner of the United Kingdom.

Regional Dimensions

Regional differences have already revealed themselves within the Celtic lands. Welsh-speaking chapels have an obvious geographical base in the Welsh-speaking parts of the country. The Highlands and Islands and the west coast of Scotland demonstrate markedly higher levels of religious practice than the southeast. And even within the relatively restricted area of Northern Ireland, the west is becoming predominantly Catholic in contrast to the rather more Protestant north and east. But the regional factor is more significant still in England, where there are considerable variations between one part of the country and another. One such has already been discussed: the far from random distribution both of other-faith communities and of Afro-Caribbean churches. (Both phenomena are relatively absent outside England.) The notion of racial or religious pluralism will resonate variously depending upon these distributions, a point nicely illustrated by the Commission for Racial Equality's Report on racism in the Southwest of England, entitled '*Keep them in Birmingham*' (Jay 1992). But other differences are equally important, for contrasting regional profiles imply divergent religious priorities in different parts of the country.

One way of considering this question lies in relatively straightforward denominational mapping, though this, in many ways, begs the essential question: why was it that certain denominations took hold in some places rather than others? Geographical contiguity forms part, but only part, of the explanation in this respect. But mapping can show more than denominational distribution; it can indicate cross-denominational patterns of religious activity including growth and decline (Brierley 1991a).[7] Demonstrable patterns emerge from this kind of analysis. Increasingly sophisticated and flexible techniques, moreover, enable a whole range of variables not only to be presented in map form but to be correlated with each other in spatial terms. But even the most sophisticated analyses need to be supplemented by a range of other sources – historical, cultural, ethnographic, linguistic even – in order to understand the significance of the regional factor for religious activity. Indeed the closer one looks, the more fascinating it becomes. Coleman (1983), for example, finds a whole range of interacting variables at a very local level – the nature of ecclesiastical provision, settlement patterns, occupational structures, variations in landownership and manorial control, the nature of population growth and redistribution – which account for the establishment of distinct religious cultures (including particular denominational combinations) even within one county. As ever, purely religious currents, if they exist at all, are moulded by an enormous variety of external factors. In this chapter, two contrasting examples will be offered of regional cultures: the far Southwest and the Northwest of England. They are selective in content but should be read as illustrations of a wider phenomenon.

First the far Southwest (Devon and Cornwall), remembering that Cornwall, strictly speaking, should be classed as a Celtic variation. It fits, moreover, the pattern that Martin discerns, for Cornwall and northwest Devon were – and culturally still are – areas of marked Protestant, more especially Methodist, presence. The inclusion of west Devon in this categorization leads to a second point. In terms of religious cultures within the Southwest the county boundaries are misleading. By the middle of the nineteenth century, tides of religious change had ebbed and flowed across the boundaries of Devon to such an extent 'that East Cornwall and West Devon were more alike than West Devon and East Devon were. The same point could be made about the eastern corner of Devon and West Dorset' (Coleman 1979: 6). Material for this kind of statement comes from Coleman's detailed work on the 1851 religious census, from which west Devon, with a distinct Methodist presence – notably the Bible Christians – emerges as a half-way stage towards Cornwall. Despite such overlaps the two counties do in 1851 demonstrate markedly different profiles. In terms of its county figures, for example, Devon was scarcely remarkable among the counties of its division and region (Coleman 1983: 169). More precisely, Devon's aggregate attendances remained above the national level and the Anglican index stronger still, though not so high as the three counties immediately to the east. Nonconformity ran well below the levels in Wiltshire and Cornwall but slightly above those in Somerset and Dorset. It was remarkably varied in content. In contrast, Cornwall was *sui generis*. It was characterized by strong Nonconformity in the context of a remarkably weak Anglicanism and only moderately high levels of aggregate attendance. Nonconformity in Cornwall was, more-over, very largely synonymous with Methodism.[8]

So much for the mid nineteenth century. What is more remarkable is the persistence of such patterns a century and a half later. Despite much-reduced levels of religious adherence of all kinds, the broad spatial dis-tributions have remained, if not completely static, then curiously enduring. Devon is still more religious than the English average while Cornwall differs little from the norm; the Church of England remains relatively strong in Devon (though more so in some parts of the county than others) and moderately weak in Cornwall;[9] Nonconformity continues to be di-verse in Devon but still dominated by Methodism in Cornwall; and the boundary between the socio-religious cultures is situated approximately where it was 150 years ago. Northwest Devon continues to lean towards the Cornish model.[10]

A particularly dramatic demonstration of the persistence of boundaries can be found in the statistically significant correlations that could still be found in the mid 1980s between the presence of Methodism in Devon and Cornwall and the Liberal vote, a fact which also illustrates the con-tinued – albeit lingering – salience of the religious factor in the determi-nation of voting behaviour in this corner of the United Kingdom. Political alignment (in geographical terms) is difficult to find for the Church of England population, but the same can hardly be said about the distribu-tion of the Methodist Church by circuit. 'This time the pattern is, frankly, quite extraordinary, showing as it does the great sweep of Methodism across North Devon and down through the whole of Cornwall corre-sponding almost exactly with the very Liberal "heartland" that was sought' (Davie and Hearl 1991: 221). Of course the correlation begs many ques-tions, for it does not demonstrate causality. There may well be a third factor which accounts for the apparent connection between Methodism and the Liberal vote. Be that as it may, the Soutwest remains distinct both religiously and politically and the two cultures appear to be related either directly or indirectly. (For a full account of the methodology used in this enquiry, see Davie and Hearl 1991.)

A final point concerns the nature of Anglicanism in Devon and Corn-wall together with the relative lack of Roman Catholicism. Once again cause and effect are difficult to disentangle but the marked presence of Nonconformity in the region cannot be dissociated surely from the Anglo-Catholic flavour of the Southwest dioceses; for rapid growth in the

Nonconformist presence has inevitably encouraged alternative (Anglo-Catholic) emphases in the Church of England, the case of the Truro Diocese being even more marked than that of Exeter. Conversely, the presence of Roman (as opposed to Anglo-) Catholicism declines the further west one goes. There has been some growth in this respect in recent years due to in-migration into the area, but it is hardly surprising that the numbers of Catholics (still for the most part urban people in contemporary Britain) remain low in these predominantly rural counties (Brierley 1991a and 1991b).

In this respect, as indeed in many others, the Northwest provides almost a mirror image of the area just described. Here the presence (rather than the absence) of Roman Catholicism – both recusant and Irish – is the notable feature. It is a presence, moreover, which has had an effect on the development of other denominations in the region, for there exists in the Northwest – in addition to considerable numbers of free churches – a distinctive Low-Church, but not necessarily evangelical, Anglicanism;[11] a regional feature which illustrates, like its Southwest counterpart, an evident adaptability within the Church of England. Two points about the Northwest are, however, important before going further. Firstly its self-definition is not so obvious as the Southwest peninsula. Following the census and government regional policy, Brierley's figures include Cheshire, Lancashire, the Isle of Man, Merseyside and Greater Manchester, a densely populated part of the country where most socio-economic indicators contrast sharply with the Southwest. Secondly, it is, of course, an enormously varied region. Rural Cheshire, for example, looks nothing like the major cities, and Liverpool, in religion as in so many ways, is a special case. This case will be the one developed here, for it embodies a second, albeit very different, illustration of the interaction between religious factors and political life; a politico-religious culture, moreover, which demonstrates dramatic change – rather than lingering survival – through the course of the post-war period.[12]

In the mid 1950s Liverpool had a Conservative city council and a majority (six out of ten) of Conservative MPs. It is hard to remember in the present political climate this presence on Merseyside of a popular Toryism that attracted a large proportion of the working-class vote. Four decades later (in 1993) Liverpool has five Labour MPs, one Lib-Dem MP and a council more or less divided between Labour (itself split into two factions) and Liberals; the Conservatives are non-existent as an effective political group. Changes in Liverpool's religious life have been equally radical. Liverpool has not only shaken off its sectarian past; it has emerged as a striking example of ecumenical co-operation. The question to address, then, is whether these two evolutions – political and religious – are in any way related to one another?

The key to understanding what one might call the traditional divisions of Liverpool's politics, that is, the pattern which prevailed until the 1950s, is the Irish factor (Waller 1981). Huge Irish immigration into nineteenth-century Liverpool had unavoidable consequences for almost every aspect of the city's life, not least its politics. Just as in Northern Ireland, political divisions along class lines were less important than sectarian splits, and the working-class vote divided. Protestants chose to vote Conservative rather than join with the Catholics in the Labour Party. Employment and housing opportunities also depended on the right denominational connections, for the sectarian divide pervaded almost every aspect of daily life. It was not until after the war that this pattern began to fade. Indeed the war experience itself contributed to the change both directly (in the form of a common enemy) and indirectly (in the massive housing programmes that followed the bombing). Populations became increasingly mixed and the ghetto mentality diminished.[13] At the same time social and economic problems began, increasingly, to dominate the agenda, and sectarian politics seemed less and less relevant. In other words the process of secularization was taking its course. But the situation in Liverpool is rather more complex than this, for the churches and their leaders remain unusually active in the political life of this city. What is more their voice is, to a very considerable extent, a united one; a point that can be illustrated at all levels but which is most easily exemplified in the high-profile partnership between the two Bishops, Archbishop Derek Worlock and Bishop David Sheppard.[14]

Why should this be the case? The local political situation provides at least part of the explanation. In the mid 1980s the normal political processes in Liverpool came close to breaking down. This was one of the most disturbing aspects of the Militant episode in the middle of the Thatcher decade (Parkinson 1985). At the same time Liverpool presented – and continues to present – one of the most severe cases of urban deprivation in contemporary Britain, an issue that has become increasingly central to the churches' agenda both locally and nationally. It was hardly surprising in such circumstances, civic and economic, that local people began to look away from conventional political leadership for an alternative way out of their predicament. The churches offered an effective resource in this respect, the more so in view of their capacity for united action. The extent of deprivation in the city is, however, the most obvious explanation for the drop in the Tory vote. Despite Liberal success at local level, Labour is undoubtedly the natural political colour of a city like Liverpool, no longer torn apart by sectarian strife. All the more reason, then, to note the absence of a strong Labour Party until the 1950s and the presence pre-war of a popular, indeed populist, Toryism. Ironically the style of this Toryism was in many ways closer to the Thatcherism so detested on Merseyside than it was to mainstream British Conservatism. Liverpool, as ever, remains a city of profound paradox.

In many respects, the contrast between the Southwest and Northwest examples can be accounted for by the first being predominantly rural and the second predominantly urban, but this is only part of the story. Distinct regional – even local – cultures cannot be ignored. Two of these have been explored in some detail to give an indication of the kind of work that is possible within this framework. But a number of further variables must also be taken into consideration. The range and complexity of such variables in the subtle and evolving relationships linking 'believing' and 'belonging' in contemporary Britain will come clearer in the following somewhat tentative typology of religious belief.[15]

A Suggested Typology of Belief

1. The typology itself

The inner city	Belief depressed
The suburb	Belief articulated
The city centre	Civic belief
The countryside	Belief assumed
The Roman Catholic Church	Belief expressed
The Afro-Caribbean churches	Communal belief
Religious education	Belief injected or rejected
Religious broadcasting	Believing without belonging *par excellence*

The above typology is neither conclusive nor exhaustive. On the contrary, its compilation is essentially pragmatic with the intention that it may be added to as necessary. It could, for example, include many more denominational illustrations. It could also incorporate some of the national or regional variations already discussed alongside additional variables such as age or gender. The typology is also pragmatic in that it is ideal-typical in the sociological sense. That is to say, the types suggested in the columns are most unlikely to exist in pure form on the ground, for in practice belief will almost always display mixed characteristics. Rather the labels are intended to evoke a distinctive characteristic, a particular flavour even, that differentiates belief in one part of society from another, and the way that this particular type of belief relates (or fails to relate) to religious practice. In this sense, the typology can become a useful tool of analysis, an example of a Weberian ideal-type, against which to measure reality.

More immediately, however, it can begin to bridge the gap between an approach based on geographical or territorial factors and one that evokes social and economic differences. The first four examples in the typology – the inner city, the suburb, the city centre (varieties of urban) and the countryside (rural) – demonstrate this point. They can be looked at either way, for it is clear that the particular locations in question are related to distinct social classes, or combinations of social classes. The salience of such social and economic differences for an analysis of religious belief and belonging – the preoccupation of this and the following section – is undeniable. The relationships between these variables are, however, complex; they are best described by illustrating the cases in question.

The discrepancy between believing and belonging, for example, is at its sharpest in urban working-class areas, and above all in the inner city. Here belief persists (albeit in a depressed form), but the expected reluctance to practise religion is compounded by a further factor, a mistrust of institutional life of whatever kind, the churches included (see Sheppard's foreword to Ahern and Davie 1987). A second point is equally significant: this situation of alienation from institutional Christianity is nothing new. Indeed some sections of the urban working class in Britain have been without any real contact with their churches for several generations. How, then, has working-class belief been able to maintain itself despite a prolonged divorce from institutional Christianity? And what effect has this divorce had on the nature of working-class belief? Part of the explanation lies in what might appear a self-contradictory statement, but it is one that begins to display the intricacies of the connections between believing and belonging. For it is at one and the same time true that higher social groupings are on average more inclined to belief and practice than lower ones, and that increased educational levels (normally associated with higher social class) have a negative effect on religious belief. In other words the nature of the relationship between belief and practice varies depending on the social class in question. In a middle-class environment people are more likely to make conscious choices about both belief and practice; if they do one, they do the other. In contrast, in a working-class environment (where levels of education are lower) there is, apparently, no perceived need to put belief into institutional or liturgical practice. Indeed it could be argued that the reverse is true; in many urban areas, churchgoing is seen as at best unnecessary and at worst hypocritical (Hoggart 1984).

The overall pattern of religious life is changing. For it appears that more and more people within British society want to believe but do not want to involve themselves in religious practice. In other words some aspects of working-class religious behaviour (notably the lack of regular religious attendance) – traditionally thought of as exceptions to the rule – are increasingly becoming the normal pattern of our society. At the same time the small number of working-class church attenders has declined even further. Practice declines in all social groups (unevenly and from different starting points), while some sort of belief persists.[16] It is easy to slip into value judgements about different types of religious behaviour and to conclude that things are not only changing but getting worse. This is not necessarily the case. Traditional working-class modes of religious behaviour may be different, but they are just as valid as middle-class ones. There are, nonetheless, important shifts taking place in our society concerning which questions should be asked. One such has already been hinted at, at the beginning of chapter 5, but arises again in the present discussion. It is this. How far can the present structures of religious life in this country maintain themselves if increasing numbers of people in British society prefer a passive rather than an active relationship to these structures? Or, in other words, is there a minimum size below which the active religious minority can no longer be effective in society? And what factors, apart from size, might determine this effectiveness?

A second set of questions runs parallel. They relate in particular to the third section of the typology. If churchgoing in its conventional sense is diminishing, through which institutional mechanisms can those concerned about the religious factor in contemporary society work outside of the church itself? Who has access to these institutions? And what, in this connection, is the role of religious education or religious broadcasting? But before turning to the final part of the typology (religious broadcasting at the end of this chapter and religious education in the next), one or two aspects of the earlier sections require further explanation.

2. *Different models of church organization*

Parochial and market models of church organization have coexisted in Britain for centuries. The Church of England worked on one model, the free churches – the 'gathered church' (the term itself is significant) – on another.[17] The contrast between the two still persists, accounting, at least in part, for the relative fortunes of each of these churches in different parts of British society. In general the parochial model has held up better in conditions of severe economic hardship, notably in the inner city. Held there by its parochial obligations, the Church of England has – unlike almost every other social institution – maintained at least a presence in these deprived communities despite increasingly difficult circumstances. The free churches have found the going harder, though it is important to note that the traditional free churches have in some, if not all, British cities been replaced by the gathered congregations of the immigrant populations, whether these be Christian in the Afro-Caribbean churches or other-faith communities. What is relatively new is the introduction of the market principle into some parts of the Church of England. This shift is best illustrated by the phenomenon noted in chapter 4, that is, the flourishing churches of suburbia which attract large numbers of like-minded individuals from a relatively wide geographical area, well beyond the parochial boundaries. These are, very often, articulate individuals who choose – for doctrinal or aesthetic reasons – the type of church to which they want to belong. Such churches are often characterized by activity, by successions of committees and by a much clearer distinction between members and non-members than is found in most Anglican churches. In other words, middle-class organizational patterns reflect middle-class ways of believing: the two variables – believing and belonging – have come much closer together than is normally the case. More rather than less hardline baptism policies tend to be a visible sign of this phenomenon.[18]

If we turn now to the rural church, it is different again. It is, moreover, a rapidly changing church; or, more precisely, one that is struggling to come to terms with a rapidly changing situation. Traditionally, the rural church has been the focus of largely unspoken corporate belief. Local people assume that they are members of this church unless proved otherwise. Their relatives are, more often than not, buried in the churchyard, and there is little reason to doubt that the same resting place will be theirs when the time comes. There is no need, in the meantime, to display church membership through specifically religious activity, though social events will often be very well supported. So too will appeals for the church building, which assumes considerable symbolic importance. Belief or membership is, essentially, experiential; it is not based on regular religious practice.[19] This long-standing unquestioned arrangement has, however, been overtaken by events in many places. Demographic shifts in contemporary society are leading to a changing rural population, as the large industrial conurbations decline in favour of the small towns and villages. As a consequence of this shift, a significant number of those arriving in the villages come equipped with habits – including religious habits – acquired in suburbia. The resulting clash between two styles of belief (rural and suburban) centred on one Anglican church (the parish church) can be very painful indeed. Articulate, often rather energetic religiosity sits uneasily alongside the largely unexpressed – or, to be more accurate, differently expressed – emotions of the rural community. Not surprisingly, this change in the rural community forms an important dimension of recent investigations, both pastoral and sociological, into the rural church, for they result in difficult situations. Such difficulties are compounded by a shortage of personnel, for very few rural parishes now have exclusive use of one incumbent.[20]

Regarding the remaining examples in this section, 'city centre' needs to be distinguished from 'inner city'. The latter has become a widely accepted concept, though it is worth underlining that the rather more precise term 'urban priority area' describes a set of social and economic characteristics rather than a particular geographical location. For the term 'UPA' was devised with the deliberate intention of including the deprived council estates which ring the larger conurbations and which are, geographically as well socially, separate from the centres of urban activity. From the point of view of pastoral care, the outer council estates are very often the hardest patches of all in that they lack even local tradition to form any kind of connection with the institutional churches. Inner city communities, in contrast, may suffer from the reverse phenomenon. They are over-provided with churches – frequently large impractical Victorian buildings erected to serve a densely populated area – in which small congregations eke out a problematic existence. But the closing of such buildings, however inevitable, has a demoralizing effect on everyone.

City centres are rather different. In many places they are served by cathedrals or large city-centre churches which become the focus of civic or public religion. It is here, for example, that the principal Remembrance Sunday parades take place or that the Assize Judge will go prior to the Assize Court's sitting. It is in these buildings that the year's turning points – some religious and some less so – are marked formally and publicly for the whole community. It is here, too, that all manner of clubs and voluntary organizations will congregate for commemoration of the past or blessing for the future. The effectiveness of such churches varies from place to place but some become a natural and effective focal point of the community; the gathering place in moments of joy, danger, doubt or sorrow (the place of mourning after a disaster, for example). Their potential as a focus for the sacred is, if anything, increasing as the century draws to a close,[21] for in many respects this kind of public marking of both expected and unexpected events is what religion seems in the present circumstances to be doing best. It is anything but privatized religion.

3. Denominational variations/minority status

The second section within the typology illustrates a rather different type of pressure on religious belief and its relationship to practice, and it is this section which could be extended considerably further bearing in mind the diversity of denominations present in contemporary Britain. It could also, with appropriate caution, provide a framework for a consideration of the other-faith populations of this country, for such communities may well be interesting precisely because the combinations of variables which they display are markedly different from those considered the norm – albeit a very diverse norm – within the various branches of Western Christianity.

In this section, however, two Christian examples, contrasting minority churches, must suffice.

The first point to grasp, in this connection, is that minorities almost always behave differently from majorities with respect to both believing and belonging. For there are, undoubtedly, certain pressures on a community which derive from its minority status; a status which poses inevitable questions about identity, about the maintenance of a tradition, about the future of the group in question. Not surprisingly, religious practice tends to be higher within such communities, who may feel a certain responsibility to encourage a continuity that is unsupported by the mainstream. We have already seen, for example, that religious practice remains high for the Roman Catholic population in this country, much higher than the norm for the British mainland in general. But in this case, there is a second, reinforcing factor coming from a rather different quarter. The obligation of practice, of Mass attendance, is far stronger in the teaching of Catholicism than exhortations to practise are in Protestant teaching. There are, therefore, theological as well as sociological reasons why the Roman Catholic community will behave differently in this respect.[22] To a certain extent the case of Northern Ireland reinforces this kind of interpretation, though in a typically Northern Irish way. Attendance is high (relatively speaking) in both Protestant and Catholic communities, but highest of all among the Catholics, reflecting the obligation to attend Mass. The parallel question of majority/minority status in this part of the United Kingdom is, however, as delicate as it is complicated. This is hardly surprising since the whole history of partition embodies as its principal *raison d'être* the establishment and maintenance of an artificial majority in Ulster. The consequences are far reaching: a Catholic feels part of a minority in Northern Ireland, of a majority in a united Ireland, of a minority within the British Isles and of a majority within Western Europe, and will act accordingly. For the Northern Irish Unionist, the reverse is true in each case, a point that cannot be overlooked if there really are signs of demographic change in the six counties (see above, p. 99) and with respect to the European debate.

A second and contrasting denominational example comes from the Afro-Caribbean churches, this time representing an immigrant community who have arrived on the British mainland comparatively recently. These churches not only draw people together for a particular type of worship but also provide a whole range of support mechanisms for the immigrant population. They are, moreover, remarkably successful in this undertaking and in so doing, the black churches appear to be reversing the traditional English connections between church and community. For many black congregations, the sense of community grows out of the church which is its principal reason for existence. In contrast, a traditional English church – and the Church of England is the most obvious example – forms a religious focus within a given community for those who wish to take up its services (in both senses of the term), bearing in mind that there are very many ways in which this take-up may be effected. Indeed, the relationships between the community and its church, or churches, are quite clearly as diverse and elusive as those between the two variables, believing and belonging.

4. Religious broadcasting: believing without belonging par excellence

What can be said, then, about the church which has no visible community at all – the church of the air – remembering that this particular form of religious activity remains relatively popular in contemporary Britain?[23] The evidence for popularity is not difficult to find, but it continues sometimes to surprise even those responsible for programming. For example, television audience figures stay high for religious broadcasting, and especially so for those programmes which aim for the mass market (the often quoted audience figures for *Songs of Praise* or *Highway* which exceed those of *Match of the Day*). Similarly the ill-fated audience poll in 1990, seeking the opinion of *Today* listeners with regard to the *Thought for the Day* slot, discovered unexpected support for the religious three to four minutes just before eight every morning on Radio Four. There were no grounds here for discontinuing this part of the programme (Bradley 1992).

Religious broadcasting – like every other aspect of religious life – has, however, evolved through the post-war period. Unquestionably Christian at the outset, it has come, sometimes reluctantly, to reflect a much greater religious diversity in which Christian views are seen as one alternative among many, including the areligious or agnostic (Winter 1988). It will also change again as the broadcasting world in general submits increasingly to the market and as technology permits an exponential growth in the number of outlets available to the average household. One understandable, though rather negative, response to the impending revolution in broadcasting is the fear that American-style televangelism may come to dominate the religious market on this side of the Atlantic. This is one possible scenario. But whether or not the British public have any taste for this type of broadcasting remains a very open question. For media portrayals of religion undoubtedly have some sort of relationship to the social reality that they try to depict, and the social reality in Britain is very different indeed from that in the United States.[24] The relationship between the media and real life is, in fact, a symbiotic one. Television and radio claim to be a mirror held up to life; at the same time the media undoubtedly fashion the images that many of us have of religion. Such images are curiously diverse and may become more so. But equally there may well be limits to what a British audience will tolerate.

In terms of this chapter, however, the most significant aspect of religious broadcasting lies in its somewhat uneasy relationship with the institutional churches. It is, in many respects, the extreme case of belief without belonging, for it seems to permit, encourage even, a rather self-indulgent form of armchair religiosity. It reflects, moreover, the wider nature of contemporary advanced industrial society where the small screen competes (often with overwhelming success) with the equivalent activity in 'real life' whether this be sport, leisure activities or religion. The idea of competition works in fact in two ways. On the one hand *Songs of Praise* audience figures hold up well against *Match of the Day*. That, the churches feel, is a good thing. But the attraction of the media presentation – whether this be of football or of religion – competes all too effectively (if this is your point of view) against the equivalent outside the studio; in this case with attendance at church services or at football matches. In consequence, both the latter, together with a whole range of similar activities, lose out to the advantage of television. On the other hand the local churches know perfectly well that the sheer professionalism of much religious broadcasting makes good a number of their own deficiencies. It is an extraordinarily effective medium. There can be little doubt that the religious broadcasters bolster the values in society on which both they and the churches depend for their survival. Religious broadcasting becomes, therefore, both friend and foe to the institutional churches: upholding the values necessary for the survival of the religious factor in contemporary society but offering a rival focus for such values.

Either way, it cannot but disturb the conventional relationship between believing and belonging, a relationship which can never be taken for granted. Bearing this in mind, two policies suggest themselves. Firstly, that a careful eye should be kept on the media with a view to monitoring exactly who has access to this important outlet. And, secondly, that the churches themselves devote considerable resources and expertise to their media presentation, for they cannot, realistically, continue to exist without this.

Notes

1   Both publications emerged from the discussions held at St George's House, Windsor (see Preface).
2   The Marc Europe figures also demonstrate differing rates of decline for each of the UK countries. Losses in Scotland, for example, have been especially heavy since 1985.
3   Equally evident, however, are the exceptions to the rule: the popular and successful city churches attracting a particular section of the population.
4   The British Euro-sceptics reflect such attitudes. They are concerned above all with the loss of British identity within the European whole.
5   Always assuming, of course, the accuracy of the figures both in this census and in previous ones, for there have been times when one or other community in Northern Ireland has – for various reasons – urged its memebers not to co-operate in their census returns.
6   The relatively high Catholic birth-rate used to be compensated by a greater tendency for Catholics to emigrate. The latter is now more difficult given the changes in the labour market on the British mainland. The number of unskilled jobs is increasingly limited. In contrast, growing numbers of Northern Irish Protestants seek higher or further education on the mainland; many of them choose to stay out of the Provice after completing their studies.
7   Cross-denominational growth and decline has become an important dimension of the Marc Europe religious censuses, material which, significantly, is produced on a regional basis.
8   The apparent homogeneity of Cornwall's Nonconformity should be treated with some caution, for there was (indeed there still is) *within* Methodism an astonishing scope for diversity.

9 For a rather different interpretation of these figures, see Winter 1991.

10 It is hardly surprising that the distinctions between the two counties become increasingly blurred the further north one goes, for the River Tamar ceases to be an effective geographical boundary.

11 Such parishes are sometimes compared in style to the Church of Ireland, itself overwhelmingly dominated by the Roman Catholic presence in the Republic.

12 The following paragraphs can be read as background to the section on the Hillsborough disaster in chapter 5. They account for the Celtic and Irish flavour present in Liverpool's religious reactions.

13 The fading of a ghetto mentality was, of course, welcome. It cannot, however, be separated from a rather more negative phenomenon: that is, the gradual fragmentation of effective neighbourhood communities.

14 The partnership is, in fact, a three-way affair, involving, in addition to the two Bishops, the leader of Liverpool's free churches. This post, however, rotates on a regular basis. Hence the difficulty of providing a third name regularly linked to those of the two episcopal leaders.

15 This typology was first suggested at a meeting of the International Society for the Sociology of Religion in Helsinki (1989). It was subsequently published in Davie 1990b, the article critiqued by Hornsby-Smith (1992) and by Short and Winter (1993).

16 The term 'belief' is, of course, a wide one; it does not imply the acceptance of particular credal statements.

17 Gill (1993) points out the negative consequences of this cohabitation. Competition between the two models of church life has led in some areas to the rampant overbuilding of churches, itself a factor contributing to church decline.

18 Suburban churches are, of course, enormously varied. Only the extreme cases conform to the type just described; many others operate – very effectively – as parish churches serving a particular suburban area regardless of churchmanship or aesthetic style.

19 Assessing the evidence of the Rural Church Project, Short and Winter (1993) maintain that the sense of 'belonging' to the rural church remains strong, a belonging which does not depend on regular practice. Hence their challenge to the formula 'believing without

116   *Believing Without Belonging*

belonging'. The debate, however, very quickly becomes semantic, for the need to find some way of understanding modern religiosity remains, whatever the formula employed to describe the non-practising attachment to the rural, or indeed to any other, church.

20 See *Faith in the Countryside* 1990, and Davies, Watkins and Winter (1991) for a full discussion of the rural church.

21 It is in this context that the current popularity of cathedrals should be considered (see chapter 4).

22 In France, in contrast, there is evidence of relatively high practice among the very small Protestant community. Here minority status outweighs theological pressures. Religious practice among French Catholics remains unusually low, however, compared with most West European countries.

23 See Svennevig et al. (1988) for a detailed discussion of viewers, religion and television, including material about the nature and size of television audiences.

24 The difference between European patterns of religiosity and those in the United States are striking. Americans not only maintain astonishingly high levels of belief, they continue to practise in considerable numbers. Nearly half the population of the United States will be in church most Sundays. And within the churchgoing constituency, it is the theologically conservative churches which are growing in popularity. The televangelists have a large potential audience.

7 Handing on the Tradition: the Significance of Age and Gender

Two further sociological variables should now be introduced: age and gender. Both are variables whose effect on religiosity is rather more straightforward than those so far considered. For women, it seems, are almost always more religious than men, as are old people compared to the young, though the figures rise again for children. These differences hold over a wide variety of indicators. This chapter will deal first with gender. Why is it that women are so consistently more religious than men? Is it possible to discover a satisfactory explanation for this pervasive phenomenon? It will then look at generational change, a discussion that picks up the themes introduced in chapter 3 concerning the shifting moods of the post-war period. In a third section the two factors will be brought together, along with some of the differences already discussed, in three short case studies. The first examines the chaplain's role in two hospitals for women in one particular city. The second is taken from the Rural Church Project and illustrates the significance of both age and gender (alongside a range of other variables) in rural religiosity. The third moves into the world of education and demonstrates the interrelationships of age and gender in a small Cornish community.[1] The final part of the chapter develops the discussion of education further, with particular reference to church schools and to religious education; a contentious area in a supposedly secular and partially pluralist society, which acts as bridge to the analysis in chapter 8 of the relationships between church and state.

Why Is it that Women are more Religious than Men?

Or to be more accurate, why are women's religious sensitivities *different* from those of men? For not only does gender almost always appear as a significant variable, often the most significant, with respect to quantitative issues (how many individuals do or do not practise, do or do not believe), it is equally true that the nature – a more qualitative measure – of women's beliefs is different from that of their male counterparts. All such differences hold throughout the age range.

The study of the most obvious and quantifiable aspect of these phenomena remains, however, paradoxical. Despite the pervasiveness of the gender variable in studies of churchgoing, no really convincing explanation for this persistent feature exists. Not surprisingly, in some respects, for the question remains curiously understudied, disappearing down the gap between two different groups of specialists. For sociologists of religion have, it seems, given a relatively low priority to matters of gender, and gender specialists appear equally unconvinced about religion. Moreover, those most likely to bring the two sides together and concern themselves with women's religiosity in this country (the Christian feminists) have become distracted. Particularly in the last two decades – when appropriate questions might have been asked – this group has been understandably preoccupied with a different issue. They have been asking (quite rightly) why it is that men dominate in the chancel. They have not, as yet anyway, addressed the equally significant, and not unrelated question: why do women so often predominate in the pews?[2] For they undoubtedly do. The evidence is overwhelming.

This is helpfully summarized in a review of the literature (such as it is) published by Walter (1990b) in which he takes three dimensions of religiosity: churchgoing, private prayer and the content of religious belief as a framework for further discussion. Each of these requires a little expansion. The disproportionate number of women going to church, for example, is amply confirmed by the figures from the 1989 Marc Europe census, from which an additional factor also emerges. Not only do the census figures underline the imbalance between the sexes, they indicate that this feature is becoming more rather than less marked in contemporary society.[3] In assessing such figures, however, it is important to keep in mind wider demographic shifts, particularly if the age variable is introduced as well. For churchgoing has, quite clearly, a particular appeal for a group that is prospering, demographically speaking, in contemporary society; that is, older women. The ratio of live females to live males increases with every step up the age scale, a difference that might account in part, though by no means entirely, for disproportionate numbers of women especially in elderly congregations. A final point concerns denomination. Here the material is complex, but – once again – it is the mainline churches that demonstrate the greatest fall-off in attendance by men. The independents, pentecostals and the Orthodox have been able to resist this trend.

The mismatch between statistics relating to religious practice and those relating to religious belief provides one organizing theme within this book. But quite apart from the discrepancy between belief and practice, there is *within* almost every question relating to religious belief a noticeable difference between the scores of men and women. For example, the Mori poll carried out in 1989 (Jacobs and Worcester 1990) – reinforcing the findings of the European Values Study already cited – discovered that 84 per cent of the women in their sample believe in God, but only 67 per cent of the men; in contrast only 9 per cent of the women say that they do *not* believe in God as opposed to 16 per cent of the men. Seventy-two per cent of the women believe in sin, 76 per cent in a soul, 69 per cent in heaven, 57 per cent in life after death, 42 per cent in the devil and 35 per cent in hell. The corresponding figures for men were 66 per cent (sin), 58 per cent (a soul), 50 per cent (heaven), 39 per cent (life after death), 32 per cent (the devil) and 27 per cent (hell), differences that are very similar to those between the age groups (see below). Walter (following Argyle and Beit-Hallahmi 1975) emphasizes the dimension of private prayer as one where the contrasting behaviour of men and women is at its most marked, prompting reflection about the relationship between the presence of men in religious activity and the extent to which this activity is designated either as public or private. If the private is beginning to predominate in some – though by no means all – aspects of contemporary religiosity, the significance of women as transmitters of that religiosity may be increasing very rapidly indeed.[4] Moreover what they choose to transmit may equally well be affected. For women, if they are asked to describe the God in whom they believe, concentrate rather more on the God of love, comfort and forgiveness than on the God of power, planning and control. Men, it seems, do the reverse. Interestingly, these contrasts show at a relatively early age, for they emerge in a number of studies of teenagers as well as in those using samples drawn from the adult population,[5] opening an inevitable but inconclusive debate about where such notions come from in the first place. Is it a question of nature or nurture?

This discussion leads into the second part of Walter's article, in which he begins to look for explanations: why are there such marked and consistent differences between men and women with respect to such a wide variety of religious indicators? The article collects together eleven social scientific theories grouped into three categories: the psychological theories (those which talk about guilt, anxiety, dependence and about God as the father figure); the deprivation-compensation theories (those concerning material poverty, status and the different opportunities that men and women have for social life); and, thirdly, a group of theories concerning the roles that women assume in society (including child-rearing, closely linked by Walter to sacrifice, the participation of women in the workforce and a section on the privatization of religion). Walter concludes, quite rightly, that it is most unlikely that any one of these 'theories' (in many cases they are little more than suggestions) is likely to hold in every case. But taken together, and in flexible combinations, they may at least begin to indicate fruitful lines of research.

My own inclination, however, is to favour those explanations which underline the proximity of women to birth and death. Understandably, these moments continue – even at the end of the twentieth century – to evoke echoes of the sacred, for they must, by their very nature, bring to mind questions about the reasons for existence and about the meaning of life itself. Very few women give birth without any reflection about the mysteries of creation and very few people watch someone die (especially a close relative) without any thought at all about why that person lived or what might happen to them after death. It is true that medical science has, up to a point, altered the way in which these events are perceived. It is usually the case, for example, that birth and death now take place in a medical rather than domestic environment and both states will be defined in medical parlance. But the giving of birth remains, despite everything, one of the most profound experiences of a woman's life, even if she is in hospital at the time, and women are still disproportionately involved in the caring roles of our society; in the care of the elderly and dying as well as in the nurture of children. Is it all that surprising, in consequence, that the nature of their religiosity is coloured by such experiences? The evidence, however, remains impressionistic; the case is far from proven.

The Generation Game

Older people have always been more religious than the young. Whether the elderly have regarded God as judgemental (the source of all their troubles) or as a father figure (a rock in the storm of life), they have always taken him more seriously than their sons and daughters. This kind of generational difference has been reflected in church membership studies for some time, and is increasingly supported by studies of religious belief. The Mori poll already quoted – once again reinforcing the EVSSG figures – illustrates this point clearly, revealing that 67 per cent of those aged between 15 and 34 believe in God as against 87 per cent of those aged over 55. Similarly only 55 per cent of the younger age-group believe in heaven as opposed to 65 per cent of the older. It seems that belief in God, and specifically belief in a personal God, declines with every step down the age scale, as indeed do practice, prayer and moral conservatism. In short, in Britain as in most of Western Europe, a religiously and morally conservative majority among the retired becomes a religiously conservative minority in the 18–24 age-group. We need, however, to pay careful attention to detail in assessing this kind of material, for a great deal depends on how the category 'young people' is defined. The recent Marc Europe census, for example, indicates that the highest percentage of English non-churchgoers is found among those in their twenties: attendance figures rise again for teenagers and even more markedly for children. It is also important to note the possibility of significant differences *within* whatever age-group emerges as the most appropriate to define the young; differences that relate to denomination, to social class and, of course, to gender. Each of these variables must be considered in relation to the others despite the perplexing nature of the results, even within the parameters of this chapter. For having touched earlier on the significance of childbirth as a moment which evokes echoes of the sacred for many women, it is disconcerting to discover that the fewest churchgoers in English society, proportionally speaking, are to be found among those of child-bearing age. There are, quite clearly, no easy answers.

There is, however, an underlying question lurking in this data; a question which parallels the rather similar point made in connection with social class in the previous chapter. It can be stated quite simply. Are we, in the late twentieth century, experiencing a marked *generational* shift with respect to religious behaviour, or are the variations so far indicated simply in accordance with the normal manifestations of the life cycle? If the former is the case – and the evidence is by no means conclusive – the implications for the future of religious life may be very considerable indeed. The point at issue has already been posed in chapter 6 but can be stated again with the particular connotations of generational change: just how far can the familiar patterns of religious life maintain themselves if more and more people (among them increasing numbers of the young) opt out of active religiosity, not only temporarily but for the greater part of their lives? In other words, at what point does the active and practising religious minority become so reduced that it ceases to have a realistic effect upon the host society?

One or two qualifications are, however, important before jumping to conclusions about possible future scenarios. The first concerns a shift that has already taken place in British society in the post-war period which, in turn, relates to the generations described in chapter 3. It is, moreover, a shift that has been accommodated by the churches, though they may not always have been conscious of the change. *Pre-war* generations in Britain, to a greater extent than is often realized, grew up under the influence of the churches, or, at least, under the influence of a wide network of para-church organizations. By no means all British people practised their faith with regularity, but they possessed, nonetheless, a degree of religious knowledge that had some sort of connection with orthodox Christianity. This connection was most obviously expressed in the possession of a shared vocabulary; a common language which could be assumed, on either side, in encounters with the churches' personnel. Since the war, this pattern has altered radically, for it is the generation born immediately after the war that has, very largely, broken the formal link with the churches: hence the marked drop in both membership and attendance figures in the 1960s. But nominal belief in God persists, partly embodied in an accepting – and in some senses grateful – attitude to the churches despite the lack of regular attendance. It is, however, a belief which is less and less influenced by Christian teaching, in the sense of shared knowledge. Orthodox Christianity and popular religion have, not surprisingly, been drifting apart, the key point of the first case study in the following section.

But before turning to this illustration an inevitable corollary suggests itself: is a further generational shift in religious behaviour upon us as the twentieth century draws to a close? In other words – following at least one line of evidence in the European Values Study – significant groups of young people (with all the provisos surrounding this problematic term) might be moving to the next stage; for them, in particular, disconnected belief is increasingly giving way to no belief at all, a conclusion for which there is a good deal of empirical support (notably in the work of Francis).[6] There is, however, another possibility; one, moreover, that reflects the character of religiosity in the 1990s. For if the definition of religion is widened to include questions about individual and social health, about the purpose of existence, the future of the planet and the responsibilities of humanity both to fellow humans and to the earth itself, we may find a rather different pattern of 'religious' behaviour among the young. Once again, the evidence remains impressionistic but it seems at least plausible that the younger age-groups may respond to these profound ecological, moral, ethical (and, surely, religious) issues much more constructively than they do to traditional religious beliefs. Their response, moreover, may be considerably more positive than that of their elders.

Of course, this line of argument begs many questions. The first of these is obvious: has the ground been shifted so completely that we are no longer talking about the same phenomenon? And even if we agree that the approach is legitimate, we obviously need to discover a great deal more about the elusive and changing links between religious and ethical behaviour. Such questions become, moreover, more urgent rather than less, in that contemporary society, almost by its very nature, throws up issue after issue which lie, precisely, on this boundary; a crucial focus of study, surely, for theoretical as well as empirical work in the sociology of religion in the 1990s. It will reappear in the discussion of religious education.

Age and Gender: Three Case Studies

1. The experience of a hospital chaplain

The following illustration of generational change emerged from the discussions held at St George's House, Windsor (see Preface). It came from the experience of a hospital chaplain responsible for the pastoral care of two hospitals in Liverpool, both of which cater exclusively for women. The first admitted patients primarily for gynaecological treatment, including substantial numbers of women in late middle age or even older. The second was the maternity unit for most of Liverpool, admitting mothers for antenatal care and delivery, for the most part women in their late teens, twenties and early thirties. For all practical purposes the constituencies of the two hospitals were similar, apart from the difference in age.

Both groups of women were equally pleased to see the chaplain. Indeed in both hospitals there were repeated expressions of gratitude that there was someone in the institution whose business it was to affirm joy, to assuage grief and to comfort in times of tribulation, though obviously the distribution of these tasks might be different depending upon the nature of the hospital. The crucial point, however, from the point of view of this chapter, was the chaplain's appreciation that in going about her task in the two hospitals, she had to make different assumptions. For in the first instance, where appreciable numbers of the patients might have had some connection with their churches at least in their youth, the shared vocabulary was evident, if not always articulated; a common language significant both in the personal encounter and in the form of worship, even informal worship, that was possible on a Sunday morning. Exactly the same routines in the maternity hospital had to be undertaken rather differently. The younger women were equally appreciative of the chaplain but unable to communicate with her in the same way as their mothers or grandmothers. Similarly such worship as took place had to be effected without the benefit (or some might say hindrance) of a half-remembered language. Ministry was not necessarily more difficult among the younger women – particularly those emerging from the experience of giving birth – but it had to be approached in a different way. New formulas had to be found for articulating the sacred, for there was nothing to fall back on in this generation of women, born for the most part since 1960.[7]

2. Age and gender in a rural community

A second example draws on the material produced by the Rural Church Project, an extensive empirical study which examined rural religiosity from multiple points of view.[8] The following quotations are selected from the section on churchgoing. They summarize a discussion which includes the key variables of age, gender and social class, as well as a range of indicators specific to this particular enquiry; the size of settlement, the degree of rurality, the presence (or otherwise) of an incumbent in the village, churchmanship, length of residence on the part of the parishioners and regional variations. (The study covered five very diverse rural dioceses: Truro, Gloucester, Lincoln, Southwell and Durham.) The significance of gender, alongside age and social class, for churchgoing is neatly caught in the following:

> If we had to draw a pen-portrait of the type of person most likely to be a regular attender, *she* would probably be aged over 45 and belong to one of the higher social classes. She would be a housewife who had not lived in the parish all her life, but had moved there at least ten years ago. Conversely, the person least likely to attend church regularly would be a young man. *He* would belong to one of the lower social classes and either have recently moved to the parish, or lived in the parish all his life. (Davies, Watkins and Winter 1991: 245–6)

The analysis of clergy responses permits the same question to be approached from another angle. Clergy were asked about possible imbalances in their congregations. Here the age variable is undoubtedly perceived as more significant than gender:

> By far the most common group to be underrepresented were young people in general, and in particular teenagers. This partly reflects the national situation, but also the more specific problems of conducting youth work in rural areas. (1991: 219)

This kind of explanation is hardly surprising in that the particular challenges and difficulties of rural ministry were the principal focus of the project. It is, however, a further reminder that spatial distinctions have to be taken into account alongside sociological ones. Further analysis of the RCP data has been carried out by Short (forthcoming). Interestingly, the emphasis in this work – particularly with reference to a sense of denominational belonging – lies on the gender variable rather than on age. All the more reason, then, to discover a convincing sociological explanation for this persistent phenomenon; the more so in a society where gender roles are evolving very rapidly indeed.

3. *Attitudes towards religion in a small Cornish town*

The interrelationships between age and gender also emerge from a case study of attitudes towards religion in a small Cornish town (Levitt 1992). In this enquiry particular attention was paid to the education – more especially the religious education – provided by a church school. In order to assess the role of such a school in this community, the study compares the attitudes of two generations of its inhabitants to various aspects of religion. More precisely, it compares the attitudes of thirty-eight mothers with those of their children at various stages in their development (the study – rare for precisely this feature – followed the families, with almost no dropouts, for six years).

For the mothers, attending church and chapel was a normal part of childhood. Only two mothers had never attended a church regularly as a child and most had attended throughout primary school. None of them described themselves as atheistic or agnostic although some described their husbands in that way. Equally clear, however, was the mothers' resistance to what they felt to be the usual meaning of the term 'religious'; in other words to anything too overt or too pressured, which they regarded as 'over the top' (this included *regular* churchgoing). The children were both similar to and distinct from their parents. Similar in that the gender variable stands out strongly in, for example, religious attendance. 'The most obvious feature of children's attendance was the difference between boys and girls, even among young children.' But distinct in that a smaller proportion of church attenders is attracted in each generation. The sample is small, but the pattern stands out in table 7.1, remembering that the children in the sample were last interviewed at the age of 16.

It is clear, moreover, that each age cohort ceases to attend at an earlier age. On the other hand, many mothers were brought back to at least occasional practice after becoming parents. It remains to be seen whether the same sort of returning occurs as the children themselves reach that stage in life. The more specific question of attitudes towards church schools and religious education will form an important focus of the next section which will also draw on this study.

Table 7.1   Churchgoing: mothers and children

Churchgoing	Mothers (%)	Daughters (%)	Sons (%)
Ever been	95	87	86
Age 5	95	80	59
Age 10	76	67	50
Age 12	73	54	23
Age 16	57	33	9
Young adult	9		
When child young	54		
When child teenage			
occasionally	30		
regularly	13		

Source: Table reproduced with permission from Levitt 1992

Educational Issues

The debate about education in contemporary society has unavoidable implications for a book about religion. For even the most abstract discussion in this area includes the perception – whether accurate or not – that the education system is a mechanism through which society's values (including religious values) are handed on from one generation to another. In other words the education system is an agent of socialization. Our schools and those who work in them should, it follows, encourage conformity to such shared values or moral codes as society deems appropriate; moral codes which are frequently seen as incomplete without a degree of religious underpinning. The debate is complicated, however, for the demands on our education system do not stop there. Schools and institutions of higher education are also expected to provide an appropriately skilled workforce for an advanced industrial society; more particularly for a society which – in the increasing absence of labour-intensive industries – is faced either with long-term unemployment for significant numbers of people or with a radical change in the way that 'work', with all the implications of this term, is both perceived and structured. And neither prospect is all that attractive, for both involve, among many other things, a rethinking of traditional values (the work ethic, the evils of idleness) passed on, supposedly, through the educational system. The ambiguities become obvious very quickly.

The general development of post-war education is, of course, beyond the scope of this book, but some issues are unavoidable. Two of these will be tackled in this section: first the whole question of denominational schools in the educational system of a modern society, and second the evolution of religious education *per se*. Both themes take place within a framework of educational legislation, the most obvious markers in this respect being the two Education Acts, Butler's in 1944 and Baker's in 1988 (the latter in fact initiating a whole series of legislation). Apart from evoking the two walk-on characters in the Genesis story – whose eventual fates were so very different – the two Acts clearly represent attempts to structure education for contrasting economic environments. The tripartite system embodied in the 1944 Act – described by Hastings as 'one of the most decisive pieces of legislation this century' (1986: 417) – still assumed the possibility of manual jobs for those who did not achieve academically (an achievement defined by success in the eleven plus and entry into the grammar school). The gradual unpicking of the tripartite system in favour of the comprehensive school through much of the post-war period reflects external pressure, for the idea of a small educated elite and large manual class became less and less appropriate as the economy developed in unpredictable ways. The 1988 Act, however, embodies a curious mixture of nostalgia and change in this respect. It anticipates the economic demands of an advanced industrial society (notably a very strong emphasis on technology), but cannot give up the idea of selection. In combining such ideas the Act draws very explicitly on the rhetoric of a consumer society, in that parents are urged to choose for themselves what they consider to be an appropriate education for their child (a choice that may or may not include a selective school). The fact that such choices – selective or otherwise – simply do not exist at all for large sections of the population reveals the yawning gap between rhetoric and reality in this as indeed in many other aspects of contemporary education.

1. Denominational schools

Where do the church schools fit into all this? The answer is far from straightforward, for sometimes the option of a church school is part of the choice open to parents, immediately raising the question of choice for whom and on what grounds; and sometimes the church school is the only school available, where for historical reasons the Church of England (primary) School is the neighbourhood school for almost all the children in the community. The implications of the two situations in terms of policy (including an admissions policy) are, of course, considerable. The situation facing a church primary school in a rural area (possibly facing closure because of falling rolls) is quite different from that of an over-subscribed secondary school in an attractive suburb trying to work out a fair (and seen to be fair) admissions policy, and very aware that decisions about its own future will have consequences for other schools in the area. All these issues have, moreover, become very much sharper in light of the opting-out debate; an issue which has, inevitably, focused the minds of those reponsible for church schools.

Before going any further, however, it is important to get an idea of the size of the voluntary sector in England and Wales. Including both aided and controlled schools,[9] the number of children in this sector is substantial, involving nearly a quarter of all pupils in the state system. In terms of institutions, the proportion is higher still, for between them the churches have a stake in well over a quarter of non-fee-paying schools in this country. The greatest share belongs to the Church of England but numbers in Roman Catholic schools, especially in the secondary sector, are also considerable. There are, however, important differences between the two denominations with respect to their educational policies, for Catholic schools have kept a much closer link with their church, a link embodied in the assumption that most staff and most pupils would be Catholics and would be looked after as such.[10] Such an assumption is, though, increasingly challenged, particularly in those parts of the country where the Catholic population is diminishing, a shift in perspective which has financial implications. For why should the Catholic Church continue to finance institutions which include not only their own church members but significant numbers of non-Catholics?

The financial situation may, however, be changing for all voluntary-aided schools. For, following the 1992 election, one of the carrots (a juicy one) offered to such schools in order to encourage them to consider grant-maintained status was an altered funding formula. No longer would the schools, or their sponsors, have to find the 15 per cent of capital costs currently expected, for under the new rules 100 per cent (rather than the presently agreed 85 per cent) of such funding would come from central government; a change which represents a significant sum of money, difficult to ignore when budgets are tight. There is, on the other hand, understandable concern on the part of those responsible for such choices about the knock-on effects of the opting-out policy and about the churches' ongoing role in the proposed system. For few church schools – indeed few schools – really want to advantage themselves at the expense of others, especially if that means in effect a two-tier system, for such a policy does little to raise educational standards. And why give up what has been, in many cases, an effective and amicable partnership between diocesan education offices and the local education authority for a system that, so far anyway, remains very largely a step into the unknown? The long-term consequences of recent legislation for church schools have been the focus of prolonged and intensive debate.[11] And given that some if not all the uncertainty persists it is hardly surprising that opinion in this area remains divided.[12]

What is absolutely clear, in contrast, is the popularity of church schools. But for what reasons? Such schools are, after all, not without their critics; there are some – including persons as distinguished as Lord Scarman – who for good reason regard church schools as a divisive element in contemporary society (an element tragically exemplified in Northern Ireland). But even the critics agree that it would be a remarkably brave politician who embraced a policy aimed at eradicating the voluntary sector, for disproportionate numbers of parents opt in favour of such schools. Why, though, should this be the case in a society where relatively few people are sufficiently concerned about religious matters even to attend a place of worship? Indeed the cart is very often placed before the horse in this respect, for there are undoubtedly families who attend their local churches for an appropriate period in their lives purely to gain access to a church school for their children. In the words of one Diocesan Director of Education, substantial numbers do this for the following reasons: 'uniform, discipline, traditional education, manners' (see Levitt 1992), not, it would seem, for religious reasons at all. Though why church schools have come to be associated with this particular formula requires in itself a certain amount of explanation. Be that as it may, whatever criteria a popular church school adopts as an entrance requirement, it is likely that those parents attracted to such a school (often a disproportionately middle-class, though not necessarily religious group) will find appropriate ways of meeting them.

There are, in fact, multiple reasons for trying to gain access to a particular school, not all of them as cynical as the example just given. Nor are all of these motives necessarily predictable. It comes as a surprise to some, for example, that many members of the other-faith communities seek education for their children in a church school. The reason, however, is straightforward enough: they are looking for a school where the spiritual dimension of life is taken seriously and where faith is nurtured, whether that faith be Christian or Muslim or anything else. These are requests to which some church schools are able (or willing) to respond more generously than others,[13] but the corollary follows naturally enough: why should the other-faith communities not have their own voluntary-aided schools? Indeed the discrimination appears very arbitrary indeed, for the Jewish community *does* have such schools (thirteen to be precise), a privilege so far denied to Muslims. The present confusing situation can be summarized as follows. On the one hand the system is at best illogical and at worst discriminatory, for it denies to some religious minorities what it allows to others. On the other hand, the argument about divisiveness is justifiable. Indeed if it were possible to start all over again in planning a system of education, this would not, surely, include the anomalies to which we have become accustomed over time, let alone extend these further. But starting all over again is not a realistic option and church schools will remain a feature of our educational system for the foreseeable future. Their extent and nature, however, may well be modified if the movement towards grant-maintained status gathers momentum, though exactly what forms such modification might take is very much more difficult to say.

2. Religious education

The developments in religious education in the second half of the twentieth century reflect a variety of pressures. The first of these – the changing nature of religious life in this country – is well exemplified once again by the assumptions underpinning the two Education Acts of the post-war period. The 1944 Act (passed, in fact, well before the war ended) had enormous consequences both for education and for the religious life of this country. With reference to religious education, its clauses included the Agreed Syllabus of Religious Instruction; a non-denominational form of teaching just about acceptable to Anglicans and Nonconformists (the

Catholics had their own syllabus), but with no anticipation that this situation might change. In other words with no anticipation that within twenty years there might be significant other-faith communities in many British cities. In this respect the Agreed Syllabus reflects a particular stage of development in inter-church relations: Anglicans and Nonconformists could find a *modus vivendi*, the Catholics were still considered separately, and no one thought beyond this.[14] The religious intentions of the Act, moreover, suffered from the fate that was to bedevil most post-war legislation in this area. It was all very well to plan for religious education in the schools of this country, whether in the state sector or elsewhere, but quite another to deliver it. For where were the schools to find sufficient numbers of enthusiastic and appropriately trained teachers to do this undoubtedly important but extremely difficult job?

Forty-four years later, the 1988 Act was grappling with precisely the same problem. This Act had, moreover, a curious evolution with respect to its religious clauses. In the early drafts, religious education – as a compulsory subject but not part of the core curriculum – occupied but a few lines of the Bill; it looked as though religious education could end by being more than ever a Cinderella subject, given the rapidly increasing pressures on the curriculum as a whole. The Bill, however, provoked vigorous protests, led for the most part by lay politicians, notably Baroness Cox and a group of supporters in the House of Lords. Discussions with the Secretary of State followed, mediated by the Bishop of London, mindful once again of who exactly was going to fulfil the rather more rigorous obligations the protesters were asking for. Baroness Cox had considerable influence. In the final draft of the Act the clauses on religious education occupied fifteen pages, including an explicit reference to the Christian content of religious teaching.[15] Such an emphasis partly reflects the growing trend towards comparative religion in the classroom, but also indicates that Christianity can no longer be taken for granted as the only world faith represented in contemporary Britain. Indeed in some schools, the majority of children will come from other-faith families. The 1988 Act entitles them to appropriate provision but only by contracting out of what was to be considered normative. The same obligation – to 'reflect the broad traditions of Christian belief' – should also characterize religious worship in county schools. (It is worth pointing out that a great deal of discussion and debate in this area confuses religious education and provision for worship. It is not uncommon, for example, to see headlines concerning religious education in the press, even the quality press, alongside a picture of a school assembly.)

Changes in the teaching of religious education have already been hinted at. Such developments can be mapped by looking at the local authority syllabuses adopted as a basis for religious teaching throughout the post-war decades. Until the 1960s such syllabuses were, quite clearly, intended to produce children with a better knowledge of Christianity, though the content of teaching was never specified (it did not need to be); there-after religious education, like so much else, altered radically. There was, first of all, a far greater emphasis on child-centred learning (reflecting wider educational methods) but this in turn led to a fully fledged phe-nomenological approach and the gradual inclusion of other world reli-gions in classroom teaching. Hence the reaction during the debate on the 1988 Act, but one that had, necessarily, to take into account the presence of several world religions within this country. It could not be total. But once again, the old problem remains: how to find sufficient teachers of high quality who can both instruct children about religion, indeed about religions, but allow them to make up their own minds about complex and difficult issues, including their own commitment, or otherwise, to faith. Are such aims compatible? This leads inevitably to the final question of this chapter: how far can religious education in general, and church schools in particular deliver their 'product' if we are still so very unclear about what they are trying to do?

3. *The effectiveness of religion in schools*

Mr Patten (Secretary of State for Education since 1992) has well-articulated views on the matter. He is greatly concerned about spiritual and moral issues throughout the education system and convinced of the importance of religious education and collective worship in addressing such matters. Moreover, the link between such teaching and subsequent behaviour is hardly to be questioned; it is made explicit in the following:

> One great difference between religious education and other aspects of the curriculum is that there is a clear intention not simply to undertake an academic study, developing a set of knowledge, un-derstanding and skills, but to develop an understanding which should

be such as to allow children to take decisions about their own life.
(*The Tablet*, 10 October 1992)

Such teaching will, of course, be reinforced by the wider ethos of the
school; an ethos which encompasses an informal or hidden curriculum
often of greater influence than the formal teaching. Bearing this in mind,
schools in the voluntary sector are, according to Mr Patten, considerably
advantaged in that such institutions are nurtured and underpinned not
only by a community of education but by a community with faith. And
those 'with a secure foundation in faith have had guides from whom to
learn, and clear signposts directing them'.

But there also exists a significant body of sociological and social-
psychological evidence – notably the work of Leslie Francis – indicating
that church schools do not find it easy to deliver at least some of their
aims, particularly if these are defined in the rather narrow sense of having a positive effect on a child's attitude to Christianity. Of course, this
immediately begs all sorts of questions about what such a positive effect
might be and how it can be measured.[16] It may, in fact, have very little to
do with Mr Patten's understanding of the question. But Francis's extensive
empirical evidence indicates that once the data have been controlled for
gender, social class, parental attitudes towards religion and the child's
own religious attendance, there is likely to be no measurable effect on
attitudes towards Christianity among children attending Church of England schools (indeed in some cases any effect that did exist was found to
be negative), though the effects of Catholic education were usually more
positive. How can this kind of data be interpreted? A variety of explanations
are possible. One of these simply admits that no amount of religious
education and no amount of exposure to a church school ethos is going to
have any lasting effect on attitudes as embedded as those concerning
religiosity in this country. Indeed it is tempting to follow this line of
argument through to its logical conclusion and to turn Francis's findings
on their head. In other words to argue that the failure of aided schools to
encourage a more positive attitude to religion is, precisely, one reason for
their popularity. Church schools are sought after because they are good
schools, and one of the reasons why they are perceived as good by parents
is their capacity to fit in with most people's perception of acceptable
religiosity.[17] A second explanation is, however, more generous; it suggests
that a positive experience at church school is something that stays with a

child but in ways that are necessarily diffuse, difficult to discern and impossible to measure. And picking up a theme from the early part of this chapter, such experiences are unlikely to be the same for boys and for girls, on which differences a great deal more work needs to be done.

At this point it may be useful to go back to the Cornish study cited earlier in this chapter and to note the ambivalence of the Cornish mothers to precisely these questions. Religious education *per se* and some form of collective worship in schools, particularly for younger children, caused no problem. There was, on the other hand, little conviction that religious education was likely to have any real effect upon moral behaviour and there was overt criticism of anything that might be called fervent or over-demonstrative, especially those aspects of religion which were public or overt but which did not help others in a practical way. The greatest hostility of all was shown towards those who tried to influence other people's religious beliefs, including, if it became too intense, those of children. Given such ambivalence, it is hardly likely that religious education, however well it is taught, is going to turn us back into a nation of churchgoers (always assuming that that is what we are after). Nor, realistically, is it likely to make very much difference to our standards of behaviour. But religious education is, surely, more than this, for it remains, above all, a carrier of tradition. Indeed at this point it is worth taking note of the French experience. In France the teaching of religion has been firmly and systematically excluded from the state schools since the beginning of this century. The consequent inability of even the most educated of French children to understand the significance of the religious factor in European art and culture, never mind the religious conflicts of the contemporary world, is becoming all too clear, prompting at least exploratory moves in a different direction (Hervieu-Léger 1992). Do we have anything more positive to offer? A little perhaps, for at the very least religious education and collective worship have helped to keep in place some sort of religious culture, however tenuous this may be. That in itself is a valuable undertaking. The potential, however, is greater than this, for it is important to remember that among a number of negative findings, the teaching of religious education can at times be excellent. Those responsible for such good practice deserve the greatest possible encouragement. The more so in that the evidence is beginning to suggest that the cultural threads are perilously close to breaking.

But however understood, these experiences contrast sharply with a type of school to be found in a different quarter. These are the growing number of 'Christian' schools – sometimes attached to house churches and sometimes of American origin – which nurture children in a convinced and articulate doctrinal environment. They are sought after by a particular group of parents in order that home and school may become mutually reinforcing. In many ways this sector is paralleled by the Muslim schools appearing in some cities, for, like them, the 'Christian' groups have to charge fees for their education – albeit modest ones – in order to survive. It was, however, part of Baroness Cox's agenda that any such group should be able to apply for aided status, thus widening the possibility of choice to parents. Whether or not such schools will become a significant part of the educational scene remains to be seen. Their promotion is, clearly, consonant with the current political rhetoric – though still resisted in some quarters – but it is much less compatible with the religious views of the majority.[18] It is not a sensible policy, however, for the majority to ignore the existence of important religious minorities, whether Christian or otherwise. Indeed, finding an acceptable framework in which those of diverse opinions (including religious opinions) can cohabit with confidence is one of the greatest challenges facing contemporary Western societies. The relationship between the churches and the state is an essential part of this framework.

Notes

1 The three studies are also complementary in that they represent very different methodologies; the first is largely intuitive, the second is based on a large-scale survey and the third combines a small survey with a detailed analysis of one particular community.

2 Such lack of interest is all the more striking given the rapid developments in feminist theology. The understanding of feminist spirituality is also a thriving area of study.

3 For example: 'In 1979 the proportion of male churchgoers was 45 per cent. In 1989 in England it had dropped to 42 per cent, nearer to the 1982 Welsh figure of 38 per cent and the 1984 Scottish figure of 37 per cent. . . . two-thirds of the change in church-going in the last decade reflects a fall-off by males' (Brierley 1991a: 79).

4 In terms of handing on the tradition, the role of women has always been important; not least the disproportionate numbers of women in

primary school teaching. For much of the post-war period, those who taught in primary schools have been some of the most well disposed both towards faith and towards religious practice (Martin 1967: 89).

5 In, for example, Martin and Pluck (1977) and Argyle and Beit-Hallahmi (1975: chapters 4 and 5).

6 There will be many references in the remaining part of this chapter to the work of Leslie Francis. This is enormously extensive. A useful summary can be found in Hyde (1990); selective references to some of Francis's publications are given in the Guide to Further Reading and References.

7 The existence of a shared vocabulary of half-remembered liturgy is frequently expressed by clergy responsible for the pastoral care of elderly people. It is not peculiar to this example.

8 The Rural Church Project (RCP) was initiated as a background study to the Archbishops' Commission on Rural Areas (1990). It has produced a wealth of empirical detail concerning the rural church, much – though by no means all – of which has been published in Davies, Watkins and Winter 1991.

9 Precise and up-to-date figures concerning church schools of all denominations are available from Culham College Institute. In February 1993, 23.6 per cent of all *pupils* in the state schools were being educated in the voluntary sector. The same sector was responsible for 32.1 per cent of all state maintained *schools*.

10 The pastoral care of many Catholic schools is outstanding; it is one reason why such schools are popular among other sections of the population as well.

11 A good summary of the issues involved in this debate can be found in the Bishop of Guildford's précis for the *Church Times* (16 July 1993) under the title 'An act that asks for decisions'. Bishop Adie is the retiring Chairman of the General Synod's Board of Education.

12 For there are some – notably Frank Field – who feel that opting-out will offer church schools distinct advantages. Others are rather more cautious.

13 There is, in practice, an enormous range in the reactions to other-faith communities and other-faith children on the part of church schools; some require participation in Christian ceremonies, others celebrate a wide variety of religious occasions, Christian and other.

14   A more general discussion of ecumenism can be found in chapter 9.
15   An agreed syllabus 'shall reflect the fact that the religious traditions in Great Britain are in the main Christian whilst taking account of the teaching and practices of the other principal religions represented in Great Britain' (Education Reform Act 1988, chapter 40, clause 1, section 8.3). Similarly, acts of worship in county schools should reflect the broad traditions of Christian belief in this country (DES circular 3/89, *Religious Education and Worship*).
16   For a good discussion of this point, see Levitt (1994), chapter 6.
17   Osmond (1993) provides further evidence on this point. Church schools are, it seems, relatively effective in the transmission of religious *knowledge*, even if they are less able to effect a change in attitudes.
18   The government's decision not to offer aided status to the Islamia Muslim school is interesting in this respect. It was refused on the grounds that there were already too many school places in the Brent area (August 1993).

8 Church and State: a Framework for Discussion

Clarity of thought – covering among other things a careful and consistent use of terms – is essential in this potentially contentious area, for discussions about church and state are likely to become confused if the terminology is inappropriately used. There must, for example, be a careful distinction between matters relating to the constitutional framework itself and the whole variety of initiatives which go on within this framework. Of course, there may be particular initiatives aimed at altering church/state relationships – the challenges to establishment are a case in point – but the underlying difference remains a crucial one. A second point concerns the term 'establishment' itself, for there are two distinct ways in which this is used. The first – probably the original meaning – refers to the complicated but definable links between the Church of England and the state. The second (a usage which became fashionable in the early post-war years) is much harder to pin down, but it evokes the pervasive but nonetheless elusive links existing in certain circles of British society, the nature of which are conveyed in the title of Paxman's book on the subject, *Friends in High Places*. The two understandings of the term are undoubtedly related, for the senior members of the Church of England certainly have been – and in some cases still are – members of this moderately exclusive club. Despite such overlap, the distinction between the two should be maintained. In this chapter, the emphasis will fall primarily on the church/state connection.

Concerning the broader use of the term, however, the plot thickens during the 1980s. For one of Margaret Thatcher's intentions was, surely, the introduction into public life of a rather different (that is, non-establishment) type of individual: those who capitalized on the virtues of enterprise, self-help and self-advancement rather than relying on a nexus of relationships whether past or present. Paradoxically, the Church resisted the more intrusive aspects of these pressures better than most, but was at the same time undergoing an internal revolution. Or to put this another way, in the 1980s the Church was continuing a gradual process of internal change, perceptible throughout the post-war period and involving, among other things, shifts in the provenance of its senior leaders. This will be a question discussed in more detail in the following chapter, but such changes should be borne in mind as a background to the present discussion. So, too, should the question of value judgements. For the established nature of the Church of England is very often regarded as either wholly right (the greatest possible advantage) or wholly wrong (the source of all the Church's difficulties). In practice it is neither. Indeed it is more sensible to start by thinking of establishment as a particular state of affairs bequeathed to us by history, and like most historical legacies it has some advantages and some disadvantages. Nor is the situation a static one; the nature of establishment has, like everything else, shifted and adapted over time and will continue to do so. It is not so much a question of asking whether establishment works or not, but of asking how it can be made to work in the last decade of the twentieth century. There may, of course, be a moment when this is no longer possible, but this is an empirical question to be decided after a careful review of the evidence. It is not a decision to be taken a priori.

Bearing these cautions in mind, this chapter will be structured as follows. The first section will review the advantages and disadvantages of establishment at a variety of levels, paying particular attention to the wider religious context of contemporary Britain, for establishment in its English as opposed to Scottish sense involves but one church within one country of the United Kingdom. The second section looks selectively at the churches' role in some of the major initiatives (mostly political ones) which have taken place within the post-war period, but with an emphasis on the Thatcher decade. It addresses one question in particular: by what authority do the churches – including the established Church – intervene in the public debate? The final section returns to the European scene, pointing out that a Church that has functioned pretty well as a representative of the nation (at least the English parts of this) may have particular difficulties in relating to the wider themes of Europe; the more so bearing in mind the Church of England's additional role as the mother church of the Anglican Communion.

Establishment: the Advantages and Disadvantages

Establishment does not mean that the Church of England is identified with the state. It does, however, signify a special relationship between that Church and the political order (at least in its English forms). But as in all relationships, there are two sides to the partnership. On the one hand the established nature of the Church of England confers upon one and only one church within the United Kingdom certain 'rights and privileges' (there can be no doubt about this); but these rights and privileges carry with them corresponding, and unavoidable, 'restrictions and limitations' (Welsby 1985: 45). The two aspects are, moreover, inextricably linked. Twenty-six Church of England bishops, for example, have the right (at any one time) to sit in the House of Lords. But this inevitably means that the state will want to maintain a certain degree of input into, if not control over, the appointment of bishops. It is unreasonable to expect otherwise. Exactly how much control and through what channels this is effected is, however, a far more flexible matter, within which considerable changes have taken place in the post-war period.[1]

Certain lines of thinking appear to follow from this balancing of rights and restrictions. For the advantage of a seat in the Lords has, it would seem, to be weighed against the restriction embodied in the appointments system. But apparently simple equations become, in real life, impossibly complicated formulae, for how is it possible to assess with any precision what the bishops are likely to achieve through the House of Lords? And even if the advantages are considerable in terms of a high-profile forum for debate, is it a sensible use of a bishop's time to spend certain weeks in the year in attendance in the House, regardless of the agenda, or mastering a difficult brief for a crucial debate at the expense of a prior diocesan commitment? These are demanding considerations that seem, in fact, to be more like restrictions than rights. A second issue concerns not so much the existence *per se* of 'rights and privileges' but how these are used. In the mid 1980s, for instance, the privilege of a seat in the House of Lords was one way – and an extremely effective one – of bringing to public attention the everyday problems of the most disadvantaged groups in British society, groups which were underrepresented in the House of Commons.

A rather more cogent line of attack on establishment comes in fact by turning the argument of the previous paragraph round the other way. For it is far more difficult to justify the limiting of this particular privilege (or duty) to the senior members of one denomination only, than it is to dismiss it as an anachronism *tout court*. In other words if a seat in the Lords is a privilege effectively used by the bishops of the Church of England, why not extend this possibility to the senior members of other Christian denominations or even to those of certain other-faith communities? For the churches are at their most influential in bringing matters of concern to public attention when they act collectively, and there is no reason to suppose that the experience and expertise from the non-Anglican churches might not be put to very good use. Indeed the position of the Lords spiritual is, even if restricted to one denomination only, no more anomalous than the present Lords temporal, and, made more representative of the current state of British religious life, it might be considerably less so. After all, church leaders do have an identifiable constituency and a large one if nominal membership is taken into account.[2]

The question of nominal membership, especially its implications for the parochial ministry, becomes, in fact, central to the debate about establishment, for the links between church and state do not only concern a set of connections at the centre of government. In terms of everyday effectiveness (or otherwise) parochial questions are probably more significant than the high-profile aspects of establishment, exemplified by the role of bishops in the House of Lords or, most conspicuous of all, by the place of the monarch as Supreme Governor of the Church of England. It is in the parishes that the multiplicity of links are made with large numbers of English people; at an individual level through the occasional offices and at a civic level through the marking of community events discussed in chapter 6. It is curious that a certain section within the Church of England seems to regard such obligations as more of a hindrance than a help, for they undoubtedly enable contact with a population that is reluctant – and increasingly so – to attend their parish churches on a regular basis. But once again there are two sides to the relationship. On the one hand, parishioners have the right of access to their parish church; a right claimed for first marriages and for funerals in particular. The clergy are obliged (and trained) to respond appropriately. On the other hand, such responses take up a considerable amount of time and are, undoubtedly, demanding and costly aspects of ministry. They provide, however, innumerable points of access to an otherwise disinterested population; points of access which, if used wisely, can lead to more permanent contact (Carr 1985). Denying such access – particularly given the prevalent patterns of British religiosity – must, surely, amount to the Church shooting itself in the foot.

Lying beneath a number of these issues, however, lies a more fundamental tension: that which arises between the actively religious minority (of which the Anglican section forms but a third) and the very much larger Anglican penumbra – the distinguishing feature of the Church of England in this country. For it is very often the most active members of certain churches who feel the constraints rather than the advantages of establishment most keenly. The parochial system, for example, implies certain restrictions; restrictions which at times conflict with the aspirations of a particular congregation to extend its ministry (in a physical sense) beyond the parish boundaries.[3] Such boundaries, it is argued, impede rather than encourage church growth. Similarly the competing demands of parish life place conflicting demands on the clergy who have at times to justify their absence from a demanding congregation in order to fulfil obligations elsewhere in the parish. Bearing these tensions in mind, the questions posed in a rather general sense at the start of chapter 5 begin to have both immediate and practical implications:

> What, for instance, is going to be the relationship between the active religious minority and the less active believing majority? How far is one dependent on the other? Does a believing majority make the work of the minority harder or easier? Do the former constitute a pool from which the latter can fish, or do they become, in part at least, a rival set-up, an alternative religious focus for society? (p. 75)

It is these implications that the parochial clergy of the established Church face every day, as they seek to edge both their not always very co-operative congregations alongside a much wider group of parishioners in what they rather hesitantly determine to be the right direction. It is not an enviable task.

One forum in which priorities are decided at local level are the Parochial Church Councils of every parish; councils which form the base of the synodical pyramid. The apex of the same system lies in the General Synod of the Church of England, the nature of which will be discussed in more detail in the following chapter. But it is important to grasp at this stage that the synodical structure concerns and represents (albeit imperfectly) the more active section of the Church of England rather than its wider membership. And in so doing it provides a significant and necessary lay voice at every level of ecclesiastical debate. The established nature of the Church of England requires, however, that some, if no longer all, decisions of the General Synod are themselves subject to approval (or very occasionally disapproval) by Parliament. And how is it possible to justify the continuation of this system when Parliament itself is made up of an enormous variety of individuals, of different faiths and none, most of whom have no interest in the internal affairs of the Church of England? The answer can only be a pragmatic one: that the system – curious though it may be – rarely causes a major problem, though the unexpected check to synodical policy can and does occur.[4] On a more theoretical level the argument becomes more difficult. It is just, but only just, possible to suggest that among the Members of Parliament there may be a sufficient number who care enough about ecclesiastical affairs to take an informed interest in what is going on, and in a certain sense to represent the wider interests of the less active adherents of the Church of England, but this isn't an easy position to sustain. At times, however, there are unexpected advantages built into the present system. Its sheer complexity, for example, provided a helpful breathing space between the passing of the legislation permitting the ordination of women to the priesthood in the General Synod and its ratification by Parliament. Some – though by no means all – of the sting went out of the debate in the intervening months.[5]

De facto, the General Synod is taking increasing responsibility for Church of England affairs. But the ultimate authority continues to lie not in Parliament, but with the Crown, for the monarch not only has to give royal assent to the canons enacted but could, ultimately, prevent the Convocation – and therefore the General Synod – even from meeting. Indeed it is in the person of the monarch that the relationship of church and state reaches its apogee, for the Supreme Governor of the Church of England must have two (and only two) qualifications: to be Head of State and to be a Protestant. The Coronation Oath requires that the Supreme Governor shall uphold 'the Protestant reformed religion established by law' and shall 'maintain and preserve inviolably the settlement of the Church of England, and the doctrine, worship, discipline and government thereof, as by law established in England' (Welsby 1985: 45). These are obligations that the present queen has fulfilled punctiliously for the past forty years.

But what seemed reasonable in 1953 is less easy to accept forty years later. And for two reasons. The first has attracted infinite media attention, though may in the longer term turn out to be relatively insignificant. On the other hand, it may not. For it is quite possible that 1992, the *annus horribilis* of the royal family, may emerge as a turning point in the history of establishment; the moment when the whole system began to unravel. It is quite clear, for example, that the less than perfect marriage arrangements of the younger royals – and in particular the separation of the Prince and Princess of Wales – have called into question the place of the royal family in the established Church, and thus of establishment itself. Is it possible for a separated, possibly divorced – or even, with the inevitable if up to now fanciful extrapolation, remarried – man to become Supreme Governor of a Church which strives to uphold the sanctity of marriage? The question is a real one (and one to which there is no easy answer), but it is more likely that the particular events of 1992 have acted as a catalyst to a more far-reaching debate, the consequences of which are not at all easy to predict. For the second, and principal, reason for calling into question the nature of establishment in the 1990s lies, surely, in the changing nature of British society. There are two aspects to this question. In the first place, we have become, many would argue, a secular society in which an established church (of whatever kind) is no longer an appropriate institution. The complexity of the secularization issue has formed a thread running through this book, and it will be discussed again in the final chapter; it should not be over-simplified. There can, however, be little doubt that Britain has become very largely an unchurched society, a trend that has increased very markedly in the post-war period. Only a very limited section of the population now visit their places of worship with any regularity (always assuming of course that this is what counts), and less than one-third of those that do attend will be found in buildings that belong to the so-called state Church. The second point follows from this. The religiously active in contemporary Britain are now very diverse;

a diversity that sits rather uneasily alongside the undeniably privileged position accorded to the established Church. There are, in consequence, a number, and among them the present Archbishop of York, an otherwise strong supporter of establishment, who are beginning to hint at the possibility of some alteration in the content of the Coronation Oath;[6] in other words at a change within the system. There are others, however, both within and outside the churches, who feel that a more radical solution is required; in other words that an established church of any kind is no longer appropriate in a secular and moderately pluralist society.

There is, however, another way of looking at the question: that is, from the point of view of the minority religions themselves. Three examples will be outlined in the following paragraphs, one Roman Catholic, one Muslim and one Jewish, though none should be read as necessarily representative of these communities taken as a whole. They are, nonetheless, instructive.

First a Roman Catholic voice. Hastings, in the published version of the Prideaux Lectures given at the University of Exeter in 1990, reviews the English experience of church and state (Hastings: 1991b). The argument is set in a long-term theological and ecclesiastical framework, examining patterns of dualism, the triumph and decline of Justinianism and the traditions of Dissent within the English experience. But the conclusion (in a postscript written just before publication and including a discussion of Archbishop Carey's appointment to Canterbury as an example of establishment in practice) is essentially pragmatic:

> The establishment of the Church of England remains, then, in contemporary terms, somewhat anomalous – both in regard to English society and in regard to the Christian church elsewhere. But as both English society and the world church are full of anomalies, it is not to be rejected on account of that. It remains adequately but not overwhelmingly defensible on grounds of doing quite a lot of good and very little harm, on being part of the wider symbolic culture of the nation which we would be fools to dismantle, and of requiring for its termination a quite excessive amount of time and energy. (Hastings 1991b: 75–6)

And as an example of 'doing quite a lot of good', Hastings cites the *Faith in the City* enterprise in the 1980s in which the full weight of establishment was invoked on behalf of those who could help themselves least.

The argument in favour of disestablishment is often cast in the following terms: the present system is no longer tenable in contemporary society, for it discriminates against religious – and particularly the non-Christian – minorities, which are and will remain an essential part of British life. It is a tempting argument and skilfully set up by Modood (a Muslim) in a masterly review of the evidence in favour of the pluralist case for disestablishment (Modood 1994). But the denouement is unexpected:

> I have to state as a brute fact that I have not come across a single article or speech or statement by any minority faith in favour of disestablishment. This is quite extraordinary given that secular reformers make the desire to accommodate these minorities an important motive for reform. (pp. 61–2)

This counter-claim may or may not be exaggerated, but it certainly requires that an alternative view be stated on behalf of the minority religions. One such view – espoused by Modood himself – is that the real danger to multi-faithism does not come from a relatively powerless national Church (not much comfort here for the Anglicans) but from 'a virtually unchallengeable and culturally insensitive secular centre which makes demands on all faiths, but especially on the least Westernised faiths at a time when the minority faiths are asserting themselves as a form of cultural defence' (1994: 66). In other words, disestablishing the Church of England will have the result of marginalizing not only the Church of England in contemporary society, but of pushing to one side *all* those who choose to take faith seriously whatever their religious allegiance. It should not be undertaken lightly. Modood underlines a further point. There is, in certain – and quite diverse – circles, considerable talk of disestablishment. In contrast there appears to be very little interest in what might replace the present system, despite the very obvious fact that the number of loose ends left dangling would, in the case of disestablishment, be considerable. (Hastings was hinting at the same question in underlining the amount of time and energy the process of dismantling the church/state relationship might take.) But surely Modood is right when he emphasizes that the creation and sustaining of a truly tolerant and pluralist society requires creative rather than destructive thinking. What, in other words, do we need to *create* in order to have a healthy pluralism and to give institutional recognition to this?

A more general approach to the issues at stake in a pluralist society formed a dominant theme within Jonathan Sacks's Reith Lectures in 1990, subsequently published in *The Persistence of Faith* (Sacks 1991). Sacks was at that time Chief Rabbi elect, a spokesman for the oldest other-faith community in this country. In a plural society, he argues, we should indeed acknowledge our differences, but alongside the local language (or languages) of community it is equally important to seek a public language of citizenship in which to express shared values and to emphasize what we hold in common; a task traditionally fulfilled in England by – among other institutions – the established Church. But times have changed and current diversity within society 'makes many people, outside the Church and within, feel uneasy with that institution'. At this point, however, Sacks's argument – rather like Modood's – changes course, for rather than benefiting the situation, disestablishment would, he claims, do the reverse, for it would symbolize 'a significant retreat from the notion that we share any values and beliefs at all. And that would be a path to more, not fewer, tensions' (1991: 68). Once again the presentation isn't all that reassuring from an Anglican point of view, for it implies that an established Church is a lesser evil rather than a positive good. On the other hand, Sacks supplies yet another voice which counsels caution concerning the process of disestablishment, indicating what might be the unintended consequences of proceeding too far and too fast down that particular road. Perhaps the greatest danger of all is a failure to face the fundamental issues. In other words to divert attention from the need to think imaginatively and creatively about the nature of pluralism in contemporary society by concentrating rather too much on dismantling a far from perfect, but nonetheless useful (and above all flexible), institution bequeathed to us by history.

A final argument provides a bridge to the following section on recent political developments in British society. For policies pursued in the 1980s, notably those regarding local government, the health service and education, have had the cumulative effect of greatly increasing the power of central, as opposed to local, government in this country. Intermediate levels of decision making have been sacrificed under the guise of radical decentralization which, *de facto*, has had the effect of aggregating power at the centre. The established Church provides a notable exception to this trend: its intermediate structures are still intact and although some dioceses have little relationship (for historical reasons) with current population distributions, others remain visible reminders of realities no longer recognized by secular authorities. The most obvious example of secular dismantling is that of the abolition of the Greater London Council; the Diocese of London – for all its internal difficulties – is still there. So it should be.

A Variety of Political Initiatives

Both the interventions of the churches, including the Church of England, into the political life of this country, *and* the lack of such, are bound to be contentious. On the one hand there are those who argue that the churches' involvement in public affairs is, simply, inappropriate. The churches' business is not of this world and in becoming involved in secular debate, of whatever nature, the churches are allowing themselves to be distracted from their primary task. They are, moreover, laying themselves open to internal divisions of a political nature, reinforcing an already over-apparent theological disunity. There are others, however, who take a different view, maintaining that a withdrawal from politics on principle endorses the status quo, at least indirectly. The prophetic voice of the churches is to be encouraged, rather than muted, though the forms that such prophecy might take are many and varied. In general, the more specific the intervention, the greater the controversy; abstract, relatively unspecific statements are, understandably, less problematic.[7]

The relationship between church and state cannot be ignored in this controversy. Indeed it raises a crucial point concerning establishment; a point underlined by Medhurst and Moyser in their conclusion to *Church and Politics in a Secular Age* (1988; see also Moyser 1985). It is this. Can an established church, obliged by its very nature to undertake a pastoral role with respect to the government of the day, combine this with an effective critical voice? In other words is it possible to both pastor and prophesy? Medhurst and Moyser for the most part conclude negatively and extend their argument to any national church, whether legally established or not. For all such churches must, they argue, envisage some ministry to their rulers, a ministry 'that will inevitably inhibit radical impulses' (1988: 358). But is this necessarily the case? We need, surely, to consider the nature and effectiveness of different kinds of political protest. For it may be that some, if not all, forms of protest – or of change – are helped rather than hindered by national or even established status.

A useful case study in this respect can be found in Davies's essay on 'Religion, Politics and the "Permissive" Legislation' (Davies 1989). Davies is concerned for the most part with the early post-war period, with debates which culminated in the 1960s, notably those related to capital punishment and homosexuality. Much of the presentation is unsurprising, for the most vigorous defenders of capital punishment and condemners of homosexuality were those most attached to the traditional and organic view of state and society (1989: 325); those, more specifically, 'who belonged to the disciplined interlocking hierarchies that made up the Establishment' (in its wider sense), among them the established churches of England and Scotland. But once again, the narrative takes an unexpected turn, for a systematic examination of the votes and speeches of the bishops in the House of Lords on the subjects of capital punishment and homosexuality since the Second World War revealed 'a gradual growth of distance between these religious leaders and the substantial body of Peers who opposed any change in the law on moral issues' (pp. 327–8). The point at issue is not so much the rights and wrongs of complex moral issues – to which there are never any simple answers – but that the expected alignments for and against such issues no longer obtained. A change in the law was advocated in the least expected quarters. Such readjustments were not, however, achieved without cost. The painfulness of this episode is told with some feeling, and from a rather different point of view, in the chapter devoted to 'Parliament and the Moral Law' in Chadwick's biography of Archbishop Ramsey. Chadwick underlines a further point with respect to the homosexuality debate in the House of Lords: the hereditary peers, with no constituents to worry about, had a greater freedom of manoeuvre than their colleagues in the Commons in what was bound to be an exceptionally delicate encounter.

This shifting of the expected alignments in contemporary society has continued throughout the post-war period. It forms the crucial thread within Martin's analysis of the Thatcher decade, that extraordinary (in its strictest sense) period in British post-war politics. Martin (1989) describes the inevitable, and at times unbelievably rapid, unravelling of earlier solidarities as the churches, the universities and the BBC emerged as the defenders of the old-left liberal consensus and the politics of welfare, joined by the ousted 'grandees' of the old Tory Party and all those attached to the ideal of 'One Nation' (1989: 340). Evidently disparate and differently motivated groups came together to defend shared values against new forms of conservatism, especially an aggressive free-market emphasis.[8] This is not the place to examine in detail the motivations, ideologies, politics and consequences of the Thatcher decade, except to stress again the unprecedented and un-British nature of what was going on. Nor is it necessary to rehearse once more the stand-off between Mrs Thatcher and the churches, and in particular the Church of England. This important debate is already well sourced, for example in Bradley (1992) and Clark (1993) and the facts are well known. (It can also be discovered – with rather different connotations – in political accounts of the period.) But it *is* necessary, and essential to the central thrust of this book, to get behind this series of episodes to discover the kind of arguments being used and their plausibility given the statistical profile of the churches that we have already established. How did it come about?

1. Faith in the City

The *Faith in the City* debate will be taken as an example of a wider process.[9] The Archbishop of Canterbury's Commission on Urban Priority Areas was established in 1983 under the chairmanship of Sir Richard O'Brien, a distinguished layman. Its vice-chairman was David Sheppard, Bishop of Liverpool, a diocese with an obvious interest in the concept 'urban priority area'; a term adapted from the educational world to include within the Commission's terms of reference the deprived estates ringing many British cities alongside the already familiar (and in some cases notorious) inner city areas. Those assembled for the task looked very similar to a Royal Commission (a concept out of fashion at the time); they were experienced, evidently able, and well-qualified individuals from a variety of backgrounds. The Commission worked under the personal authority of the Archbishop of Canterbury (not the General Synod). Its report, *Faith in the City*, was published in December 1985. Not only did it provoke a considerable reaction at the time, it also spawned a whole series of subsequent studies.[10] The first point to note, however, is that this report was not the first of its kind. The Methodists, for example, had already embarked on their Mission Alongside the Poor Programme which included a series of publications,[11] whose conclusions were not so very different from *Faith in the City*. Nor was the Anglican version solely concerned with the political dimension of the debate, for more than half of its recommendations were directed to the Church itself. The political repercussions were, however, considerable. For an established church can, it seems, still create an impact denied to other denominations and bring to the attention of the nation as a whole the plight of those living in the most deprived areas of Britain's larger conurbations. The Church of England had in fact achieved what the Labour Party had so conspicuously failed to do; that is, to push issues of deprivation – and in particular urban deprivation – to the top of the political agenda.

The paradoxes in this achievement abound, some of which are caught in the cartoon in the introductory chapter to this book. For the established Church found itself speaking for precisely those elements of society least likely to be found in its pews, a point fully acknowledged by the Commission itself. Why, then, was it possible for the Church to do what the political opposition could not? And how could a Church so apparently out of touch with ordinary people speak on behalf of those who had for several generations excluded themselves from its worshipping congregations? Part – if not all – of the answer must surely lie in the parochial structure of the established Church, stretched to its limit in some parts of the country but nonetheless extant. For in many of the most problematic areas of British cities it is not an exaggeration to say that the clergy are the only professionals still resident (in the sense of living as opposed to working) in the community concerned. The Anglican priest has a legal obligation to live in the parish; it is very exceptional for him (or her) to commute in and out of the area. And though living over the shop imposes a very great strain on the individuals and families in question, it provides a network that is invaluable for the gathering of accurate information if for nothing else. Indeed it was this unique source of firsthand information which gave the Commission's Report a quite distinctive authority. The government had chosen to pursue particular economic policies; the Church's personnel found itself experiencing the consequences of such policies firsthand in the communities in which they lived; and they – through the Commission – declared those consequences unacceptable.

The fact that those most likely to suffer were not churchgoers was immaterial.

It would seem from this episode that an established church can still utter a prophetic voice, thus challenging Medhurst and Moyser's assertion that this is unlikely to occur when the ties between church and state are close. But there is another side to this question, discovered in the form of a persistent ambiguity which needs to be properly articulated. For an all too evident ambivalence bedevils a great deal of the discussion surrounding *Faith in the City* (both in the Report and thereafter); a discussion which hovers between a radical rejection of the capitalist system as such and a more pragmatic approach which sought to ameliorate the worst effects of what was going on, but stopped short of total condemnation. Critique there certainly was, but a critique restrained by the system. Bearing this dimension in mind, Medhurst and Moyser are, perhaps, partly if not wholly correct in their assertion that there are inevitable limits on what a national church can or cannot say. Paradoxically, however, this ambivalence matched a similar equivocation on the other side of the argument, an equivocation revealed by Plant et al. (1989) in a subsequent essay on the theological and moral challenges of conservative capitalism. For if the Commission itself stopped short of a radical critique of the whole economic system, it also failed to realize the radical nature of the policies that they were confronting. Not surprisingly the Commission continued to make the traditional assumptions that governments exist, among other things, to ensure social justice, that is to say, an equitable distribution of resources between citizens. But Plant's argument challenges precisely this point. The New Right regard the pursuit of social justice as a mirage; it is beyond both the concern and competence of government. There is, in consequence, an unmet challenge at the heart of the social theology of *Faith in the City* and 'one which goes to the centre of its presumed view about the nature and the role of government' (1989: 71). Had this challenge been met head-on, the debate might have been quite other. But the Commission, like almost everyone else, failed to appreciate in the early 1980s the unprecedented nature of the New Right's ideology.

It is important not to exaggerate the effectiveness of the churches in the *Faith in the City* episode. They were successful (considerably more successful than the opposition parties) in some respects, for the concept 'urban priority area' became current in political circles and grave injustices had to be acknowledged. But acknowledging injustices did not remove them, a point all too evident to anyone with firsthand experience in the inner city. Nor, it must be stressed, were all those in the churches equally enthusiastic about what was going on, an ambivalence which needs some elaboration. It is quite clear, for example, that the critique offered by the Archbishop's Commission, if relatively restrained from some points of view, was still too much for many regular worshippers; notably those – probably a majority – who were unlikely to have had any real contact with the areas in question and for whom the notion that unemployment (to take but one example) might have structural rather than individual causes was not an easy idea to accept. It contradicted too many embedded assumptions. In this respect, however, the *Faith in the City* debate simply reveals a more persistent trend in Church life in the later post-war decades; namely, that the Anglican laity were proving themselves considerably more cautious, more conservative and indeed more Conservative than their clergy. In many ways such differences of opinion were hardly surprising, for an essentially pragmatic alliance between supporters of a leftish liberal consensus and One Nation Tories does not imply convergence of ideas. And within this rather unlikely coming together (evident within the Church as well as outside it), it becomes increasingly clear that the clergy lean rather more to the liberal consensus than the Anglican laity, who – despite everything – maintained their predilection to vote Conservative for most of the post-war period.[12]

2. Political behaviour

Having said this, the connections between denomination and voting behaviour – never a major feature of British political life – are becoming more and more difficult to discern. Some links can still be determined, particularly those between Roman Catholicism and the Labour vote; though, following Hornsby-Smith, the distinctive political identity of Roman Catholics in this country is just as much altered as other aspects of Catholicism in the gradual – and, in many ways, welcome – assimilation of Roman Catholics into British society. Likewise the traditional association between Nonconformity and the Liberal Party now hardly exists except in regional pockets, one of which was described in chapter

6. It is hardly surprising, therefore, that the description of the Church of England as the Tory Party at prayer has an equally dated ring, particularly from the point of view of its clergy. Life has, quite simply, moved on. Discerning the collapse of previous religio-political collusions is, however, considerably easier than discovering what has emerged to replace these. Doubly so in that the political agenda has also altered dramatically in the post-war period. Indeed, the two shifts are quite possibly related, for if it is the case that the most distinctive differences in church life (including political inclinations) now lie across denominational lines rather than between these, this feature is also true of the political system. It is indisputable, surely, that some of the major divisions within politics now lie across rather than between the conventional parties, the 'denominations' of British political life.

Secondary analyses of the 1981 European Values Study data corroborate the relatively weak connections between religion and politics in this country (Abrams, Gerard and Timms 1985); results that seem to be confirmed by the as yet tentative analyses of the 1990 findings (Hornsby-Smith and Proctor 1993). The European data reveal, however, the religious factor as stubbornly salient in a rather different, though not unrelated, way. It becomes a highly significant indicator both of moral outlook (on the level of attitudes) and of involvement in the caring organizations (on the level of action). Such evidence has been examined in some detail by Gill in *Moral Communities* (1992: 17–21). Probing the question, Why Care? Gill finds the evidence from both the 1981 and 1990 surveys persuasive: not only do the two samples show that those who go regularly to church have distinctive positions both on standard items of Christian belief and on a variety of moral concerns, they also show 'that those involved in unpaid voluntary work are typically more religious in terms of both belief and practice than those who are uninvolved' (1992: 17). Of course this does not imply that many other, less overtly religious people are not involved in this kind of activity, for they most certainly are and in considerable numbers. Gill simply states that the actively religious are *disproportionately* present in unpaid voluntary work in this country. And given the increasing significance of this sector in many aspects of contemporary British society, the evidence should, perhaps, be pondered. It offers some indication of altruism in outlets other than overtly political channels; outlets which, very frequently, provide the last line of defence for the most vulnerable in the community.

3. *A 1990s postscript*

The report of the Archbishop's Commission on Urban Priority Areas was published in 1985; its terms of reference and style of reporting reflected the concerns of the mid 1980s. Five years later, a parallel Commission (this time 'owned' by both Archbishops) reported on rural areas. *Faith in the Countryside* was both similar and different to the earlier undertaking. Similar in that it operated more or less like a Royal Commission and once again reported to both Church and nation; but markedly different in its political colour (wet Tory rather than left of centre) and in the fact that its motivation came more from the internal concerns of the Church than from any political urgency about rural matters. Its content, moreover, began to reflect issues pertaining to the 1990s rather than the 1980s – notably a preoccupation with environmental concerns and a greater awareness of the European dimension. Such interests were partly driven by subject matter but were also evidence of changing social and political conditions: justice and peace issues (that familiar duo) were, it seems, no longer separable from 'the integrity of creation' and all three increasingly transcended national boundaries.

There were other indications of a change in mood by the time the rural report was published. Mrs Thatcher had resigned; so too had Dr Runcie. They had been replaced by John Major and George Carey respectively. The newly appointed leaders of church and state were in fact remarkably similar: both were relatively young; neither acquired academic qualifications at the conventional stage in life; and neither has the remotest establishment connections. In other respects, however, the appointments should be viewed differently. Mrs Thatcher saw in John Major the most likely candidate to continue what she had set in motion. The Church on the other hand was looking for something rather different in Dr Carey's appointment; an Archbishop who could pilot the Church decisively after ten rather diffident years. Neither scenario has proved entirely accurate. Dr Runcie's achievements, for example, as an admirable foil to Mrs Thatcher's divisiveness have been more appreciated in retrospect than they were at the time; not least his careful pastoring of that very English individual, the wistful seeker after truth, to be found on the edge rather than at the centre of church life. Dr Carey, constrained maybe by his office, does not seem anxious to abandon this role. The political debate, on the other hand, has revealed Mrs Thatcher's articulate opposition to Mr Major's policies on Europe, the dominant question of the 1990s. It is to this question that we must now turn.

European Issues

The European dimension has already been raised in connection with the non-English parts of the United Kingdom. Their responses (both religious and secular) to this unavoidable issue were, not surprisingly, indicative of underlying preoccupations. The rather more complicated English situation has been deferred until now, in that it follows rather than precedes the discussion of church and state which forms the early part of this chapter. It also picks up the themes of the middle section on religion and politics, which revealed a persistent paradox in English society: namely that an ill-attended established church can still at times articulate the concerns of a nation. There is, however, a further point. For not only has the Church of England remained, albeit spasmodically, a vehicle for the expression of Englishness at home, it has also been inextricably linked to a long and geographically extensive colonial history. Missionaries have followed the flag (or vice versa) in large parts of the world. This pull overseas, away from Europe, has had profound and long-term effects on the organizational nature of the Church of England. It has become the centre of an Anglican Communion, an important international grouping even at the end of the twentieth century, but one which has been shaped first by the British Empire and then by the Commonwealth. It is anything but European in its emphases. Anglicanism is centred in Canterbury; it has no home on the European mainland. We find, then, a Church of England still capable, if pushed, of expressing significant aspects of English life alongside an expanding role as the mother church of the Anglican Communion. But neither of these attributes – the essential Englishness of the domestic Church nor the imperial connections of the wider communion – are going to be much help in forming creative and effective links with Europe; they may well in fact be a hindrance. Or to put the same point in a rather different way, there is no avoiding the fact that Anglicanism remains marginalized in Europe, numerically, organizationally and geographically. What, then, are the most likely outcomes for the English churches regarding the increasing, if disputed, importance of European affairs in the life of the nation? There are, I would argue, three possible scenarios.

The first is the most negative, but ought to be mentioned. It envisages the Church of England as the spiritual arm of English (if not always British) isolationism from Europe. The second possibility is more positive but it remains problematic. It suggests that the Church of England might be prepared to stand back a bit and to allow the minority churches – notably the Roman Catholics and those of the reformed tradition – to make a more significant contribution. Both, after all, form part of the major Christian traditions of mainland Europe. The role of Catholicism could be particularly valuable in view of its organizational links with the Continent.[13] Perhaps the crucial question to ask in this respect is how far the Catholic Church might be permitted to fulfil a bridge-building role into Europe, bearing in mind that Protestant identity remains a curiously significant issue for many British people even in the late twentieth century. The third scenario stresses the potentially positive attributes of Anglicanism itself in this whole debate. There are three of these that come to mind.[14]

The first concerns the distinctiveness of the Church of England, combining as it does both catholic and reformed traditions (that is, both dimensions of West European Christianity). Or put differently, the essence of the Church of England is accurately conveyed in the phrase 'a largely Catholic church within a predominantly Protestant country'. Bearing this in mind, might it not be possible to see a positive way forward for the Anglican Church as the *via media* within European church life, a contribution that no one else can make? It would be good to think so. But the compromise at the heart of Anglicanism – an issue to be considered more fully in the following chapter – is an uneasy one and it would, surely, be unwise to build too much on these rather shaky foundations. The second possibility, however, looks further afield, for the Church of England has relatively good relations with the Orthodox churches, a dimension that can only grow in importance as Eastern Europe develops closer links with the European Union. Unlike many churches of the Continental Reformation, the moderately hierarchical nature of Anglicanism offers something recognizable to the Orthodox but without being associated with the ancient and persistent division between Rome and Constantinople. Here there is certainly room for manoeuvre.[15] The final suggestion concerns the Anglican Communion just as much as the Church of England itself. For there can be no doubt that the global nature of Anglicanism can bring to Europe a whole series of international linkages, many of them in developing parts of the world. Such global emphases are particularly attractive to those within the European Union who wish to avoid a 'fortress Europe' mentality. All the churches of Europe offer an important contribution in this respect, but it is a role in which the British churches can share with proven competence and particular enthusiasm. It draws on long-term experience.

The pivot, however, of the whole undertaking – that is, the bringing together of church and state in this country, the delicate political manoeuvres that go on within this framework, the extensive and expanding nature of the Anglican Communion and the relatively new dimension of Europe – lies very largely in the role of the Archbishop of Canterbury. Is it surprising, therefore, that growing numbers of commentators are beginning to conclude that the resultant combination dictates an impossibly demanding agenda for any one individual, however gifted? More specifically there are those who feel that the time has come to look elsewhere for the leadership of the Anglican Communion, in, for example, a Province where membership figures are expanding rather than contracting? For an effective prophetic voice at home can, surely, be muted as much by overwork as it can by the closeness of church/state relations. In other words, a certain amount of decoupling may indeed prove helpful in the not too distant future, but not necessarily that which involves the disestablishment of the Church of England from the English state.

Notes

1 The most decisive change came in 1977, following the Report of the Chadwick Commission. The initiative for appointing bishops now lay with the Church, more especially with the Crown Appointments Commission; the state could reject the names proposed by the Commission but could not suggest alternatives beyond those already offered. Should no name be acceptable to the state, the system would start again.

2 This argument assumes the present constitutional arrangements concerning the House of Lords. The possibilities will be very different

indeed if the second chamber changes its nature; as it surely must, sooner rather than later.

3   Aspirations epitomized by the debate about church 'planting'.

4   For example, in the rejection first time round of the Clergy Ordination Measure concerning the ordination of divorcees and those who marry divorcees (July 1989).

5   The Ecclesiastical Committee of Parliament (composed of representatives from both the Lords and the Commons) took an active role in this particular debate. How this role was perceived depended considerably on the point of view of the observer: those in favour of the ordination of women felt the restrictions of the system; those against made the most of a further opportunity to put their case. The issue itself will be discussed in more detail in chapter 9.

6   Such changes were proposed in the course of a television interview (24 January 1993). A considerable correspondence followed in the press.

7   A dilemma admirably captured by Martin in his awareness that a bishop should indeed speak out; but what should he say? (*The Times*, 15 November 1975, quoted in Habgood 1983: 1.)

8   Such groupings imply a certain amount of generalization. There are, of course, certain sections of the churches which espouse rather than reject a free-maket emphasis.

9   The following discussion concerns the sociological rather than the theological aspects of the *Faith in the City* enterprise. The theological arguments have been rehearsed elsewhere (A. Harvey 1989).

10 Many of these are listed in *Living Faith in the City* (1990: 168–74). Important among them are the whole series of case studies on different British cities, which adapted the overall framework of the original report to the particular situations of individual conurbations.

11 Among them *Two Nations, One Gospel* (1981), *What Churches can Do* (1983) and *Gospel from the Poor* (1984), all published by the Urban Theology Unit in conjunction with the Methodist Home Mission.

12 A 1988 poll (*The Times*, 14 November 1988) revealed that 63 per cent of active churchgoers voted Conservative in the 1987 General Election, as opposed to 43 per cent of the population as a whole.

13 Hornsby-Smith is, however, right to point out the essential Irishness of the English Roman Catholic Church. Its links with the European mainland are limited.

14 Two of these are closely related to ecumenical issues, which will be discussed more fully in the following chapter. The link between ecumenism and Europe is hardly surprising given the relationship between theological argument and geographical shape in the history of Europe. Conversely the coming together of Europe offers particular opportunities for ecumenism.

15 Though less than there used to be, given the decision to go forward with the ordination of women in the Church of England.

9 Religious Professionals: Lay and Ordained

The previous chapter ended with a discussion of European issues, including the suggestion that in many respects European questions are closely related to the ecumenical debate. An important corollary followed from this: namely that the last decade of the twentieth century might offer a particular opportunity for progress in both areas. But alongside the developing links across the Channel, there are domestic dimensions to this discussion. Post-war ecumenical endeavour – including the emergence of a new set of 'ecumenical instruments' in the British Isles – will form the first part of this chapter. A second section looks at a rather different feature of the ecclesiastical landscape: the membership and staff of the Church of England's General Synod and the organizational style embodied therein. Finally the discussion turns to the ordained clergy in more detail, gathering together a variety of sources on what must be the most significant group of religious professionals in this country. The post-war period has, however, seen considerable changes in the size and social make-up of this professional body, including latterly the decision to include within parts of it women as well as men, a change accepted relatively easily within the free churches but rather less so elsewhere. Such changes bring the argument full circle in that ecumenical issues form an unavoidable thread within this debate. For there are those who maintain that the existence of women as priests within the Church of England cannot be reconciled with its inclusion in the one, holy, catholic and apostolic Church.

Looked at from a different point of view, the chapter raises – from a variety of perspectives – a persistently problematic question for religious organizations: the nature of authority. How, for example, can churches with very different authority structures collaborate together when their modes of legitimation lead them, it would seem, in opposing directions? Nor are such questions limited to inter-church relationships, for they can, equally well, bedevil internal attempts both at making and enforcing decisions. The Church of England is the most obvious example of manifest confusion in this respect, but no church is entirely free from the problem. Some (though by no means all) house churches, for example – for all their congregational emphases – can be ferociously authoritarian in the way that they operate, notably in the system known as 'shepherding'. And at the other end of the ecclesiastical spectrum, many Roman Catholics quite clearly choose to ignore the teaching of the hierarchy on matters of contraception. The selective nature of responses in this area is probably more corrosive of Roman authority than many care to admit, for it initiates an insidious process of choosing rather than accepting doctrinal commitments. Understandable enough in itself, the *de facto* rejection of papal teaching on birth control cannot be other than the thin end of the wedge.

Ecumenical Developments in the Post-war Period

When David Sheppard (already consecrated Bishop of Woolwich) was appointed Bishop of Liverpool in 1975, his first congratulatory telegram came from the Roman Catholic Archbishop already resident in that city, Andrew Beck (Sheppard and Worlock 1989: 39). That gesture proved a foretaste of things to come, for Sheppard's partnership with Beck's successor, Archbishop Derek Worlock, has become nationally – and indeed internationally – famous. Liverpool, a city dominated by sectarianism until well into the post-war period now finds itself at the forefront of practical ecumenism. So much so that the Bishops are seen together in public more often than they appear separately and their joint presence has become as embedded in Scouse humour as jokes about the ferries and the football clubs. But the religious life of Liverpool is *sui generis*, and it would be foolhardy to deduce any general trends from this most Irish of British cities. It is clear, nonetheless, that one factor among many which enabled such an outstanding Christian partnership in Liverpool was the transformation in the ecumenical climate of the country as a whole. For what was totally impossible in Liverpool in the immediate post-war decades was very nearly impossible almost everywhere else.

Sociologists differ in their interpretation of ecumenical developments. There are those, first of all, who see ecumenism as a sign of strength on the part of the churches in that they have the confidence to engage in dialogue. But there are just as many others who see ecumenical initiatives as a sign of weakness; in other words, all churches now have their backs against the wall and may as well co-operate in their efforts to stave off disaster. There is probably a certain amount of truth in both explanations, but either way, the shift from mutual hostility towards active co-operation – never mind toleration – on the part of most, if not quite all, of the churches in contemporary Britain is one of the most remarkable stories of the post-war decades. It should not be taken for granted. How has such a transformation come about?

In many ways, the answer to this question is paradoxical. On the one hand there has been more than one false start. Indeed there have been some spectacular and painful failures, notably the collapse of the Anglican–Methodist Unity Scheme in 1972 and the less than enthusiastic reception of Covenanting for Unity in 1980. On the other hand, the gradual *rapprochement* of the various Christian churches has continued throughout this period despite, rather than because of, such organizational initiatives. It could, in fact, be argued that the whole enterprise begins to take off precisely when organizational schemes cease to dominate the agenda. Left to itself, the centre of gravity gradually but irrevocably begins to shift, away from the separate identity of individual churches – still very prevalent in the immediate post-war period – towards an awareness that there might be different ways of expressing what is essentially a common message. The change occurs at different times in different places, but a decisive moment arrives when the minority who have always looked for ecumenical opportunities turn themselves, almost imperceptibly, into a majority. For reasons that remain very difficult to determine, the middle ground begins to shift and those who resist begin to look increasingly out of place. Nowhere more so than in Liverpool where the tired demonstrators of militant Protestantism still emerge on ecumenical occasions but are unable to attract more than a handful to their cause.[1] The vast majority are, each Whitsunday, following their Bishops from one Liverpool cathedral to the other along the length of the appropriately named Hope Street.

Such a shift is crucial to the ecumenical process but we need to be clear about its implications. One of these is only too apparent: relatively successful ecumenical occasions do not imply unanimity among British church people. Far from it. Many issues – for example the split between those who feel that the churches should play a prominent part in public debate and those who resist this trend – continue to divide Christian thinking in this country. Similarly evangelicals from a whole variety of denominations will assert priorities rather different from other Christian groups, who feel at best uneasy and at times distinctly embarrassed by their rather more zealous co-religionists.[2] In other words controversies, of whatever kind, will remain and they may at times be heated. But they result, for the most part, in splits which lie across rather than between the major denominations in this country. The unpredictable and shifting nature of these alliances is a point already discussed in the concluding section of chapter 4. The most successful combinations are very often those which unite people of relatively disparate backgrounds around more rather than less specific issues and for a relatively short space of time.

Essentially pragmatic and short-lived alliances are one thing, but centuries-old religious cultures are quite another. For old habits regarding the latter die particularly hard and it may be several generations before they disappear completely, if ever. To be more precise, a certain kind of Protestant identity – muted rather than militant – may turn out to be an enduring feature of British society, for we have already seen that the acceptance of Catholicism as a valued and integral part of British culture does not imply the welcoming of papal *authority* in this country. Important boundaries remain and this, clearly, is one of them. The internal changes within the Catholic Church are, however, one (if not the) key factor in the ecumenical process. For, as Hastings points out, the Second Vatican Council – the 'Protestantization' of the Roman Church – not only permitted Catholics to take part in ecumenical dialogue; at one and the same time, it altered the whole context in which such initiatives take place. And to exemplify, from an English point of view, the change in mood that had taken place between 1962 and 1965 – the years of the Council's deliberations – Hastings compares the visits to Rome of two English Archbishops. In 1960, Dr Fisher paid a highly significant, yet private (almost furtive) visit to Pope John XXIII. Six years later, Dr Ramsey made a similar journey. This time, though, the visit was an immensely public occasion, including a jointly led ecumenical service in

St Paul's Basilica in Rome. Hastings concludes: 'Here was both a deliberate example of prayer in common and a degree of mutual recognition
which would have seemed unimaginable a decade earlier' (1986: 530–1).
The papal visit to Britain in 1982 was but the culmination of this process.
What was unthinkable in the immediate post-war period has become
almost commonplace as the century draws to a close.

Given the magnitude of such changes, it is hardly surprising that
progress has been, and continues to be, uneven. There is still, for example, no prospect of organic unity between the major branches of Christendom, nor is there likely to be in the foreseeable future. Nor is the
present (as opposed to the period immediately following the Vatican
Council) outlook among the Catholic leadership all that encouraging as
far as Anglicans are concerned. For the Roman reaction to the long-
drawn-out process known as ARCIC (the Anglican Roman Catholic International Commission) has been profoundly disappointing. The response
to ARCIC I came in December 1991; it confirmed that there had been
'notable progress' in the dialogue between the two communions, but did
not accept that this amounts to 'substantial agreement'. The tone of the
response was, moreover, revealing; indicating a relationship in which a
dominant sibling urges its considerably smaller and somewhat wayward
younger sister to return to the fold. It was not a dialogue between equals.
On the British scene, however, a significant step occurred in 1990. This
was the creation of a new set of ecumenical instruments – the Council of
Churches for Britain and Ireland (CCBI) – under which four partially
independent bodies operate at national level.[3] The complexities of these
arrangements are unlikely to catch the imagination of even the most
regular churchgoer, never mind the man in the street, for they are very
much the work of professionals, but behind the jargon a crucially important change occurred at this moment (a change already referred to in
chapter 4). That is, the inclusion within the new instruments of the
Roman Catholic Church as a full participating member, a role never
achieved within the British Council of Churches. This, surely, must be
considered a positive if rather bureaucratic step forward and one, perhaps,
that was made in the nick of time. For following the establishment of the
CCBI, moderately rapid advances in the ordination of women debate in
the Church of England have had a more negative effect on relationships
between Canterbury and Rome.

We will return to the ecumenical implications of this particular issue in the final section of this chapter. But a change in the nature of priesthood inevitably raises deeper questions of ecclesiastical authority; questions which reveal persistent and unresolved tensions not only between Rome and Canterbury but within the Church of England itself. It is important, therefore, to look initially at the issue of authority within the Church of England and, more especially, at the emergence in the post-war period of fully fledged synodical government.

Synodical Government: a Bureaucratic Church?

Synodical government came into being in the Church of England in 1970; it represented a new stage in the life of the established Church. But 1970 was a date of significance in church/state relations for other reasons as well. For the inauguration of the General Synod coincided with the Report of the Chadwick Commission on Church and State, the principal recommendations of which effectively transferred the responsibility for the appointment of bishops within the established Church from the Prime Minister to the Church itself; in other words to a suitably constituted committee.[4] These multiple shifts in responsibility have had important repercussions for the way that the Church conducts its business. On the one hand, it has become an organization with far greater control over its own affairs; that is generally thought to be a good thing. But equally inevitably it now sets about its work in a style rather different from that which predominated in the immediate post-war period. For better or for worse, it has become a more bureaucratic institution with all the ambiguity that the word 'bureaucracy' implies. It is, moreover, an area where value judgements abound, for – rather like establishment – people respond to synodical government in either black or white terms. A rather more realistic approach, however, recognizes that the synodical system – like most efforts at better representation – offers some advantages and some disadvantages. It is not, as some of its instigators believed, 'a panacea for the many ills which beset the Church' (Welsby 1984: 208), but then, nor were the combinations of Convocations and Church Assembly that preceded it. Indeed synodical government represents a genuine attempt to overcome the most obvious defects of the previous system.

What, then, are the advantages of the new arrangements? Welsby (1985: 51) outlines four of these. First, that all matters affecting the Church, including doctrine and worship, now come before one body instead of three,[5] a move which undoubtedly enhances the participation of the laity in such matters (probably the biggest single advantage of the new pattern). Secondly, the General Synod is considerably smaller than its predecessor (the Church Assembly) and is correspondingly more manageable. Thirdly, less time is involved in meetings, though still, in the opinion of some, too much. Lastly, there is built into the system a much closer link between the General Synod and the dioceses and parishes, achieved through the electoral college of the Deanery Synods and through the mechanism of referral. The latter demands that certain measures be sent to the Diocesan Synods for approval before a final decision can be made by the General Synod. It is a mechanism which emphasizes the position of the General Synod at the apex of a much larger system, a framework in which information works its way up as well as down (more or less) through the parishes, deaneries and dioceses.[6]

The setting up of synodical government has engendered some heated debates; central among these is the question of 'representativeness'. The focus of such discussions tends, however, to be rather narrow, targeting the General Synod in particular (rather than the whole synodical system) in a series of sociological enquiries carried out since 1970 (Jones 1971 and 1976, Moyser 1979 and 1982, Medhurst and Moyser 1988, Davie and Short 1993). Such enquiries have, nonetheless, produced a body of material that is gaining in value with each survey achieved, in that it is now becoming possible to plot changes over time with some accuracy.[7] The question of representativeness is, moreover, a real one; if the General Synod is to operate as a mechanism through which the voice of both clergy and laity is expressed, it is important to know what kinds of people find themselves in that body. The question of the laity needs, however, to be posed in two ways. Firstly, with respect to the relatively active churchgoer, who – presumably – would like to feel that his or her voice is heard at the centre of Church government. We shall come back to this point shortly. But there is, in addition, the much more problematic issue of the very large number of Anglicans who rarely practice. For it is almost impossible to see how any sort of representative body can be formed to convey the opinion of this sizeable group of English people to those responsible for decision making in the Church. The solution, of course, is simply to exclude the Anglican fringe from the synodical process. Such a decision is reasonable enough but, like every other decision, it has consequences. For those who attend irregularly are likely to have rather different priorities, regarding – to give but a few examples – liturgy, the occasional offices, parochial structures and, most of all, regarding buildings.

More immediately, the narrower question of representativeness needs further attention, for it is important to discover to what extent the General Synod is likely to reflect the opinion of ordinary churchgoers. But even this question is not entirely straightforward, for representativeness can be understood in different ways. With reference to the General Synod, there are – and, as Jones (1976) points out, there always have been – two possible interpretations of the term; interpretations that are not *necessarily* in conflict, but which pull, it seems, in rather different directions. Jones describes the two models in the following:

A. that the General Synod, as the senior policy-making body of the Church, ought to represent the wisest heads and the broadest spread of talents which the Church has at its command.

B. that the General Synod, as the senior policy-making body of the Church, ought to be a microcosm of the whole Church – that is, that it should be representative in terms of age, sex and social class with a membership which changed at every election to prevent the formation of a closed elite. (1976: 152)

The five General Synod 'classes' elected since the inception of synodical government in 1970 have all, not surprisingly, fallen somewhere between the two ideal-types, reflecting a compromise between wisdom and diversity. It seems reasonable to suggest, however, that over the past twenty years, the Synod has gradually, if not always very steadily, encompassed rather more of Model B. To be more precise and to give the most obvious example, the far better representation of women in recent years, and notably in the Synod elected in 1990, gives considerably greater credence to the idea of a microcosm. An immediate caveat is, however, important: the greater number of women in the Synod does not imply correspondingly fewer wise heads or a narrower spread of talent. Indeed the reverse is likely to be the case in that the pool of experience is, by definition, extended. The shift, moreover, has been displayed in two ways: firstly in the greatly increased proportion of women present in the House of Laity (rising from 22 per cent in 1970 to 52 per cent in 1990), but also in the influx of women into the House of Clergy. Interestingly, the latter innovation preceded the decision to ordain women as priests within the Church of England, for ten women deacons were admitted to the House of Clergy in 1987 following the first ordinations of women as deacons.[8] But whether in the House of Clergy or in the House of Laity, the significant number of women now taking part indicates one way in which the General Synod reflects its constituency far more adequately than its most obvious political equivalent.

There is, however, no getting away from the fact that the House of Laity remains essentially a middle-class body, filled with well-educated individuals who are prepared and able to offer a great deal to the Church in the form of talents and time. The age range, predictably enough, is heavily skewed.[9] In other words there is a good deal of Jones's Model A that persists: considerable experience and a broad, or moderately broad, spread of talent.[10] In many respects this is hardly surprising, for the General Synod can be an intimidating place in which both experience and expertise are necessary for survival. And it is bound to attract a certain type of individual, one all too easy to stereotype. Such individuals are not necessarily unrepresentative of churchgoing opinion even if they fall short of a perfect microcosm. The much-publicized final vote on the ordination of women, for example, seems to have reflected the opinion of the active churchgoer pretty accurately.[11] A close analysis of the Synod's opinion on a diverse range of issues in 1993 revealed, however, that the General Synod membership had a rather greater confidence in the Church's capabilities than the average churchgoer. Table 9.1 compares a set of questions taken from the European Values Study, which were re-used in an enquiry directed to the Synod's membership (Davie and Short 1993). Bearing the inevitable methodological difficulties of such a transfer in mind (and they are considerable), the results remain significant. Members of the General Synod's House of Laity are, it seems, rather more ready than either the general public or the regular church attender for the Church to speak out – to prophesy – and on a dauntingly wide range of issues.

There was, however, a paradoxical aspect to these findings, for the previous question in this survey revealed a House of Laity that was, by implication at least, critical of the Church's existing responses to a variety of contemporary problems. In other words the precedents for effective prophecy were dubious. The two questions need to be seen together: there can be no doubt that the Synod affirmed the reponsibility of the

Table 9.1 Support for the churches' voice

Topic	Population (%)	Church attender (%)	House of Laity (%)
Disarmament	55	60	79
Abortion	53	71	94
Third World problems	74	83	93
Extra-marital affairs	49	70	92
Unemployment	45	56	93
Racial discrimination	65	75	94
Euthanasia	57	73	96
Homosexuality	43	58	89
Ecology and environmental issues	60	68	87
Government policy	34	42	80

Source: Table adapted from Timms 1992: 73 and reproduced from Davie and
Short 1993

Table 9.2 General Synod membership: voting in 1992 election

Party	House of Clergy (%)	House of Laity (%)
Conservative	23	44
Labour	30	24
Liberal	46	30
Other	2	2

Source: Figures (rounded up) reproduced from Davie and Short 1993

Church to speak out; the difficulties arise in deciding what, precisely, her representatives are supposed to say. For a full discussion of these data, see Davie and Short 1993.

The same enquiry probed the vexed question of the Synod's political views (see table 9.2), the subject of ongoing and rarely accurate speculation. The results[12] in this case are interesting in that they indicate contrasting profiles for the House of Clergy and the House of Laity; they reveal moreover a 1990s Synod whose political views are distinctive but certainly not extreme. To be more precise, the most notable feature to emerge from these data is the persistent predilection of the synodical clergy for a party of the political centre (a fact already observed by Medhurst and Moyser ten years earlier) alongside the relative Conservatism of the laity.

All investigations of this type are, however, bedevilled by a persistent lack of information; not so much about the members of the General Synod itself (by now a well-studied species), but about the ordinary churchgoer or the clergy that these people are supposed to represent.[13] The problem, moreover, becomes even more acute with reference to the intermediate stages of synodical life, about whose sociological make-up we know virtually nothing. It would, for example, help to discover at which stage of the synodical process the idea of a microcosm begins to give way to one based on expertise. In that relatively few churchgoers are attracted by committee, let alone synodical life, it seems likely that this shift occurs at or near grassroots level. If this is so, there is, surely, little point in castigating the General Synod for a bias which enters the system very much closer to home.

Be that as it may, synodical government embodies a particular approach to church life; one that has, in theory at least, constructed a 'rational, administrative and representative system of synods and committees' (Habgood 1983: 115) in which matters important to the church can be thoroughly discussed and from which the necessary decisions will emerge. It is an essentially democratic process in which information passes in two directions and follows a pattern adopted by the majority of reformed churches. The Church of England is, however, both catholic *and* reformed, a tension revealed organizationally as well as theologically in that synodical government is not the only decision-making process which it observes. For alongside the pattern already described, there continues to exist within the Church of England a 'traditional, pastoral, hierarchical system, staffed by the clergy, and finding its fullest expression in the – largely undefined – authority of bishops' (p. 115). These citations are taken from the present Archbishop of York, but in this analysis, Dr Habgood is drawing very directly on an earlier sociological study of the nature of authority in the Church of England (Thompson 1970). Thompson, in turn, links his argument to Weber's distinction between different types of authority. In other words he is looking at the bases of legitimation underlying the competing structures within the Church of England: the rational-legal authority underpinning synodical government and the traditional authority embodied above all in the episcopate. The crucial point to grasp is that not one but two organizational systems continue to coexist within the Church of England, each with its own claim to authority.[14]

The results can be confusing, but to a considerable extent both Thompson and Habgood start by emphasizing the positive aspects of the dual system, maintaining that a wholly rational church structure could never be so resilient as the present system of checks and balances, complex though they may be. More precisely, both authors emphasize that the dual system is particularly necessary in a church which contains within itself a bewildering number of different parties, interests and shades of belief; indeed within a church that claims to be both catholic and reformed. In theory, at least, the Church of England has evolved an arrangement in which each of its organizational systems can 'compensate for the major operational deficiencies of the other – the potential impersonality of bureaucracy and the potential authoritarianism of hierarchy' (Habgood 1983: 117).

The Archbishop, however, goes further than this and reinforces the sociological justification of the dual system with a theological argument; an argument which concerns the very nature of a church. In so far as churches are operating as secular or temporal institutions, rational and representative forms of organization (based on rational-legal authority) are entirely appropriate. But churches are, surely, more than this; they are called to live under the gospel, deriving their ultimate authority from God. Furthermore, and crucial to the Archbishop's argument, they claim to embody their message as well as to transmit it. And it is in this embodiment that the traditional hierarchical structure finds its ultimate justification:

> The parallel existence of two types of structure, therefore, the rational and hierarchical, is not just the end-product of a series of political compromises. It is a valid expression of the nature of the church itself, an institution but claiming to be more than an institution. This is the crucial theological point. (1983: 117)

It provides, in addition, a framework in which the nominal Anglican, the fringe member of the Church of England, can be much more easily included, for activity, including synodical activity, ceases to be the sole criterion of membership.

But how does the dual system work in practice. Like so much within the Church of England, it all depends on your point of view, for neither the system nor its results are equally pleasing to everyone. The final section of this chapter – the case study on the ordination of women to the priesthood – will provide an example of Anglican decision making in practice. But first, what is the nature of the priesthood to which some women aspire?

Priests and Ministers

The nomenclature surrounding religious professionals is full of subtlety. Bearing this and the dangers of over-simplification in mind, this section – following definitions offered in the *Oxford Dictionary of the Christian Church* – suggests that there is a crucial distinction between the term 'minister', used primarily in non-episcopal churches, and the term 'priest', traditionally associated with the Mass. Somewhere between the two, the Anglican formula 'clergyman' can be pushed in either direction (or, at the extremes, superseded), depending on the churchmanship of the parish or individual in question.[15] Such distinctions are primarily theological. They have, nonetheless, important practical implications for the way that the role is carried out; implications that will become apparent in the latter part of the discussion. Initially, however, the emphasis will be on the pressures common to all those engaged in the professional ministry of the churches, using this term in its widest sense. It will also extend, at times, to the religious professionals of the other-faith communities, for they – just as much as their counterparts in the host society – are obliged to conduct their ministry in a rapidly changing context.

Broadly speaking, the pressures to which an ordained minister must respond can be divided into two distinguishable though interrelated areas: those which derive from the external environment and those which come primarily from within the churches themselves. Taking the external pressures first, the argument develops aspects of the discussion initiated in chapter 2, though with a narrower focus. The impact of increasing consumerism and of a changing economic structure affects the very nature of religious institutions; such changes are, therefore, unavoidable for everyone involved in the religious sector, whether lay or ordained. Some aspects of these changes, however, do have a particular effect on those engaged in the professional ministry, notably – to develop one among many possible illustrations – the restructuring of the economy in favour of the service sector, within which a whole range of 'new' professions have emerged in the post-war period. The counselling indus-try, for instance, has become a dominant feature of contemporary society and one that impinges on the clerical role in two rather contradictory ways: firstly, in usurping some of the traditional functions of a pastor and, secondly, in obliging that pastor – if he wishes to keep on terms – to ac-quire skills (including an extensive vocabulary) of a novel and essentially unreligious nature.[16]

These twin pressures are, of course, nothing new. Such changes are an inevitable part of a long-term process of increasing social differentiation, itself one of the least controversial aspects of the term 'secularization'. A whole range of functions traditionally undertaken by the churches' per-sonnel have become, bit by bit, the responsibility of widely diverse and non-religious professionals. The important point to grasp in this section, however, is the particular forms this process has taken since 1945, which relate in turn to the evolution of advanced capitalist society. The trend, however, predates the post-war period, which has simply reinforced an existing and seemingly irreversible situation: that is, the inevitable loss of confidence which derives from the fact that a clergyman's role is increas-ingly characterized 'by marginality to the mainstream concerns of ordinary people' (Russell 1980: 262). For modern or post-modern individuals now turn to other experts for the particular skills that they require and for counsel.

But do they? For the later decades of the post-war period have, in some respects at least, seen a counterveiling trend; a trend that began in the mid 1970s with the retrenchment in public spending but which gathered not only momentum but ideological underpinning as the New Right began to dominate under Margaret Thatcher. Welfare (including professional advice), education and health – to state but the most obvious cases – were themselves shifting (or shifted) from a production or supply mode to a consumption model. One, that is, in which clients, parents or patients select or choose the service packages that suit them best and use their own resources to buy what the state no longer offers. A full discussion of the profound transformation currently taking place in British society is beyond the scope of this chapter, but within this wide-ranging debate one point is crucial: the existence of particular groups within society who are effectively denied the choices open to the majority, or – quite simply – who find themselves without any provision at all. The effect on the religious professional (of any faith) in certain parts of society is only too obvious; he or she becomes the *only* available person to whom the most vulnerable turn when there is no apparent alternative. The urban priority area is the most obvious example of need in this respect, but the withdrawal of services in rural areas – particularly in the privatization of transport – should not be ignored simply because the rural population is relatively small. The suspension of a bus service on the grounds that it is uneconomic will have a devastating effect on the most vulnerable members of a rural community.

So, in a certain sense, the clergy become once again the generalists of our society; the first port of call in an emergency who offer both immediate care and considered advice about what to do next.[17] No wonder the strain is considerable. But the strain is greatly exacerbated by a second set of factors which in some senses are internal to the churches, but which also reflect – all too obviously – the marginalization of the religious professional (Russell 1980, Towler and Coxon 1979). Cause and effect are, of course, interrelated but the net effect of what is happening is both serious and undeniable; the numbers of clergy in almost all denominations in this country have diminished steadily in the post-war period, and dramatically so since the 1960s (see table 4.1, p. 46). The vicious circle of marginality and declining vocations can, moreover, be illustrated in any number of ways: statistical profiles, age distributions, the number of training colleges, remuneration (or the lack of it), qualifications for entry (widening all the time), the strain in the parochial network, teams and group ministries and a wonderful tapestry of make do and mend in the form of unpaid, retired or part-time workers. There is, in short, a crisis, though not always as severe in Britain as it is elsewhere in Europe.[18]

There is, of course, a rather more positive way of looking at this issue. For gifted individuals do still come forward to serve in the ministry whether full time or in addition to another job, and a whole range of priestly functions can, it seems, be undertaken just as well by the laity, if not better. In other words, the show goes on. Lay people of most denominations, for example, now frequently administer the chalice at the Eucharist (or its equivalent), a practice which has much to recommend it theologically. But, and this is the crucial point, the theology has evolved of necessity in that there simply were insufficient professionals to carry out the task; a situation exacerbated in the Church of England by a much more frequent celebration of the Eucharist in recent years.[19] A more fundamental issue lurks, however, beneath these adjustments, for they pose in a particular form a question introduced in earlier chapters. It can be restated quite simply. Just how far can the sacred – in this case the sacred role – be adapted or superseded without losing its integrity, in other words its sacredness? The perplexing boundary between the sacred and the profane is, as ever, under review. Hence inevitable and heated controversies, revealing among other things – in the shorthand of this chapter – the fundamental difference between priest and minister, for the priest cannot so easily be substituted.

There are, in addition, important denominational differences in this respect; both in the form in which the ministerial crisis occurs and in the manner in which it is confronted. Catholics, for example, have had to cope with the changes already mentioned, but at the same time (indeed as part of the same process) with the transformation brought about by Vatican II, including its reappraisal of the priesthood. For some older priests this has caused acute difficulties. Quite apart from this, the peculiarly Roman issue of celibacy has faced significant numbers of gifted men with an agonizing conflict of loyalties. Anglicans, on the other hand, are mindful of the particular reponsibility they have for maintaining a viable and recognizable parochial structure, itself caught between historical legacies and the need to adapt to population movement. Their resources are stretched to the limit, sometimes straining marriages as well as the clergy themselves. The free churches have had to face a situation in which they have nothing very much to fall back on once the gathered congregation (and its finance) starts to melt away. And those responsible for other-faith communities nurture vulnerable minorities, some of them existing in far from favourable conditions. It has not been easy for any of them.

Turning now to a rather different – though by no means unrelated – aspect of clergy life, Towler and Coxon's study of the Anglican clergy raises the whole question of clergy careers, at least in the Church of England. Using a sample of clergy ordained between 1934 and 1969 as a basis for their analysis (see 1979: appendix I), Towler and Coxon construct the likely career paths of a hypothetical hundred clergy ordained in the Church of England in the mid twentieth century. Their breakdown postulates the following. Of the hundred clergy, thirty-nine will remain throughout in the parish ministry; a further seventeen will spend most, but not quite all of their working lives in that way and seventeen more will remain incumbents but achieve additional minor honours. (A further three more or less fit these categories.) Two clergy will achieve senior honours (that is, they will become canons or archdeacons) and three will gain preferment, becoming either deans or bishops. Four will serve abroad, four will become specialists, five will demonstrate no discernible pattern, four will drop out of the ministry and two will disappear from the record (1979: 180). In other words, the parochial ministry will absorb the greater part of the working lives of a very large majority of these people; it is the core of Anglican ministry.[20] The authors proceed to a further question. Is it possible to predict which of these individuals might reach the senior posts and at which point in their careers (always assuming the clergy are permitted such) do their choices become significant? It seems that the choice of a post immediately following a curacy remains an important indicator in this respect, for those who achieve high honours in the Church are less likely than their contemporaries to go straight from a curacy to a benefice; they move, instead, to a non-parochial job (1979: 184). Such moves are, one assumes, related to the gaining of particular kinds of experience; those, perhaps, thought to be of value in obtaining preferment in the long term. If this is the case, they need to be set against a second set of data: those which indicate ongoing changes within the episcopate itself.

Medhurst and Moyser (1988) document this question in considerable detail, drawing on a range of historical and sociological studies but also on their own interviews with a complete generation of bishops. Much of their material – historical as well as contemporary – is organized around a moderately long-term evolution in the role of an English bishop: from, that is, the traditional model of 'prince bishop', through the transitional era of 'prelate' to the emergence of the modern bishop, the 'pastor'. The authors locate the second of these shifts (from prelate to pastor) firmly in the 1960s; it was, in fact, part of a whole series of interrelated changes which led – among other things – to the Chadwick Commission on Church and State, which proposed new arrangements for appointments to the Bench. But quite apart from the *mode* of appointment it is hardly surprising that the preparation considered most desirable for a pastor-bishop at the end of the twentieth century involves considerable hands-on experience in the parish ministry rather than anything else.[21] The parochial emphasis is, however, at least partly balanced by an interesting evolution in episcopal patterns of working. For both within the dioceses and among the bishops as a whole (both diocesans and suffragans) there is a move away from what might be termed 'line-management', culminating in the role of the senior bishop or archbishop, and towards a markedly more collaborative style. From which shift there emerges, inevitably, a growing emphasis on the complementarity of skills: those skills that can be contributed to the diocese or that offer particular expertise to the wider church become, therefore, in addition to parochial experience, a significant factor in the appointment process.[22]

Such occupational shifts are matched by a social evolution already mentioned in an earlier chapter: that is, the gradual, but quite evident movement in the social provenance of the Anglican elite;[23] a change that indicates – to a certain extent at least – an episcopal Bench which is rather less closely identified with the establishment, in the broader sense of the term, than it used to be. The process can, however, be looked at in two ways: negatively in that it is part of the decline in social prestige suffered by the clergy as a whole (part, in other words, of their social marginalization), but positively in that gifted and sensitive priests, from whatever background, can be promoted to positions of high authority in the established Church. Their authority, moreover, is crucial, for it remains the apex of one system of legitimation within the Church of England. It forms in addition one strand in the complex debate about the ordination of women to the priesthood, a debate to which we must now turn.

The Ordination of Women: a Sociological Case Study

The problematic issue of women's ordination draws together the threads of this chapter, notably the theme of authority. For at the heart of the matter lies the question of who (or which body), precisely, possesses the authority to make decisions of this nature and how can such decisions, once made, be enforced. It reveals, therefore, in an unusually visible form, an unresolved question that lies at the heart of Anglicanism, notably in its English form; an ambiguity that bedevils, among other things, the relationship between Anglicanism and the other Christian churches.

The issue needs, however, to be placed in its proper context. It arises – and there can be no doubt about this – because there have been profound and irreversible changes in secular life; changes that predate the war but which have gained enormously in momentum since then. They concern the evolving role of women in Western society; a far from simple process prompted by a wide range of economic, demographic, social and ideological factors. They have resulted in very different patterns of life for many, if not most, women in the late twentieth century, who more often than not combine their domestic responsibilities – themselves changing – with increasing participation in the labour market. It is true that women's careers still look very different from those of men, but it no longer causes surprise when women rather than men are discovered in positions of responsibility across a wide range of professions. Indeed – and this is the point at issue – it is beginning to be noticeable when the reverse is the case; that is, when a profession contains no women at all.

Such a situation is bound to place the guardians of the sacred in a difficult position, for the nature of the sacred for which they are responsible, in this case the Christian tradition, has maintained an exclusively male priesthood from the days of the early church. So what are such guardians to do in contemporary Western society? Should they preserve the tradition as they received it, or should they begin to reconsider not so much the tradition itself but the grounds on which it is based; in other words to ask questions about the nature of the society from which the early church emerged. Was it a question of universal forms, of undisputed patterns established for all time, or was the early church just as much as its possible successors coloured by a particular culture? If the latter is the case, the contemporary guardians of the sacred are free, or at least freer, to think through questions of gender (or indeed any other question) in relation to changing circumstances. They are not bound for all time.

Not surprisingly, different Christian churches have come to different conclusions when faced with a question of this magnitude. In Britain – and indeed in most of the Western world – a wide range of Protestant churches (for example, Baptist, Congregationalist, Lutheran, Methodist, Moravian, Pentecostal, Presbyterian, Unitarian and United Reformed) now ordain women to their official ministries. Smaller groups such as the Salvation Army and the Society of Friends have been similarly welcoming within the limits of their leadership structures. In other words, those Christian groups whose religious professionals are normally termed 'ministers' rather than 'priests' do not seem to have found the inclusion of women in their professional ministries all that problematic. There are, however, important exceptions even in this group, for resistance to change comes from two quarters: the Christian communities that put the strongest emphasis on either scripture or tradition. Hence the particular – and in some respects unusual – combination of churches that challenge 'the admissibility of women to an office which until recent times has been the prerogative of males [and] even now remains so among seventy-five per cent of the world's Christians' (Langley 1989: 299–300). The last point should not be forgotten, for in world terms, it is still a minority of Christians who have chosen to accept women into their ministries. More precisely, both the Roman Church and the Orthodox churches maintain their traditional policies, a situation unlikely to change in the immediately foreseeable future.

So where does this leave the Anglican Church? The answer, as ever, is not entirely clear, for some Anglican Provinces have taken this step and some have not. In other words there have been different solutions within a Communion which looks for guidance in three directions, that is, to scripture, to reason and to tradition, and which embodies the principle of provincial autonomy. The Church of England, however, as Mother Church of the Anglican Communion, has been watched with particular attention in this respect, for a change here would undoubtedly have a far-reaching effect on ecumenical as well as internal relationships. Two preliminary points are crucial in the Anglican debate. First, it is worth repeating that its churches are both catholic and reformed and in so being Anglicanism straddles a very deep divide in Christendom. Second and following the discussion earlier in this chapter, the Church of England possesses more than one framework within which to decide policy; frameworks which are legitimated by different forms of authority. There is, however, no neat or tidy fit between the decision-making systems and the two sides of the ordination of women debate. For both the advocates of change within the Church of England and those who resist it use the synodical process to promote their point of view; and most – if not quite all – of the present Bench (the embodiment of traditional authority) are in favour of ordaining women to priesthood, more so very often than either the clergy or the laity, a discrepancy revealed in synodical voting.

The first ordinations of women to the priesthood within the Church of England took place in March 1994. The progress towards that point has, however, been a gradual one. As long ago as 1975 the Synod accepted that there were 'no fundamental objections to the ordination of women to the priesthood'; the problem (if so perceived) lay in the matter of timing. A number of subsequent debates concerned a seemingly minor issue; the admissibility or otherwise of the ministries of women who had been ordained to the priesthood in an Anglican Province overseas. The issue was, nonetheless, problematic and took up a good deal of synodical time. In the mid 1980s the discussion focused on the ordination of women as deacons, as a result of which many parishioners had their first direct, and clearly formative, experience of a woman's ministry, and following which a significant number of women became members of the Synod's House of Clergy. It also provoked a more general debate about the nature of the diaconate. It is, however, the ordination of women to the priesthood that causes the greatest controversy and raises most sharply the legitimacy of the Church of England to make this decision unilaterally. For the core of the resistance undoubtedly lies in the conviction among most, though by no means all, Anglo-Catholics that the Church of England alone (never mind the General Synod) is, quite simply, not empowered to make a decision affecting the threefold ministry belonging to the one, holy, catholic and apostolic Church. It follows that women who take holy orders as a consequence of the Synod's decision cannot be full members of the priesthood.

Legitimately or not, the Synod did, on 11 November 1992, vote in favour of the ordination of women to the priesthood in the Church of England, after a protracted process of referral to the dioceses and deaneries, and in which vote the final figures seemed to indicate proportions in favour and against rather similar to those ascertained by opinion polls among churchgoers. These figures need underlining, notably the size of the majority. It was a two-thirds majority in each house of the General Synod voting separately, and considerably more than this in the House of Bishops and the House of Clergy. The margin in the House of Laity was, however, extremely narrow. Hence the following day's headlines which produced every possible variant of 'Synod votes by a whisker to ordain women,' implying a result rather different from that which obtained in practice. More precisely, the resistance had come from two quarters: a sizeable group of Anglo-Catholics, both lay and ordained, concerned primarily about the legitimacy (or rather illegitimacy) of a unilateral decision; and a rather smaller group of conservative evangelicals, stressing above all the immutability of scripture. In other words two groups came together for very different reasons, a good example of the single-issue campaign already referred to in previous chapters.[24] The *committed* nature of this opposition is also important, for resistance, it seems, diminishes as one moves away from the centre or core. In so far as their opinion can be canvassed, the majority of Anglicans (the less rather than more regular churchgoers) are not overly opposed to change in this respect; many, moreover, overcome whatever scruples they do have once they have experienced a woman's ministry first hand. There remains, nonetheless, a sizeable minority who are visibly distressed by what is taking place; not surprisingly, for the vote undermined their understanding of Anglicanism.

The reactions to the Synod's decision were immediate. The responses of three Anglicans quoted in *The Tablet* (21 November 1992) very soon after the vote illustrate both the strong emotions that surround the decision and the incompatibilities within Anglican thinking, a particularly problematic combination as far as future policy is concerned, for compromise doesn't come easily in such circumstances. First a voice in favour, though an unusual one since it comes from an individual (a woman) nurtured in and nourished by the Catholic tradition:

> Last Wednesday's vote, then, broke a vacuum and let in a gush of fresh air. One deacon in Dean's Yard said to me that she felt as though she could breathe again for the first time in years. The Church of England as an *institution* – with all the implications for our corporate life as a Church – had said 'yes'.

The second illustrates the shock felt by those for whom the Synod's vote was nothing short of a betrayal of the Church of England's true nature:

> The overwhelming sense of devastation has taken me by surprise. At a stroke, through the changing of minds by a group of laity counted on the fingers of one hand, the General Synod has destroyed the faith of the Church of England. Catholic faith and order has been sold for a quick fix of popularity, for a seven-hour wave of celebrity status in the national press, for a temporary appeasement of shrill feminism.

The third adds a more personal postscript. Visiting a new grandson born that morning in a London hospital, the writer sought out the Church of England chaplain:

There was a notice on his door: 'I am with the Roman Catholic chaplain.' In his office we found two Catholics, one woman Methodist minister and one Anglican. They were together toasting the courage of the synod. They shared their glasses with us and we prayed together for the ministry of the future to serve all the world's grandchildren.

So which was it: the end of the Church of England as we know it or a welcome breath of new life into the Mother Church of the Anglican Communion? An effective end to an already faltering ecumenical relationship (at least as far as Rome is concerned) or a new ecumenism 'full of promise and adventure' embodied in a new partnership between men and women? It all, as ever in the Church of England, depends on which foot you kick with.

What, though, will happen next? Will the Church of England be able – as it has done so many times in the past – to ride out the storm and maintain within itself diverse, even opposing points of view? Or will this issue be the proverbial straw that breaks not only the camel's back but the Church of England in its present form? Only time will tell. But the question raises immediately the second aspect of authority suggested in the introductory paragraph to this section, for if it is one thing to make a decision (and that was hard enough), it is quite another to enforce it. More specifically, it isn't at all easy to see how the twin authority structures within the Church of England will work out their respective roles over this issue; an ambivalence epitomized in the ongoing debate concerning the rights (both short- and long-term) of those bishops opposed to the ordination of women, but repeated at every level of the synodical structure. For who will take precedence in the inevitable decision making: the diocesan bishop or the Diocesan Synod, parish priest or the Parochial Church Council and what happens when agreement between them is, quite simply, not possible? The notion of alternative oversight, moreover, for those priests no longer able to accept the pastoring of their diocesan bishop, strikes at the heart of traditional priestly legitimation. So, too, do no-go areas in certain dioceses; either within the diocese where the bishop is no longer made welcome by his priests or across a whole diocese where women – legally ordained in the national Church – exercise their ministry, as it were, on sufferance. None of these questions will be solved by the escape formula of the 'Bishops in Synod' for they threaten the core of the

Church's structures. Finding acceptable solutions is, surely, the task of the next generation of Anglicans both in this country and overseas.

In the meantime, it is inevitable that some will look elsewhere for both spiritual oversight and pastoral care. Such searchings will take a variety of forms: high-profile conversions, quieter shifts of allegiance in more than one direction and, possibly, group as well as individual movement. One way of looking at this process is that of boundary adjustment, particularly the boundary between different types of Catholicism, remembering the peculiarly English nature of Anglo-Catholicism.[25] Such adjustments will not, however, be easy; indeed they raise almost as many problems as they solve. Is it really possible, for example, for Rome to welcome significant numbers of priests from the Church of England, albeit re-ordained, when these priests are allowed to pursue their clerical functions within marriage when Roman priests cannot? Nor can prospective Roman Catholics pick and choose about what they are embracing, for the package includes Roman doctrine in its entirety. Not an easy commitment, one would think, for a generation nurtured on consumerism, though one – it seems – that some find attractive for precisely that reason. This more general point raises wider sociological questions about the nature of religious life in late or post-modernity. To be better understood, they require a rather more rigorous theoretical framework; this will be one focus of the following, concluding chapter.

Notes

1 The last real success of the militant Protestants occurred in Lent 1982, when Dr Runcie – as Archbishop of Canterbury – visited Liverpool Parish Church shortly after announcing the forthcoming visit of the Pope to Britain. The protest was such that the Arch-bishop was unable to continue with his sermon. At Pentecost, when the Pope finally came to Liverpool, Protestant sabre rattling came to nothing. The visit was a huge success.

2 Indeed there are ongoing controversies, sometimes heated ones, between different groups of evangelicals.

3 There are four national bodies: Churches Together in England, Action of Churches Together in Scotland (ACTS), Churches Together in Wales (CYTUN) and the pan-Irish Irish Council of Churches and Irish Inter-Church Meeting.

4 See chapter 8, note 1.

5 That is, the Convocations of Canterbury and York and the Church Assembly.

6 The 'more or less' caveat concerns, in particular, the position of the deanery, which has no decision-making capacity. It is, moreover, relatively rare to discover a deanery that has any real local resonance, for in most cases it is formed from a rather arbitrary group of parishes, and survives simply as a talking shop.

7 These studies provide a complete, if not always consistent, set of data concerning Synod membership, apart from one Synod 'class', that operative between 1985 and 1990. The last of these studies (Davie and Short 1993) has not yet been published. I am grateful to the Secretary-General of the Synod for permission to reproduce some of the data from this enquiry.

8 These deacons were admitted in a special women deacons constituency. In 1990 that constituency was abolished, following which women competed with men for places in the House of Clergy. The 1990 election returned twenty-three women (still as deacons) to the House of Clergy.

9 And getting more so; figures from the 1993 survey indicate a reduced proportion of members (both lay and ordained) in the under 40 age-group compared with earlier surveys. This may not, however, indicate reduced representativeness; it might well indicate the ageing of the actively religious constituency taken as a whole.

10 The Synod – or perhaps the Church as a whole – seems to attract disproportionate numbers from certain occupational groups, notably education. For further details, see Davie and Short 1993.

11 That is, two-thirds in favour of the change and one-third against. Among the less active churchgoers, it is becoming increasingly clear that there is very little resistance to change.

12 These should be interpreted with care, for not all Synod members were prepared, even anonymously, to disclose their voting preferences. The bishops are not included in the table in that significant numbers of them are barred from voting in a general election due to their membership of the House of Lords.

13 The Rural Church Project (see Davies, Watkins and Winter 1990) partially filled this gap for rural populations. Elsewhere there is little in addition to Brierley's statistical documentation and the two European Values Studies.

14 See Avis 1992 for a full and helpful discussion of this issue.

15 Following Russell (1980), the term 'clergyman' denotes an occupa-
    tional – rather than theological – role; hence Russell's *sociological*
    examination of *The Clerical Profession*.

16 An alternative way of looking at such changes stresses the merging
    of boundaries characteristic of contemporary society; a wide range of
    alternative therapies, for example, include some aspects of spiritual-
    ity, though the stresses will be rather different from those tradition-
    ally associated with the churches. Bereavement counselling often
    involves a variety of professionals, including clergy from the mainline
    churches.

17 The number of calls made to clergy doors becomes in fact an accu-
    rate indicator of the degree of deprivation in any particular area.

18 The West European picture is, in fact, enormously varied, ranging
    from the catastrophic collapse of the professional ministry in France
    (where vocations per year have dropped from around 1,000 to less
    than 100 in the post-war period), to the abundance of relatively well-
    paid religious professionals anywhere where a system of church tax
    remains in place, notably the Scandinavian countries. The partial
    collapse of Church of England finance in the 1990s needs to be seen
    in this perspective as well as in a purely domestic one.

19 The Rural Church Project found a curious resistance to this wide-
    spread practice; quite different, for example, from the readiness of
    rural people to accept the ministry of women. But rural parishioners
    have a particular subtext to their arguments; they are understand-
    ably reluctant to demonstrate too great an independence in Eucha-
    ristic practice, or indeed in any other respect, for that might pave the
    way for the withdrawal of professionals from rural ministry alto-
    gether. *Ordained* women are welcomed for precisely the same reason.

20 For a full discussion of this point both in connection with the sup-
    posed popularity of sector ministries and with respect to generational
    changes, see Towler and Coxon 1979: 179–81.

21 A trend both noticeable and empirically verifiable through the analysis
    of pre-episcopal appointments.

22 See, for example, one of the conclusions of the 1983 Report on a
    research training programme for bishops in the Church of England
    (produced jointly by the Urban Ministry Project and the William
    Temple Foundation). The Report is entitled *Episcopacy in the 80s*
    and asks for a register of episcopal skills and experience in view of

the increasingly 'strong sense of mutuality and complementary skills' that is emerging among the episcopate.

23   A trend noticeable in educational backgrounds; the numbers of bishops coming from public schools and Oxbridge has diminished in the post-war period. The following figures are selective; nevertheless, in 1960, 85 per cent of diocesans had attended a public school, in 1984 the figure had dropped to 65 per cent; in 1960, 89 per cent had attended Oxbridge, in 1984, 72.5 per cent.

24   An attempt to involve the membership of the Prayer Book Society in the debate concerning the ordination of women proved hopelessly divisive. It was not possible to extrapolate from one issue to another.

25   Hence in Britain, the use of the term *Roman* Catholic to make the required distinction.

10 Religion and Modernity: a Theoretical Postscript

The religious life of Britain in the final decade of the twentieth century – with all its ambivalence and internal contradiction – is wonderfully captured in the following, almost poetic citation:

> We in England live in the chill religious vapours of northern Europe, where moribund religious establishments loom over populations that mostly do not enter churches for active worship even if they entertain inchoate beliefs. Yet these establishments guard and maintain thousands of houses of God, which are markers of space and time. Not only are they markers and anchors, but also the only repositories of all-embracing meanings pointing beyond the immediate to the ultimate. They are the only institutions that deal in tears and concern themselves with the breaking points of human existence. They provide frames and narratives and signs to live by, and offer persistent points of reference. They are repositories of signs about miraculous birth and redemptive sacrifice, shared tables and gift-giving; and they offer moral codes and exemplars for the creation of communal solidarity and the nourishment of virtue. They are places from which to launch initiatives which help sustain the kind of networks found, for example, in the inner city; they welcome schools and regiments and rotary clubs; they celebrate and commemorate; they are islands of quietness; they are places in

which unique gestures occur of blessing, distribution and obei-
sance; they offer spaces in which solemnly to gather, to sing, to lay
flowers, and light candles. They are – in Philip Larkin's phrase –
serious places on serious earth. (Martin 1991: 1)[1]

No wonder the domain is so difficult either to summarize or to theorize.
It is, simply, too elusive. Indeed it might be better not to try. Sidestepping
the issue is not, however, a viable option, for the evidence of the previous
chapters reveals in the closing decades of the twentieth century a critical
moment in the religious history of this country, and one which we would
do well to ponder. They are, first of all, decades in which both traditional
institutions and traditional certainties struggle, in secular as well as religious
life. The documentation from chapter 4 was unequivocal; so, too, the
evidence from other areas of society. But other passages, including the
one above, describe a society in which 'spiritual stirrings' – of a widely
diverse, not necessarily conventional and frequently contradictory nature
– are widespread; activities or sensibilities which show little sign of diminishing, and which have provoked considerable discussion in the public arena. Examples are not difficult to find. They include the renewed
interest among politicians of all persuasions in the problematic relationship between religion and morality, a controversy seldom out of the
news;[2] a growing list of ethical questions many of which are thought
to include a religious dimension; and – on a rather different tack – an
evident incapacity among most British people to understand the upsurge
in conservative religiosity, both in Britain and elsewhere.

How, then, should the sociologist proceed? For almost at once the
argument discloses the complexities of contemporary society, so much so
that the standard frameworks simply do not work. Conventional classifi-
cations, such as those of politics or industrial life, are becoming increasingly confused as social realities alter; divisions run through the political
parties rather than between them and the traditional rhetoric of industrial
relations fails to resonate in the post-industrial workplace. Equally faltering are the classic (in the sociological sense) explanations of religion,
formed for the most part in an emergent industrial society,[3] for the evidence no longer fits. The data demand, in fact, a new start, an altogether
more constructive frame of reference. Is it possible, then – and the question has a degree of urgency – to rework if not a fully fledged theoretical
framework for the sociology of religion (for that is probably too ambitious),

then at least some sociological ground rules within which to consider the nature and forms of religious life at the end of the twentieth century? That is the task of the following section.

Theoretical Suggestions

One way into the debate is through the concept of modernity; not a new idea in sociological thinking but one which has been considerably sharpened in recent controversy as modern or industrial forms of society are contrasted with *post*-modern or *post*-industrial mutations. Emerging from such discussion is a difficult and frequently confusing terminology, beneath which it is possible to discern two distinct phenomena: on the one hand, shifts in the way that society itself is ordered; on the other, changes in the cultural forms that have become associated, rightly or wrongly, with particular economic and social structures. In both respects, cultural as well as structural, this debate has critical implications for the way that we understand religion. But the whole process of relating particular forms of the society to particular cultural expressions, including expressions of the sacred, begs a number of questions. Each stage in the argument requires further explanation.

The plan below offers a schematic representation of some of the ideas in question, but like the typology in chapter 6, it must be treated with caution. It is, as before, an essentially pragmatic device. It neither postulates nor establishes a set of necessary relationships – indeed such links will be firmly denied – but attempts to separate out elements that are frequently muddled.[4] A second point requires equal stress: the plan is schematic, and indicates in outline form what, in reality, are profound, complex and confusing changes experienced not only by particular individuals but also by the communities and societies in which they live. They should never be taken lightly.

Before embarking on the schema itself, however, an important preliminary presents itself: namely the form of society that precedes modernity. In other words, should the plan contain three rather than two columns, the left-hand one referring to pre-industrial and pre-urban society; a society which was primarily agricultural and in which religion – or at least certain forms of traditional religion – appeared to be far more secure than they have been ever since? The question is well put and the following

Religion and Modernity: a Schematic Representation

Modernity	Post-modernity
Industrialization	Information technology
Urbanization	De-urbanization
Production	Consumption

Both modernity and post-modernity
are problematic for religion
but in different ways

Modernism	Post-modernism
The grand narrative: religious or anti-religious	Fragmentation/decentring of the religious narrative but also of the secular; i.e. of the scientific,
Progress	rational or anti-religious narrative e.g. rationalism/communism
Secularization	A space for the sacred but often in forms different from those which have gone before
God the Son	The Holy Spirit
The institutional churches	Varied forms of the sacred
Medical Science	Healing
Agribusiness	Ecology

discussion will bear this dimension in mind. But the question is also problematic in that it raises the difficult issue of time-scale that bedevils a great deal of the discussion in this area. For when precisely does one form of society give way to another and when (if ever) do these shifts have discernible and corresponding effects on particular cultural forms? Or to put the problem more directly, some observers would discover the beginnings of modernity long before others; indeed well before most of Western Europe became an industrial or production-based society.[5] The important point to grasp, however, is the need for a longer-term perspective, particularly in the study of contemporary religion. For much of what exists today looks back to the past. Indeed I would argue that the combination of believing without belonging is better understood as the residue of former, pre-industrial patterns of religious organization than it is as a fragmented or consciously post-modern form of religious activity.[6]

But this statement jumps far too quickly to one possible conclusion about the nature of religiosity in contemporary Britain. We need instead to go back to the plan and to work through the stages in the argument. The plan indicates, albeit in simplified form, the metamorphosis which provides the background to the discussion in each of the previous chapters; that is, the shift from an industrial to a post-industrial society, characteristic not only of contemporary Britain, but of much of the Western world in the later decades of the twentieth century. It also suggests that it is not only possible but necessary to distinguish the changes that have occurred in the way that society is structured from those that have taken place in the cultural or ideological sphere and to look at these one at a time. A second, and often misunderstood, point follows from this: change does not imply that things are – from the point of view of either the more or the less organized aspects of religion – getting worse or getting better. They are simply changing.

To be more precise and starting with societal structures rather than cultural forms, both modern (industrial) and post-modern (post-industrial) societies make heavy demands on most forms of organized religion *but in different ways*. The movement, for example, of large sections of the population away from the countryside to the large centres of population associated with certain kinds of industry was, clearly, disruptive to patterns of religious life established for many centuries all over Europe. It was, moreover, this shift that the classical sociologists observed in considerable detail – indeed it was the motivating force for a great deal of their work – and led, among other conclusions, to their generally pessimistic predictions about the future of religion in Western society.[7] Getting on for a century later, however, religious organizations – much reduced, though not always in ways that the classical sociologists had anticipated – find themselves in a rather different situation. The larger industrial conurbations, so often the focus of apprehension on the part of the churches, are declining alongside the industries that brought them into existence: so, too, proportionately, are the social class or classes traditionally most reluctant to attend their churches. But the corollary is far from straightforward, for, following the evidence of chapter 6, patterns of working-class religion – that is, relatively high levels of belief alongside low levels of practice – instead of disappearing, have become ever more prevalent in contemporary society. So much so that other factors must, surely, be taken into account. One of these concerns the nature of religiosity itself, within which an undeniable evolution has occurred. No longer perceived as a duty, religious activity has become, for an increasing proportion of the population, a *leisure* pursuit; one, moreover, which competes for the public's attention alongside all sorts of other pastimes, including the ever more pervasive and ever more technologically advanced small screen.[8]

But precisely those pressures that have been brought to bear on the religious life of this country are equally present in other dimensions of contemporary society (political, industrial and sporting, to give but three examples). Indeed it was this linking of religion to broader societal change that Beckford insisted upon in the passage already quoted in chapter 2, but worth repeating in a more theoretical context: namely 'the important observation that religious believing seems to have become detached from religious belonging . . . should be understood in relation to the observation that virtually all voluntary associations have been finding it difficult in the last few decades to attract and recruit members.' In other words it is the nature of society which is changing, rather than – or at least just as much as – the nature of religiosity. Technological innovations have enabled, indeed they have required, with both positive and negative consequences, profound and irreversible shifts in the way that society is ordered; religious institutions and those who work in them are part and parcel of these developments, but are not in themselves responsible for them.

Two non-religious examples will clarify the argument before returning to the central theme. The first comes from the world of sport where it is obvious that the popularity of sport on television has an ambiguous – if not a negative – effect on attendance figures and, therefore, on the financial health of sporting organizations. Persistent wrangling between the major football clubs and those competing for the television franchise is the most obvious example of this phenomenon. Another lies in the scheduling of major sporting events to coincide with viewing times on a variety of national networks. But more profoundly, the nature of what is understood by the term 'sport' has itself metamorphosed in recent decades, as self-fulfilment (rather than, or at least alongside, the competitive instinct, both individual and collective) becomes an increasingly prevalent feature of modern recreation.[9] The parallels with the changing nature of religiosity are obvious. The second example elaborates the theme. In the immediate post-war period, particularly in those years still dominated by austerity and rationing, the provision of household needs was for the vast majority in the population dominated by necessity. Shopping – the activity through which such needs were met – was, almost always, the *task* of women undertaken while their menfolk were at work. Not often was it associated with pleasure or with an excess of choice (in 1950, for example, Sainsbury's stocked only 550 products). For a significant proportion of British people – though not, it should be stressed, of all of them – the situation is now very different. Particularly for the better-off, shopping (like religion) has become, increasingly, a *leisure* activity, undertaken by the family (itself much altered) as a whole and at times and in places convenient to both partners or to the single parent and his or her dependants. Choice, moreover, has proliferated almost out of control (in Sainsbury's alone the shopper now selects from approximately 11,700 items).[10]

One consequence of these changes concerns the religious sector very directly: that is, growing pressure for extended opening hours, notably at weekends, with the inevitable competition with religious organizations for the 'use' of Sunday mornings. This, surely, is one reason for the heatedness of the debate concerning Sunday opening (echoing a rather similar debate concerning sporting fixtures), but it has as much to do with societal evolution as it has with the process of secularization itself. The increasing detachment of many British people from their regular contact with their churches is undoubtedly part of this process, but over-simplified cause-and-effect arguments are as misleading as they are unhelpful. In short, the pressures of post-industrial society are indeed problematic for religious life, itself enormously diverse, but in ways rather different from those of the immediate post-war period. Or, to make the same statement more positively, by recognizing the specific and changing nature of recent social and economic development, those responsible for religious institutions become better able to understand the tensions of their own role and the difficulties facing those to whom they minister. Among the latter, one section of society merits particular attention; the sizeable minority, excluded for whatever reason, from the evident advantages of a consumer society. For them (and more especially for those unable to find employment), Sunday – in its traditional form as a day of rest, or in its emergent form as a day of diverse spending – is like any other day: a struggle.

The same sort of analysis can, in many ways, be applied to the lower half of the plan; that is, to the cultural rather than the structural layer of contemporary society, remembering that the links between the two halves are by no means proven. The following discussion will, in addition, reintroduce the concept of secularization, one of the most pervasive terms in the sociology of religion. Initially, however, it builds on the lines of thought established in chapter 3, for it reflects the changing moods of post-war society (not only in Britain), particularly those feelings which became increasingly prevalent as the implications of the oil crisis were recognized. The certainties of the 1960s, the notion that economic growth would sustain itself, thereby benefiting increasing numbers of people, gave way to a rather different mood; one, more precisely, in which questions rather than answers dominated the public agenda. Intellectual corollaries appeared to follow, not least those which have become associated with the term 'post-modern'; in other words those which began to probe the whole notion of progress itself. The 'Enlightenment Project' and all that this represented was subject to penetrating scrutiny, relentlessly so in many cases.[11] So, too, were other supposed certainties, as neither the Eastern bloc nor the Western world seemed able to sustain the optimism of an earlier period. It was hardly surprising, given such an intellectual climate, that the mood infected religious as well as secular life; here, too, post-modern approaches to theology and all that these implied, both began and continue to undermine the traditional formulas, substantive as well as methodological.

The situation that emerges becomes, therefore, not only complex, but qualitatively different from that which preceded it. For the competition of varying creeds, secular (in its Western form of rationalism or in its Eastern form of communism) and religious, gives way to a pervasive self-questioning on each side of the classic divide. The locus of the debate alters as each profession or ideology struggles with the disturbing ideas introduced under the catch-all banner of post-modernism. One illustration must suffice. It is taken from Harvey's classic discussion of the subject, *The Condition of Postmodernity*, from a passage which portrays very aptly the changing relationship between theology, liberal secularism and Marxism. Harvey reviews the various and diverse fields in which post-modern influences have become visible in the later post-war decades. He continues:

In philosophy, the intermingling of a revived American pragmatism with the post-Marxist and post-structuralist wave that struck Paris after 1968 produced what Bernstein calls 'a rage against humanism and the Enlightenment legacy'. This spilled over into a vigorous denunciation of abstract reason and a deep aversion to any project that sought universal human emancipation through mobilization of the powers of technology, science, and reason. Here, also, no less a person than Pope John Paul II has entered the fray on the side of the postmodern. The Pope 'does not attack Marxism or liberal secularism because they are the wave of the future', says Rocco Buttiglione, a theologian close to the Pope, but because the 'philosophies of the twentieth century have lost their appeal, their time has already passed'. (1989: 41)

Clearly such a statement begs many questions, for its inferences are equally applicable to religious as to secular philosophies, an extrapolation that Buttiglione does not seem to perceive. The essential point, nonetheless, is clearly made; the secular certainties, the erstwhile competitors of religious truth, are themselves under attack.

If this is the case – and in the long run only time will tell – we need, surely, to look again and in a rather different way at the concept of secularization. Historically, the debate concerning this problematic term has taken a wide variety of forms. Some of these have been difficult to distinguish from the more ideological term 'secularism' (in the sense that it is used in the quotation above); others are more nuanced, by means of which much valuable work has been and will continue to be achieved within the sociology of religion.[12] There has, notably, been an increasing recognition of the different dimensions of religious life, some of which may prosper as others decline (Dobbelaere 1981). The present argument builds on the latter idea in particular, underlining the diversity within contemporary religiosity, but it suggests a further stage of development. A stage, that is, which stresses the shift *away from* rather than *into* industrial society (the classic focus of the debate), thus enabling a closer study of the evolving role of religion within new forms of economic order. Bearing such a framework in mind, two points both draw the threads of this section together and point the way forward for sociological investigation: first, the fact that the structural pressures brought to bear on the religious sector of society also operate elsewhere (in other words some manifestations of secularization may have non-religious as well as religious causes); second, that the cultural climate of recent decades has been as hard on secular certainties as it has on religious ones. The sociological focus alters accordingly. Religious life – like so many other features of post-industrial or post-modern society – is not so much disappearing as mutating, for the sacred undoubtedly persists and will continue to do so, but in forms that may be very different from those which have gone before. The empirical question follows naturally enough. What, then, *are* these forms in contemporary British society; in, that is, a society caught up in a changing global economy, but which has a deeply rooted Christian tradition, shared for the most part with its European neighbours, but experienced in a particular and historically definable way?

The final pairings of the diagram indicate some of the possible mutations that might be occurring within this situation, two of which (the medical and the ecological) were fleshed out in some detail in chapter 3. The others require further explanation. The notion of God the Son juxtaposed with God the Spirit, for example, is taken once again from an idea quoted in Harvey (1989: 43). The original juxtaposition is, however, rather different from that which is proposed here, for it opposes God the Father (modern) with the Holy Ghost (post-modern); God the Son is absent. But it is at this point, surely, that the longer-term view becomes crucial, for God the Father encapsulates a pre-modern world view just as much as, if not more than, a modern one; an outlook which was challenged by the scriptural emphases of the Reformation with all its subsequent developments.[13] (The links with the Weber thesis on the development of capitalism become as immediate as they are obvious; so, too, the connection with rationalism and the Enlightenment.) Harvey's *post*-modern emphasis on the Spirit or Holy Ghost is rather less controversial, for it undoubtedly catches something of the decentred, discontinuous and fragmented nature of contemporary culture; a form prefigured often enough in European thought (it isn't altogether new) but finding itself towards the end of the twentieth century very much centre-stage, whether in art and architecture, in planning, in diverse forms of literature or in philosophy.

Be that as it may – for such suggestions remain speculative rather than proven – the longer-term perspective is also important in a different way and one that relates rather more directly to a central theme of this book. For it is tempting to see believing without belonging, or the prevalence of unattached religion in contemporary society, as a typical form of post-modern behaviour; one, that is, that enables the believer to select at will from the religious goods on offer and to mould these into personal packages that suit a variety of lifestyles and subcultures (the phenomenon known as supermarket religion).[14] Such an assumption seems reasonable enough, given the analysis so far suggested. It becomes, however, a conclusion increasingly difficult to sustain, the harder one looks at the evidence. For in reality believing without belonging rarely represents a consciously selected personal package. It reflects instead the fall-back position acquired by British people when they simply do nothing; an *ordinary* God indeed. It becomes, in other words, not so much a choice, but the backdrop against which other decisions are made. Hence the notion, already hinted at, that it represents the residue of the past (what is left of pre-modern religion after the toll taken by both industrial and post-industrial developments), rather than the emergence of a post-modern future.

The consequences of such a situation are, however, crucially important for the argument of this chapter, for a lack of attachment to religious organizations implies for the great majority of people a lack of discipline in their spiritual orientation. They are, therefore, very much open to the widely diverse forms of the sacred which appear within contemporary society, encouraging rather than discouraging the heterogeneous beliefs of the British described in chapter 5; a heterogeneity which has included, in certain circles at least, a number of manifestations of New Age religion, themselves enormously diverse.[15] One element of religious choice, therefore, seems to mirror the post-modern emphasis on fragmentation, self-selection and self-fulfilment. In other words it follows, indeed it encourages, the wider trends of contemporary society, each of them feeding upon the other. But – and once again the qualification is crucial – this is only half the story, for an equally prevalent feature of contemporary religion does precisely the reverse. It resists all that is encapsulated in contemporary culture and reasserts – often with great vigour – the traditional certainties, however these are perceived; a reassertion (and the reactive quality is a pivotal feature of what is going on) which provides at least one explanation for the undeniable popularity of conservative religiosity in contemporary Britain, and indeed in the contemporary world.[16] For one way of enduring in a fragmented and rapidly changing context (global or otherwise) is to embrace an all-encompassing world view and to live – often in an admirably disciplined way – within this. Or to put this in a different and perhaps more provocative way, the believer not so much rejects fragmentation as takes this to its logical conclusion; selecting one particular fragment of what is on offer and expanding this to form a complete world view. Taken to extremes this tendency results in a series of competing fundamentalisms, a feature of late capitalist development, though one that bewilders many of its commentators. Such fundamentalisms take a variety of forms: some religious, both Christian and non-Christian, and some secular, including within the latter category – to give but two examples – certain types of feminism or radical expressions of regional identity.[17]

The last point, the whole question of identity and within this regional or national dispositions, picks up a second theme within this book: the considerable variety of cultures in the United Kingdom and the role of religion both within their historical development and, in a rather more muted way, in their continued existence as part of a rapidly changing European framework. It is, moreover, an area within which the state churches can still serve a demonstrable function (the case of Scotland is even clearer than that of England). In other respects, however, the parochially based churches (state or otherwise) find themselves uncomfortably squeezed between the two tendencies outlined above; trying to resist both the excessive fragmentation of modern culture and an over-rigorous reaction to this. Indeed in many ways they fit awkwardly into the whole schema, for they continue to provide – and many would endorse such an aspiration in the strongest possible terms – a production rather than consumption version of religion; providing, that is, a consistent pattern of worship and pastoral care, dictated by the obligations of their role, with little regard for whim or fashion. The pressures on those responsible for such endeavours are bound to be considerable.

The European dimension of this question furnishes, however, a broader example with which to conclude this chapter, for it illustrates in a whole variety of ways the relationships suggested in the plan on p. 192. It raises, for a start, the delicate relationship between the economic and cultural dimensions of society. Clearly interrelated, do they necessarily move in the same direction? (A crucial sociological question that demands empirical just as much as theoretical answers.) At the same time, the European dimension offers an alternative frame of reference within which to appreciate the continued significance of the religious factor within the cultural sphere itself. The persistent differences within the four countries of the United Kingdom regarding their attitudes to Europe lead me to argue that this significance has, like so much else within contemporary society, mutated rather than disappeared. The necessary task, in consequence, is to discover the precise forms of these cultural variations and to set them into their sociological framework; a task which the preceding chapters have attempted.

The final link of the chain places such material within a wider context. The following illustrations, for example, cite two English commentators from the same church regarding the role of religion in contemporary Europe, each of whom comments on the advantages and disadvantages of larger economic units. (In so doing, they pick up the theme of the first question outlined above: the unpredictable – and above all evolving – nature of the relationship between the economic and cultural dimensions of society.) Edwards, the first of these, in a book published as soon as was reasonably possible after the 1989 metamorphoses in Europe (Edwards 1990), develops the controversial notion of a 'single market' in European religion, arguing that the exchange of spiritual goods will prove as beneficial to the religious life of the continent as the exchange of commodities has been for the economy.[18] In many ways this notion – essentially an optimistic one – reflects the date of writing, for it assumes a willingness to move into and take advantage of larger units of exchange. It also depicts a cultural sphere moving in the same direction as the economic and glad to do so. A year or two later, as economic recession began to bite, the Archbishop of York offers a rather different approach, one which emphasizes the contradictory pressures of the two spheres both in Europe and elsewhere. On the one hand there are the demands of trade, economic stability and power, factors which require larger and larger economic units in order to survive and which look to the international order for security and justification. But for many people precisely the opposite inclinations – the reassertion of local and national identities and the need for psychological security and rootedness – remain paramount: in other words 'the need to know that we and our heritage, our language and our culture, count in the scheme of things, and that we are free to make our own choices' (Habgood 1992).[19] The Archbishop continues by setting the argument into a global framework:

> These conflicting pressures, manifesting themselves in local earthquake and continental drift are shaping the new world. It is not about whether individual politicians like or dislike Europe. It is about the forces at work in an era of world interdependence, easy communication and disorienting change. (1992)

A theoretically informed observation of these pressures, and within them a sensitive awareness of 'the religious', sets a demanding agenda for the sociology of religion in the 1990s. The British case, examined above, is but one of many; to be appreciated fully it requires a comparative framework.

Notes

1   The provenance of this passage is explained in the Preface.
2   During the writing of this book, for example, both the political left (Bryant 1992) and the political right (Anderson 1993) have demonstrated their anxiety to gain the moral high ground in this respect, reflecting an evident and continuing public anxiety – for whatever reason – about the religious condition of the nation. The debate has received considerable attention from journalists.
3   The mismatch between the classic sociological explanations of religion and the pressures of post-industrial society forms a key theme within Beckford's analysis of religion in advanced industrial society (Beckford 1989).
4   The complexity of the relationships between particular economic and social structures and specific cultural forms has bedevilled a great deal of sociological thinking. All that can be said so far is that the gradual shift from one form of capitalism to another (Lash and Urry 1987) seems to have been accompanied by specifiable changes in the cultural sphere, including a significant evolution in the attitudes of both individuals and societies to the religious dimension.
5   The discussion about modernity is frequently linked to the age of

discovery, to the Enlightenment and to the emergence of the nation-state in Europe. For many European societies, industrialization came considerably later. Hall and Gieben (1992) provide an excellent introduction to this debate. Indeed the whole of this four-volume Open University series is a useful resource for this chapter.

6 See Davie (1993b) for a full discussion of this point.

7 Given similar preoccupations, the classic sociologists – Marx, Weber and Durkheim – differ in their precise conclusions about religion. Marx predicted its eventual demise, thus enabling the liberation of society from delusion; Weber (a substantive sociologist) also predicted decline but with considerable unease about the future; Durkheim (a functionalist) took a rather different view, for the *function* of religion was a requirement of social life whatever its particular form or content. Some of his ideas were discussed further in chapter 5.

8 The evidence is overwhelming. In 1950, television hardly existed; only 2 per cent of households owned one and on Sundays there were but three programmes to distract such pioneers from other pursuits. In 1993, 79 per cent of the population indicated that they watched television on Sundays (Mori poll, 1993, on behalf of Sainsbury's *The Magazine*).

9 The shift in sporting emphases is neatly caught in the following French phrase, 'la spiritualité du sport: du marathon au yoga'. For a fuller discussion on this point, see Vigarello 1988.

10 A further twist in the argument is just beginning to manifest itself; namely the facility to purchase by phone and credit card following the display of goods on television. Television – always a powerful medium of advertising (in other words the friend of consumerism) – now competes with rather than supports conventional retail outlets.

11 The novelty of such scrutiny should not be exaggerated; indeed the inevitability of progress had already been difficult for many people given the devastation of two world wars and the holocaust.

12 Lyon (1985) provides a useful introduction to this debate and the various points of view within it. Wallis and Bruce (1989) develop the discussion further.

13 This argument is developed further by Turner (1991: xvi–xxii), a passage in which the long-term historical view becomes paramount.

14 Interestingly, the assumption of a post-modern framework was the

immediate reaction to the first presentation of the 'Believing without Belonging' paper (Davie 1990b).

15   A more developed argument connecting post-modern ideas specifically with those of the New Age can be found in Lyon (1993).

16   The encyclical *Veritatis Splendor* (October 1993) is a very obvious example of the reassertion of traditional values; it contains an explicit rejection of moral relativism.

17   In other words, fundamentalisms should be seen as a societal feature just as much as a religious one. They emerge as reactions to the pressures of late capitalist development.

18   A further dimension of this discussion elaborates the connection between ecumenical development and the gradual emergence, or re-emergence of European identity. There were references to this connection at the end of chapter 8.

19   Religion, surely, remains a crucial factor in this heritage. The connections between collective memory and the religious have been elaborated from a theoretical point of view by a French sociologist of religion, Hervieu-Léger (1993).

Outline Chronology

	Prime Ministers	Archbishops of Canterbury	Archbishops of Westminster	Chief Rabbis
	Winston Churchill	William Temple		Joseph Hertz
1945				
	Clement Attlee		Bernard Griffin	
1950				
	Winston Churchill	Geoffrey Fisher		
1955				
	Anthony Eden			Israel Brodie
1960	Harold Macmillan		William Godfrey	
			The Second →	
	Alec Douglas-Home		Vatican Council	
1965				
	Harold Wilson	Michael Ramsey		
1970			John Heenan	
	Edward Heath			
1975	Harold Wilson			
	James Callaghan	Donald Coggan		
1980				Immanuel Jakobovits
1985	Margaret Thatcher	Robert Runcie	Basil Hume	
1990				
	John Major	George Carey		Jonathan Sacks
1994				

Guide to Further Reading

The following bibliographical suggestions are referenced in full on p. 210; a list which includes, in addition, every work cited in the main text. The intention of this bibliography is to introduce the reader to the range of sources available. In order to do this, it pays particular attention to key books from which a useful start can be made. It is by no means exhaustive; nor does it cover every issue in equal detail. In both respects, therefore, it should be seen as complementary to the systematic citation provided in the main body of the text.

The introductory chapter to this book has already pointed out the most obvious imbalance in the sociological material relating to religion in this country; that is, the relative abundance of evidence – some of it excellent – about small pieces of the sociological jigsaw, not least the work on new religious movements, but a corresponding lack regarding the beliefs of ordinary people and the significance of such beliefs for everyday life. Such evidence as exists with respect to the latter has been reviewed in Ahern and Davie (1987); it is not repeated here. The previous chapters attempt, nonetheless, to develop this discussion in more detail, in that they offer a broad brush approach to religious issues in the post-war period and concentrate in particular on the growing mismatch between belief and practice in contemporary Britain; a theme developed by Davie (1990a, 1990b, 1993a, 1993b and 1993c), which has provoked comment and/or elaboration in Hornsby-Smith (1992), Short and Winter (1993) and Martin (1991).

In developing this approach, the book depends on adequate statistical sources, provided in the main by the range of publications edited by Peter Brierley and colleagues, first of all under the Marc Europe imprint and latterly under that of the Christian Research Association. The various editions of the *UK Christian Handbook* and the range of church censuses published by Marc Europe, notably *Prospects for the Eighties*, *Prospects for the Nineties* and *Christian England* are an obvious starting point. The introductory sections of the Handbooks also provide some help with the interpretation of such data. For earlier periods, these sources can be supplemented by Currie, Gilbert and Horsley (1977), remembering that the *interpretation* of these figures has been strongly challenged by Gill (1993). A third statistical source can be found in Maunder (1987), which reviews both recurring and non-recurring data for religion in the United Kingdom. Statistical work concerning young people and their religious inclinations is well covered in the prolific output of Francis. The *British Journal of Religious Education* carries a good deal of this; other aspects are covered in Hyde (1990). The European framework set out in chapter 2 relies heavily on the European Values Study. This is usefully summarized in Barker, Halman and Vloet (1993), which also contains a full list of references relating to the study. The detailed work on the 1981 survey can be found in Abrams, Gerard and Timms (1985) and Harding and Phillips with Fogarty (1986).

The analysis which has been offered in the previous chapters is sociological rather than historical, vertical rather than horizontal. It should, however, be read alongside two other sources of information: the straightforward historical accounts of religion in the post-war period and the range of books which review the vicissitudes of each denomination or faith group in this country. In the former category, Hastings (1986) is outstanding but the scope is limited to a discussion of Christianity in England. Welsby (1984) on the Church of England from 1945–80 is also useful. Up to a point, equivalents for Scotland and Wales can be found in Brown (1987) and Williams (1991), though their time-scales are much longer. On the question of national differences as such, Jenkins (1975) offers the classic discussion. Northern Ireland raises particular issues: Hickey (1984), Bruce (1986) and Fulton (1991) provide a starting point. The regional case studies draw on Brierley's statistical breakdowns and a series of local studies; full references were given in chapter 6.

Denomination by denomination overviews can be found in Winter (1988) and Badham (1989), both of which include material on the Celtic countries as well as England. Specific religious communities vary in the amount of material which is available on them. Noteworthy in this respect – at least in terms of sociological coverage – is the Roman Catholic case, for Hornsby-Smith's string of publications provides an unrivalled source of data on the sociological make-up of this community. Some of the same themes can, however, be absorbed from the novels of David Lodge which span at least three of the post-war decades. Work on the free churches, including material on Wales, Scotland and Northern Ireland is well referenced in Badham (1989), which also covers the major other-faith traditions of Britain and includes bibliographies (for other-faith communities, see also the discussion on pluralism below). Walker (1985) has become the standard text on house churches. Rather more thematic approaches to contemporary religion can be found in Bradley (1992) and Thomas (1988). The latter brings together a valuable collection of essays, notably the two by Knott (those on new religious movements and on the other-faith communities of Britain, both with excellent bibliographies) and the one by Thompson on broader patterns of belief. The growing diversity of British religion is admirably covered in Parsons (1993) and Wolffe (1993).

New religious movements can be approached from a variety of angles. Knott's relatively short discussion offers one way in, but Barker's invaluable *New Religious Movements: a practical introduction* (1989a) is the obvious source of reference. Alternative possibilities include Barker (1982b), Barker and Dyson (1988), Beckford (1985), Wilson (1990 and 1992), who provide a variety of frameworks for discussion and/or useful collections of articles. There are, in addition, numerous case studies. For the most part these approaches are rigorously sociological. Less so the flood of publications concerned with the New Age in all its diversity, a prominent section in any high street bookshop. More immediately appropriate in this respect is the work of Heelas (1991 and 1992) together with a collection of articles in a theme issue of the journal *Religion*, 1993 (volume 22), entitled 'The New Age in Context'. Material on religious experience and its role in contemporary society can be obtained from the Alister Hardy Centre, Westminster College, Oxford.

The secularization issue has provided one organizing theme for the sociology of religion in post-war Britain. Lyon (1985) provides a helpful introduction to this debate in which the work of Martin (1978) and Wilson (1982) dominates. Further discussions can be found in Gilbert (1980), Dobbelaere (1981), Wallis and Bruce (1989), Wilson (1992) and in Barker, Beckford and Dobbelaere (1993). Bruce (1992) gathers together useful historical and empirical sources as well as more theoretical papers. The concept of secularization raises complex issues, among them the question of pluralism. The connections are immediate, for there are those who maintain that a greater degree of religious pluralism leads – through progressive relativization – to an increase in secularization. Others are less sure as the tenacity of other-faith communities appears to contradict this tendency. Pluralism itself prompts further reflection concerning a crucial aspect of contemporary society: that is, the capacity of communities of widely different origins to live alongside each other within a society dominated, historically, by one world faith in particular. Modood (1990 and 1994), Webster (1990) and Sacks (1991) provide thought-provoking discussions of the implications of this situation; implications raised but not resolved by the Rushdie controversy.

Habgood (1983) collects together a useful set of essays including a discussion of establishment and of bureaucracy within the churches. More detailed questions of church and state and of a range of political issues in the post-war period can be found in Moyser (1985), in Medhurst and Moyser (1988) and in Nicholls (1990). The Church of England's own reports concerning church/state relations (notably that of 1970) are a parallel source of data. The *Faith in the City* debate occupied much of the 1980s and spawned a whole series of publications on individual cities. A thorough coverage of this literature can be found in *Living Faith in the City* (1990). The debate itself is covered in detail in Clark (1993). *Faith in the Countryside* and Davies, Watkins and Winter (1991) raise equivalent issues for the rural community. Both urban and rural initiatives merge into discussions of ministry more generally, which are enlarged in Ranson, Bryman and Hinings (1977), Russell (1980) and Towler and Coxon (1979). The ministry of women raises very particular issues. Once again the flood of writing on this debate tends to be polemical rather than scholarly but Aldridge (1989 and 1992) has initiated sociological work in this area.

Placing this material within a broader sociological context isn't easy, for there is a dearth of good sociological writing on advanced capitalist societies which takes proper account of religion. Beckford's succinct account (1989) of recent theoretical work in the sociology of religion is a notable exception; so, too, the contributions of Bocock and Thompson (1985 and 1992). In the latter volume the chapter by Thompson himself is particularly helpful. Wider statistical comparisons can be made using *Social Trends, Regional Trends* and the *Annual Abstract of Statistics*.

References

Abercrombie, N., Baker, J., Brett, S. and Foster, J. 1970: Superstition and religion: the God of the gaps. In D. Martin and M. Hill (eds), *A Sociological Yearbook of Religion in Britain*, 3, London: SCM, 91–129

Abrams, M., Gerard, D. and Timms, N. (eds) 1985: *Values and Social Change in Britain*. London: MacMillan

Ahern, G. and Davie, G. 1987: *Inner City God: the nature of belief in the inner city*. London: Hodder and Stoughton

Aldridge, A. 1989: Men, women and clergymen. *Sociological Review*, 37, 43–64

—— 1992: Discourse on women in the clerical profession. *Sociology*, 26, 45–57

Anderson, D. (ed.) 1993: *The Loss of Virtue*. London: Social Affairs Unit

Appignanesi, L. and Maitland, S. 1989: *The Rushdie File*. London: Fourth Estate

Argyle, M. and Beit-Hallahmi, B. 1975: *The Social Psychology of Religion*. London: Routledge and Kegan Paul

Ashford, S. and Timms, N. 1992: *What Europe Thinks: a study of Western European values*. Aldershot: Dartmouth

Avis, P. 1992: *Authority, Leadership and Conflict in the Church*. London: Mowbray

Badham, P. (ed.) 1989: *Religion, State and Society in Modern Britain*. Lewiston/Lampeter/Queenston: Edwin Mellen Press

Barker, D., Halman, L. and Vloet, A. 1993: *The European Values Study 1981–1990. Summary Report*. London/The Netherlands: Published by the European Values Group

Barker, E. 1982a: A sociologist looks at the statistics. In P. Brierley (ed.), *The UK Christian Handbook 1983 edition*, London: Marc Europe, 5–9

——(ed.) 1982b: *New Religious Movements: a perspective for understanding society*. Lewiston/Lampeter/Queenston: Edwin Mellen Press

——1989a: *New Religious Movements: a practical introduction*. London: HMSO

——1989b: Tolerant discrimination: Church, state and the new religions. In P. Badham (ed.), *Religion, State and Society in Modern Britain*, Lewiston/Lampeter/Queenston: Edwin Mellen Press, 185–208

Barker, E., Beckford, J. and Dobbelaere, K. (eds) 1993: *Secularization, Rationalism and Sectarianism*. Oxford: Oxford University Press

Barker, E. and Dyson, A. (eds) 1988: Sects and new religious movements. Special issue of the *Bulletin of the John Rylands University Library of Manchester*

Beckford, J. 1985: *Cult Controversies*. London: Tavistock

——1989: *Religion and Advanced Industrial Society*. London: Unwin Hyman

——1991: Politics and religion in England and Wales. *Daedalus*, 120, 179–201

——1992: Religione e società nel Regno Unito. In *La religione degli europei*, Turin: Edizioni della Fondazione Giovanni Agnelli, 217–89

Bocock, R. 1985: Religion in modern Britain. In R. Bocock and K. Thompson (eds), *Religion and Ideology*, Manchester: Manchester University Press, 207–33

Bocock, R. and Thompson, K. (eds) 1985: *Religion and Ideology*. Manchester: Manchester University Press

——(eds) 1992: *Social and Cultural Forms of Modernity*. Oxford: Polity Press / The Open University

Bowie, F. 1993: Religion and Language in Wales. *Informationes Theologiae Europae. Internationales ökumenisches Jahrbuch für Theologie*, 2 Jahrgang

Bradley, I. 1992: *Marching to the Promised Land*. London: Murray

Brierley, P. 1980 and 1983: *Prospects for the Eighties*, vols. 1 and 2. London: Marc Europe

——(ed.) 1982: *The UK Christian Handbook 1983 edition*. London: Marc Europe

——1991a: *Christian England*. London: Marc Europe

——1991b: *Prospects for the Nineties* (11 volumes). London: Marc Europe

Brierley, P. and Evans, B. (eds) 1983: *Prospects for Wales*. London: Marc Europe

Brierley, P. and Hiscock, V. (eds) 1993: *UK Christian Handbook 1994–5 edition*. London: Christian Research Association

Brierley, P. with Longley, D. (ed.) 1988: *UK Christian Handbook 1989/ 90 edition*. London: Marc Europe

Brierley, P. and Longley, D. (eds) 1991: *UK Christian Handbook 1992/93 edition*. London: Marc Europe

Brierley, P. and McDonald, F. (eds) 1984: *Prospects for Scotland*. London: Marc Europe with the National Bible Society of Scotland

Brown, C. 1987: *The Social History of Religion in Scotland*. London: Methuen

Bruce, S. 1985: *No Pope of Rome. Militant Protestantism in modern Scotland*. Edinburgh: Mainstream

—— 1986: *God Save Ulster. The religion and politics of Paisleyism*. Oxford: Clarendon Press

—— (ed.) 1992: *Religion and Modernization*. Oxford: Clarendon Press

Bryant, C. (ed.) 1992: *Reclaiming the Ground: Christianity and Socialism*. London: Spire

Carr, W. 1985: *Brief Encounters*. London: SPCK

Chadwick, O. 1990: *Michael Ramsey: a life*. Oxford: Oxford University Press

Church and State: report of the Archbishops' Commission: 1970. London: Church Information Office

Clark, H. 1993: *The Church under Thatcher*. London: SPCK

Coleman, B. 1979: Religious worship in Devon in 1851. *The Devon Historian*, 18, 3–7

—— 1983: Southern England in the census of religious worship. *Southern History*, 5, 154–88

Currie, R., Gilbert, A. and Horsley, L. 1977: *Churches and Churchgoers*. Oxford: Clarendon Press

Davie, G. 1990a: 'An Ordinary God': the paradox of religion in contemporary Britain. *British Journal of Sociology*, 41, 395–421

—— 1990b: Believing without belonging. Is this the future of religion in Britain. *Social Compass*, 37, 456–69

—— 1992: God and Caesar: religion in a rapidly changing Europe. In J. Bailey (ed.), *Social Europe*, London: Collins, 216–38

—— 1993a: You'll Never Walk Alone: the Anfield pilgrimage. In I. Reader and T. Walter (eds), *Pilgrimage and Popular Culture*, London: MacMillan, 201–19

——1993b: Religion and modernity in Britain. *International Journal of Comparative Religion*, 1, 1–11

——1993c: Believing without belonging: a Liverpool case study. *Archives de Sciences Sociales des Religions*, 81, 79–89

Davie, G. and Hearl, D. 1991: Politics and religion in the South West. In M. Havinden, J. Queniart and J. Stanyer (eds), *Centre and Periphery: Brittany and Devon and Cornwall compared*. Exeter: University of Exeter Press, 214–32

Davie, G. and Short, C. 1993: Church of England General Synod 1990–95. Analysis of Membership. Report presented to Secretary-General of the Synod in September 1993. Publication is under discussion.

Davies, C. 1989: Religion, politics and 'permissive' legislation. In P. Badham (ed.), *Religion, State and Society in Modern Britain*, Lewiston/Lampeter/Queenston: Edwin Mellen Press, 319–40

Davies, D. 1990: *Cremation Today and Tomorrow*. Bramcote: Grove Books

Davies, D., Watkins, C. and Winter, M. 1991: *Church and Religion in Rural England*. Edinburgh: T. and T. Clark. A longer 4-volume typescript version of this material is available from the Centre for Rural Studies, Royal Agricultural College, Cirencester, Glos.

Diamond, I. and Clarke, S. 1989: Demographic patterns among British ethnic groups. In H. Joshi (ed.), *The Changing Population of Britain*, Oxford: Blackwell, 177–98

Dobbelaere, K. 1981: Secularization: a multi-dimensional concept. *Current Sociology*, 29/2

Douglas, M. 1973: *Natural Symbols: explorations in cosmology*. London: Barrie and Jenkins

Edwards, D. 1990: *Christians in a New Europe*. London: Fount Paperbacks

Faith in the City: 1985. The Report of the Archbishop of Canterbury's Commission on Urban Priority Areas. London: Church House Publishing

Faith in the Countryside: 1990. The Report of the Archbishops' Commission on Rural Areas. London: Church House Publishing

Forster, P. 1989: *Church and People on Longhill Estate*. Occasional Paper 5, University of Hull, Department of Sociology

Francis, L. 1984: *Teenagers and the Church: a profile of churchgoing youth in the 1980s*. London: Collins Liturgical Publications

——1985: *Rural Anglicanism: a future for young Christians?* London: Collins

———1986: *Partnership in Rural Education: church schools and teacher attitudes.* London: Collins

———1987: *Religion in the Primary School: partnership between church and state.* London: Collins

Francis, L. and Lankshear, D. 1992: *Continuing in the Way: children, young people and the church.* London: The National Society

Fulton, J. 1991: *The Tragedy of Belief: division, politics and religion in Ireland.* Oxford: Oxford University Press

Fulton, J. and Gee, P. (eds) 1991: *Religion and Power.* BSA Sociology of Religion Study Group

Gilbert, A. 1980: *The Making of Post-Christian Britain.* London: Longman

Gill, R. 1992: *Moral Communities.* Exeter: Exeter University Press

———1993: *The Myth of the Empty Church.* London: SPCK

Gorer, G. 1955: *Exploring English Character.* London: Cresset Press

———1965: *Death, Grief and Mourning in Contemporary Britain.* London: Cresset Press

Habgood, J. 1983: *Church and Nation in a Secular Age.* London: Darton, Longman and Todd

———1992: Viewpoint. *The Independent,* 12 March 1992

Hall, S. and Gieben, B. (eds) 1992: *Formations of Modernity.* Oxford: Polity Press / The Open University

Halsey, A. H. 1985: On methods and morals. In M. Abrams, D. Gerard and N. Timms (eds), *Values and Social Change in Britain,* London: Marc Europe, 1–20

Hammond, P. 1985: *The Sacred in a Secular Age.* Berkeley: University of California Press

Harding, S., Phillips, D. with Fogarty, M. 1986: *Contrasting Values in Western Europe.* London: MacMillan

Harvey, A. (ed.) 1989: *Theology in the City.* London: SPCK

Harvey, D. 1989: *The Condition of Postmodernity.* Oxford: Blackwell

Hastings, A. 1986: *A History of English Christianity, 1929–1985.* London: Collins

———1991a: *Robert Runcie.* London: Mowbray

———1991b: *Church and State.* Exeter: Exeter University Press

Heelas, P. 1991: Cults for capitalism? Self religions, magic and the empowerment of business. In J. Fulton and P. Gee (eds), *Religion and Power,* BSA Sociology of Religion Study Group, 27–42

———1992: The sacralization of self and new age capitalism. In N.

Abercrombie and A. Warde (eds), *Social Change in Contemporary Britain*, Oxford: Polity Press, 139–66
——(ed.) 1993: The New Age in context. Special issue of *Religion*
Hervieu-Léger, D. 1992 (ed.): *La Religion au Lycée*. Paris: Cerf
——1993: *La Religion pour Mémoire*. Paris: Cerf
Hickey, J. 1984: *Religion and the Northern Ireland Problem*. Dublin: Gill and MacMillan
Highet, J. 1972: Great Britain: Scotland. In H. Mol (ed.), *Western Religion: a country by country sociological inquiry*, The Hague: Mouton, 249–69
Hobcraft, J. and Joshi, H. 1989: Population matters. In H. Joshi (ed.), *The Changing Population of Britain*, Oxford: Blackwell, 1–11
Hoggart, R. 1984: *The Uses of Literacy*. Harmondsworth: Peregrine
Hornsby-Smith, M. 1987: *Roman Catholics in England*. Cambridge: Cambridge University Press
——1988: Into the mainstream: recent transformations in British Catholicism. In T. Gannon (ed.), *World Catholicism in Transition*, London/New York: MacMillan, 218–31
——1989a: *The Changing Parish: a study of parishes, priests and parishioners after Vatican II*. London: Routledge
——1989b: The Roman Catholic Church in Britain since the second world war. In P. Badham (ed.), *Religion, State and Society in Modern Britain*, Lewiston/Lampeter/Queenston: Edwin Mellen Press, 85–98
——1991: *Roman Catholic Beliefs in England*. Cambridge: Cambridge University Press
——1992: Believing without belonging? The case of Roman Catholics in England. In B. Wilson (ed.), *Religion: contemporary issues*, London, Bellew Publishing, 125–34
Hornsby-Smith, M. and Proctor, M. 1993: Religion and Politics in Britain: Evidence from the 1990 European Values Study. Unpublished paper, presented at the BSA Sociology of Religion Study Group Conference, University of Bristol
Hyde, K. 1990: *Religion in Childhood and Adolescence: a comprehensive review of research*. Birmingham, Alabama: Religious Education Press
Jacobs, E. and Worcester, R. 1990: *We British: Britain under the MORI-scope*. London: Weidenfeld and Nicholson
Jay, E. 1992: *'Keep them in Birmingham': challenging racism in the South West*. London: Commission for Racial Equality

Jenkins, D. 1975: *The British: their identity and their religion.* London: SCM

Jones, K. 1971: The House of Laity in the General Synod. *Crucible,* July-August, 104–8

——1976: The General Synod: 1975 version. *Crucible,* October–December, 152–8

Joshi, H. (ed.) 1989: *The Changing Population of Britain.* Oxford: Blackwell

Jupp, P. 1990a: How cremation came into fashion. The *Guardian,* 30 May 1990

——1990b: *From Dust to Ashes: the replacement of burial by cremation in England 1840–1967.* London: The Congregational Memorial Hall Trust

Knott, K. 1983: Conventional religion and common religion in the media. Transcript of a talk given at the IBA Religious Broadcasting Consultation, April 1983. Religious Research Papers 9, University of Leeds, Department of Sociology

——1988a: Other major religious traditions. In T. Thomas (ed.), *The British. Their religious beliefs and practices 1800–1986,* London: Routledge, 133–57

——1988b: New religious movements. In T. Thomas (ed.), *The British. Their religious beliefs and practices 1800–1986,* London: Routledge, 158–77

Krarup, H. 1982: Conventional religion and common religion in Leeds. Interview Schedule: Basic frequencies by question. Religious Research Papers 12, University of Leeds, Department of Sociology

Langley, M. 1989: Attitudes to women in the British churches. In P. Badham (ed.), *Religion, State and Society in Modern Britain,* Lewiston/Lampeter/Queenston: Edwin Mellen Press, 291–318

Lash, N. and Urry, J. 1987: *The End of Organized Capitalism.* Oxford: Polity Press

Leaman, O. 1989: Taking religion seriously. *The Times,* 6 February 1989

Lerman, A. 1989: *The Jewish Communities of the World.* London: MacMillan

Levitt, M. 1992: Parental attitudes to religion: a Cornish case study. Unpublished paper presented at the BSA Sociology of Religion Study Group, St Mary's College, Twickenham

——1994: The influence of a Church of England primary school education on children's religious beliefs and values. Unpublished doctoral thesis, University of Exeter

Living Faith in the City: 1990. A progress report by the Archbishop of Canterbury's Group on Urban Priority Areas. London: General Synod

Lodge, D. 1965: *The British Museum is Falling Down*. London: Penguin
——1980: *How Far Can You Go*. London: Penguin
——1991: *Paradise News*. London: Penguin
Longley, C. 1991: *The Times Book of Clifford Longley*. London: Harper Collins
Lyon, D. 1985: *The Steeple's Shadow*. London: SPCK
——1993: A bit of a circus: notes on postmodernity and the New Age. *Religion*, 23, 117–26
Martin, B. and Pluck, R. 1977: *Young People's Beliefs*. A report to the Board of Education of the Church of England.
Martin, D. 1967: *A Sociology of English Religion*. London: Heinemann
——1969: *The Religious and the Secular*. London: Routledge and Kegan Paul
——1972: Great Britain: England. In H. Mol (ed.), *Western Religion: a country by country sociological inquiry*, The Hague: Mouton, 249–69
——1978: *A General Theory of Secularization*. London: Blackwell
——1989: The churches: pink bishops and the iron lady. In D. Kavanagh and A. Seldon (eds), *The Thatcher Effect*, Oxford: Clarendon Press, 330–41
——1990: *Tongues of Fire*. Oxford: Blackwell
——1991: Believing without belonging: a commentary on religion in England. Unpublished paper
Mass Observation 1948: *Puzzled People: a study of popular attitudes to religion, ethics, progress and politics in a London borough*. London: Victor Gollancz
Maunder, W. F. (ed.) 1987: *Religion*, Reviews of United Kingdom Statistical Sources, 20. Oxford: Pergamon Press
Medhurst, K. and Moyser, G. 1988: *Church and Politics in a Secular Age*. Oxford: Clarendon Press
Michel, P. 1991: *Politics and Religion in Eastern Europe*. Oxford: Polity
Modood, T. 1990: British Asian Muslims and the Rushdie affair. *British Political Quarterly*, 61, 143–60
——1994: Ethno-religious minorities, secularism and the British state. *British Political Quarterly*, 65, 53–73
Moorman, J. 1980: *A History of the Church in England*. London: A. and C. Black
Moyser, G. 1979: Patterns of representation in the elections to the General Synod in 1975. *Crucible*, April-June, 73–9

——1982: The 1980 General Synod: patterns and trends. *Crucible*, April–June, 75–86

——(ed.) 1985: *Church and Politics Today*. Edinburgh: T. and T. Clark

Nicholls, D. 1990: Politics and the Church of England. *Political Quarterly*, 61, 132–42

Northcott, M. 1993: Identity and decline in the Kirk. In D. McCrone, W. Storrar, M. Northcott, N. Shanks, J. Harvey and I. Swanson, *Seeing Scotland. Seeing Christ*, Edinburgh: Centre for Theology and Public Issues, University of Edinburgh, 43–64

Obelkevich, J. 1976: *Religion and Rural Society*. Oxford: Oxford University Press

Osmond, R. 1993: *Changing Perspectives. Christian culture and morals in England today*. London: Darton, Longman and Todd

Parkinson, M. 1985: *Liverpool on the Brink*. Hermitage: Policy Journals

Parsons, G. 1993: *The Growth of Religious Diversity: Britain from 1945*: Vol. I, *Traditions*; Vol. II, *Issues*. London: Routledge/Open University.

Patten, J. 1992a: Mocking God. The *Spectator*, 18 April 1992

——1992b: Don't sell pupils short. *The Tablet*, 10 October 1992

Paul, L. 1964: *The Deployment and Payment of the Clergy*. London: Church Information Office

Paxman, J. 1991: *Friends in High Places*. London: Penguin

Pilkington, A. 1984: *Race Relations in Britain*. Slough: University Tutorial Press

Plant, R. et al. 1989: Conservative capitalism: theological and moral challenges. In A. Harvey (ed.), *Theology in the City*, London: SPCK, 68–97

Poulat, E. 1987: *Liberté, Laïcité: la guerre des deux Frances et le principe de la modernité*. Paris: Cerf

Ranson, S., Bryman, A. and Hinings, B. 1977: *Clergy, Ministers and Priests*. London: Routledge and Kegan Paul

Reid, I. 1989: *Social Class Differences in Britain*. London: Fontana Press

Robertson, R. 1991: The globalization paradigm: thinking globally. In D. Bromley (ed.), *Religion and the Social Order. New developments in theory and research*. Greenwich, Connecticut: JAI Press, 207–24

Rushdie, S. 1989: *The Satanic Verses*. London and New York: Viking-Penguin

Russell, A. 1980: *The Clerical Profession*. London: SPCK

Sacks, J. 1991: *The Persistence of Faith*. London: Weidenfeld

Sheppard, D. and Worlock, D. 1988: *Better Together*. London: Hodder and Stoughton

——— 1989: Asking for a little resurrection now. The *Independent*, 29 April 1989

Short, C. forthcoming: Religiosity in rural England: the existence of Towler's conventional religious types. Open University M.Phil. thesis in progress

Short, C. and Winter, M. 1993: Believing and belonging: religion in rural England. *British Journal of Sociology*, 44, 635–51

Simons, J. 1986: Culture, economy and reproduction in contemporary Europe. In D. Coleman and R. Schofield (eds), *The State of Population Theory: forward from Malthus*, Oxford: Blackwell, 256–78

Stoetzel, J. 1983: *Les Valeurs du Temps Présent*. Paris: Presse Universitaire de France

Svennevig, M., Haldane, I., Spiers, S. and Gunter, B. 1988: *Godwatching: viewers, religion and television*. London: John Libbey/IBA

Thomas, K. 1971: *Religion and the Decline of Magic*. London: Weidenfeld and Nicholson

Thomas, T. (ed.) 1988: *The British. Their religious beliefs and practices 1800–1986*. London: Routledge

Thompson, D. 1989: The free churches in modern Britain. In P. Badham (ed.), *Religion, State and Society in Modern Britain*, Lewiston/Lampeter/Queenston: Edwin Mellen Press, 99–118

Thompson, K. 1970: *Bureaucracy and Church Reform*. Oxford: Clarendon Press

——— 1988: How religious are the British? In T. Thomas (ed.), *The British. Their religious beliefs and practices*, London: Routledge, 211–39

——— 1992: Religion, values and ideology. In R. Bocock and K. Thompson (eds), *Social and Cultural Forms of Modernity*, Oxford: Polity Press / The Open University, 321–66

Timms, N. 1992: *Family and Citizenship: values in contemporary Britain*. Aldershot: Dartmouth

Towler, R. 1974: *Homo Religiosus*. London: Constable

——— 1982: Conventional religion and common religion in Britain. Religious Research Papers 11, University of Leeds, Department of Sociology

Towler, R. and Coxon, A. 1979: *The Fate of the Anglican Clergy: a sociological study*. London: MacMillan

Turner, B. 1991: *Religion and Social Theory*. London: Sage

Veritatis Splendor: 1993: London: Catholic Truth Society

Vigarello, G. 1988: *Une histoire culturelle du sport: techniques d'hier et d'aujourd'hui.* Paris: Laffont

Walker, A. 1985: *Restoring the Kingdom.* London: Hodder and Stoughton

Walker, D. (ed.) 1976: *A History of the Church in Wales.* Cardiff: Church in Wales Publications

Waller, P. 1981: *Democracy and Sectarianism. A political and social history of Liverpool.* Liverpool: Liverpool University Press

Wallis, R. and Bruce, S. 1986: *Sociological Theory, Religion and Collective Action.* Belfast: Queen's University

—— 1989: Religion: the British contribution. *British Journal of Sociology,* 40, 493–519

Walter, A. 1990a: *Funerals and How to Improve Them.* London: Hodder

—— 1990b: Why are most churchgoers women? *Vox evangelica,* 20, 73–90

—— 1991: The mourning after Hillsborough. *Sociological Review,* 39, 599–625

Waterman, S. and Kosmin, B. 1986: *British Jewry in the Eighties.* London: Research Unit, Board of Deputies of British Jews

Webster, R. 1990: *A Brief History of Blasphemy.* Southwold: The Orwell Press

Welsby, P. 1984: *A History of the Church of England 1945–80.* Oxford: Oxford University Press

—— 1985: *How the Church of England Works.* London: Church Information Office

Wickham, E. R. 1957: *Church and People in an Industrial City.* London: Lutterworth

Williams, G. 1991: *The Welsh and their Religion.* Cardiff: University of Wales Press

Wilson, B. 1982: *Religion in a Sociological Perspective.* Oxford: Oxford University Press

—— 1990: *The Social Dimensions of Sectarianism.* Oxford: Clarendon Press

—— (ed.) 1992: *Religion: contemporary issues.* London: Bellew Publishing

Winter, D. 1988: *Battered Bride. The body of faith in an age of doubt.* Eastbourne: Monarch

Winter, M. 1991: The twentieth century. Part 1: Cornwall. In N. Orme (ed.), *Unity and Diversity: a history of the Church in Devon and Cornwall,* Exeter: Exeter University Press, 157–74

Wolffe, J. 1993: *The Growth of Religious Diversity in Britain from 1945: A Reader.* London: Hodder and Stoughton Educational/Open University.

Index

Abercrombie, N., 9, 79
Abrams, M., 27, 153
Afro-Caribbean, 60, 63, 69, 100, 105, 108, 111–12; *see also* immigration
age, and religiosity, 106, 117, 119, 121–7, 169
Ahern, G., 30, 76, 77, 88, 91, 106
Anderson, D., 202
Anfield, 90–1; *see also* Hillsborough; Liverpool
Anglicanism, 45, 47, 48, 51–6, 59, 61, 65, 69, 81, 82–3, 87, 96, 101–2, 103, 108, 109, 131–2, 141, 143, 147, 148, 152, 157, 158, 165, 168, 173–4, 177, 181, 183, *see also* Church of England
Anglican–Methodist Unity Scheme, 34, 164
Anglican–Roman Catholic International Commission, 166
Anglo-Catholicism, 102–3, 182, 185
Appignanesi, L., 64
Argyle, M., 119, 137
Ashford, S., 27
Avis, P., 187

Bangladeshis, 64, 65
baptism, 52, 53–4, 56, 81, 109
Barker, D., 13, 27, 72
Barker, E., 38, 71
Beck, A., 163
Beckford, J., 16, 18–19, 43, 92, 194, 202
Beit-Hallahmi, B., 119, 137
Bible Christians, 101
Bocock, R., 31, 86, 87
Bowie, F., 96
Bradley, I., 112, 151
Brierley, P., 45, 53, 56, 57–8, 61, 62, 64, 66, 72, 95, 100, 103, 136, 186
British Council of Churches, 60, 166
Brown, C., 17–18, 28, 95
Bruce, S., 7, 95, 96, 97, 98, 203
Bryant, C., 202

Calvinism, 96, 98, 99; *see also* Presbyterianism
Canning Town, 34
Canterbury, Archbishop of, *see* Carey, G.; Fisher, G.; Ramsey, M.; Runcie, R.
Carey, G., 146, 156
Carr, W., 143

Chadwick, O., 150, 159, 167, 178
Charities Law, 68
Chesterton, G. K., 32
Church in Wales, 51, 94, 96;
    see also Wales
Church of England, 6, 16–17, 31,
    32, 38, 49, 72, 81, 102–3, 108,
    112, 187; Board of Social
    Responsibility, 70; clergy of,
    177–9; disestablishment of,
    147–8, 159; and Europe,
    140–1, 157–9; General Synod
    of, 144, 151, 162–74, 181–3,
    186; membership of, 51–6; and
    politics, 154–7; schools, 129,
    134; and the state, 56, 70,
    86–7, 117, 136, 139–59, 167;
    see also Anglicanism
Church of Ireland, 51, 115; *see also*
    Northern Ireland
Church of Scotland, 17, 51, 81, 95;
    and the state, 86, 150, 200; *see*
    also Scotland
civil religion, 74, 75, 86–8
Clark, H., 151
Clarke, S., 24
Coleman, B., 101
Commission for Racial Equality,
    100
common religion, 74, 75–7, 79,
    82–3
Commonwealth, 28, 157
Conservative government, 31, 39,
    105, 152, Conservative Party,
    103–4, 105
Cornwall, 101–3, 114–15, 117,
    126–7, 135
Coronation Oath, 145, 146
Council of Churches for Britain and
    Ireland, 166
Covenanting for Unity, 164

Cox, Baroness, 132, 136
Coxon, A., 176, 177–8, 187
cremation, 82, 92
Currie, R., 47, 53, 61

Davie, G., 19, 30, 76, 77, 88, 89,
    91, 102, 106, 115, 168, 170,
    171, 186, 203, 204
Davies, C., 150
Davies, D., 82, 116, 125, 137, 186
demographic changes, 21–4, 109,
    180
Devon, 101–3
Diamond, I., 24
Dissent, 15, 16, 61, 62, 63, 94–5,
    96, 146; *see also* free churches;
    Nonconformity
divorce, 24; *see also* demographic
    changes
Dobbelaere, K., 197
Dorset, 101
Douglas, M., 35
Durham, diocese of, 125
Durkheimian, 22, 84, 86, 203

East End, 34
Ecclesiastical Committee of
    Parliament, 160
ecumenical developments, 34, 51,
    59–60, 138, 158–9, 161, 162–7,
    184, 204
education, 6, 65, 77, 105, 107, 108,
    117, 123, 126, 127–36, 186,
    188; Education Acts, (1944),
    128, 131–2, (1988), 128,
    132–3, 138; in France, 135;
    religious education, 128,
    131–5; Secretary of State
    for, *see* Patten, J.; *see also*
    schools
Edwards, D., 201

Elizabeth II, 31, 86–7; Coronation of, 31–2, 86–7; Jubilee of, 87; Supreme Governor of the Church of England, 142, 144–5
Elizabethan Settlement, 16
Europe, 2, 3, 8, 10–18, 24, 67, 88, 96, 157–9, 162, 176, 200–1; Britain and, 10–18, 114; immigration in 26
European Community, 2; *see also* European Union
European Union, 26, 158–9
European Values Study (EVSSG), 11, 12, 14, 16, 27, 28, 71, 72, 77, 79, 119, 121, 123, 155, 170, 186
evangelicalism, 8, 62, 70, 165, 182, 185
Exeter, diocese of, 103

Faith in the City, 146–7, 151–3, 160
Faith in the Countryside, 156
Falklands conflict, 87
Field, F., 137
Fisher, G., 165
Fogarty, M., 11, 12, 27
France, 64, 67, 73, 116, 135, 187
Francis, L., 123, 134, 137
free churches, 60–3, 69, 103, 108, 115, 162, 177; *see also* Dissent; Nonconformity
fundamentalism, 43, 200, 204
funerals, 56, 72, 81–2, 92, 142

gender, and religiosity, 106, 117–21, 124–7, 169
gender roles, 23–4, 33, 126, 179–80; *see also* ordination of women

generational shifts, 4, 29–30, 117, 118–19, 121–4; *see also* demographic changes
Gerard, D., 27, 155
Gieben, B., 203
Gilbert, A., 47, 53, 61
Gill, R., 115, 155
Glasgow, 64
Gloucester, diocese of, 125
Greater London Council, 149
Gulf War, 64

Habgood, J., 146, 160, 172–3, 201–2
Hall, S., 203
Halman, L., 13, 27, 72
Halsey, A. H., 10, 28
Hammond, P., 44
Harding, S., 11, 12, 27
Harvey, A., 160
Harvey, D., 196–7, 198
Hastings, A., 29, 31, 32, 34–5, 53, 57, 128, 146, 147, 165–6
Hearl, D., 102
Heelas, P., 44, 67
Hervieu-Léger, D., 135, 204
Highet, J., 17
Hillsborough, 75, 88–91, 115; *see also* Anfield; Liverpool
Hindus, 66
Hiscock, V., 45, 57–8, 62
Hobcraft, J., 21
Hoggart, R., 32–3, 107
Hornsby-Smith, M., 35, 57, 58, 82, 94, 115, 154, 155, 160
Horsley, L., 47, 53, 61
house churches, 60, 62–3, 136, 163
House of Commons, 142, 160
House of Lords, 132, 141–2, 150, 159–60, 186
Howe, Lady, 72
human potential movement, 43, 67

immigration, 24–6, 28, 33, 37, 58, 60, 66, 95, 98, 104, 108, 111–12; Immigration Acts, 25
inner city, 27, 63, 105, 106, 108, 109, 110, 151–2, 189; *see also* urban priority area
Irish Republic, 97, 98
Islington, 9, 79,
Israel, 64

Jacobs, E., 119
Jay, E., 100
Jehovah's Witnesses, 67
Jenkins, D., 31
Jones, K., 168, 169, 170
Joshi, H., 21
Judaism, 64, 65, 146; schools, 131
Jupp, P., 82

Knott, K., 63, 66
Kosmin, B., 64

Labour Party, 53, 95, 100, 103, 104, 105, 152
Langley, M., 181
Lash, N., 202
Leaman, O., 65
Leeds, 64, 77, 83
Lerman, A., 64
Levitt, M., 126–7, 130, 138
Lincoln, diocese of, 125
Liverpool, 88–91, 115, 124, 163–4, 185; Bishop of, 70, *see also* Sheppard, D.; politics in, 103–5; *see also* Anfield; Hillsborough
London, 64; Bishop of, 132; diocese of, 30–1, 149
Lyon, D., 203

Maitland, S., 64
Major, J., 156–7
Manchester, 64
Martin, D., 7, 9, 14, 15, 16, 66, 72, 77, 84, 94, 95, 98, 101, 137, 150, 160, 189–90
Marxism, 197, 203
Mass Observation (1948), 77
Maunder, W. F., 71
Mayflower Centre, 33–4
Medhurst, K., 149–50, 153, 168, 171, 178
Methodism, 61, 62, 72, 101–2, 115, 152, 180, 184
Methodist Home Mission, 160
Michel, P., 27–8
middle class, 107, 108–9, 130, 170
Militant, 104
Mission Alongside the Poor Programme, 152
modernity, 190–4, 198–9, 202–3
Modood, T., 64–5, 68
monarchy, 86–7, 92, 144–5
Moorman, J., 16
morality, 3, 84, 88, 133, 134
Mori poll, 119, 121
Mormons, 67
Moyser, G., 149–50, 153, 168, 171, 178
Muslims, 28, 64, 65, 73, 76, 146; schools, 131, 136, 138

New Age, 14, 41–3, 44, 67, 83–4, 92, 199, 204
New Right, 153, 175
Niebuhr, R., 32
Nonconformity, 61, 63, 101–3, 131–2, 154; *see also* Dissent; free churches
Northcott, M., 95

Northern Ireland, 76, 88, 94, 96–100, 104, 111; church membership in, 47, 96–100; demographic changes in, 99; education in, 130; political problems in, 36, 97–100, 104, 111, 114; Roman Catholicism in, 57, 99; *see also* Church of Ireland; Unionism

Obelkevich, J., 92
O'Brien, R., 151
oil crisis (1973), 36, 196
ordained ministry, 174–9
ordination of women, 160, 161, 162, 166, 170, 179–85
Orthodox, 26, 60, 119, 158, 181
Osmond, R., 138

Paisley, I., 97, 99
Pakistanis, 64, 65
Parkinson, M., 104
Parliament, 144; *see also* Ecclesiastical Committee; House of Commons; House of Lords
Parochial Church Councils, 144, 184
Patten, J., 84–5, 132, 133–4
Paxman, J., 139
Phillips, D., 11, 12, 24–6, 27
Pilkington, A., 65
Plant, R., 153
Pluck, R., 137
pluralism, 51, 63–4, 65, 66, 68, 94, 100, 117, 146, 147–8
Pope John XXIII, 35, 165
Pope John Paul II, 59, 197
post-modernity, 191–3, 196–9, 203–4
Poulat, E., 15

Prayer Book, 34
Presbyterianism, 61–2, 95, 96, 98, 180; in Europe, 61, 96
Prideaux Lectures, 146
Prince of Wales, 145; *see also* monarchy
Proctor, M., 155
Protestant, 11, 13, 16, 17, 34–5, 59, 61, 67, 76, 92, 94, 95, 96, 97, 98, 100, 101, 111, 145, 158, 164, 165, 180, 185

Ramsey, M., 150, 165
Reid, I., 65
Reith Lectures, 148
religious broadcasting, 105, 108, 112–14
Robertson, R., 41
Roman Catholicism, 34–5, 46–51, 53, 65, 69, 76, 82–3, 90, 92, 95, 96, 97, 98–9, 102–3, 105, 111, 114, 115, 146, 154, 160, 163, 165, 166, 177, 181, 184, 185, 188; and Europe, 158; membership, 56–60; schools, 129, 131–2, 134, 137; and society, 57
Runcie, R., 59, 151, 156, 185
Rural Church Project, 115, 117, 124–5, 137, 186, 187
Rushdie affair, 7, 26, 64–5, 68, 69
Russell, A., 175, 176, 187

Sacks, J., 148
St George's House, Windsor, 114, 123
Salvation Army, 180
Satanic Verses, The, 65, 69; *see also* Rushdie affair
Scarman, Lord, 130

schools, 126, 128–31, 134–5, 137;
   denominational, *see* Church of
   England; Roman Catholicism;
   Judaism; Muslims; *see also*
   education
Scotland, 17, 18, 28, 43, 81, 88, 94,
   95–7, 98–9, 100, 114, 140;
   Roman Catholics in, 95, 96;
   see also Church of Scotland
Second Vatican Council, 34–5,
   58–9, 165–6
secularization, 12, 18, 43, 76, 85,
   98, 104, 117, 145, 146, 175,
   192, 195–8
Sheffield, 32–3, 89
Sheppard, D., 32, 33–4, 70, 90–1,
   104, 106, 151, 163
Short, C., 94, 115–16, 125, 168,
   170, 171, 186
Sikhs, 66
Simons, J., 22
Single European Act, 15; *see also*
   Europe; European Union
Social Trends, 28
Society of Friends, 180
Somerset, 101
South Africa, 97
Southwell, diocese of, 125
Soviet Union, 64
Stoetzel, J., 13
Svennevig, M., 116

Thatcher, M., 39, 104, 105, 139,
   140, 150–1, 156–7, 175
Thomas, K., 92
Thompson, D., 61
Thompson, K., 31, 86, 172–3
Timms, N., 27, 71, 155
Tory Party, 151, 155, 156; *see also*
   Conservative government
Fowler, R., 176; 177, 8–147

trades unions, 20
Treaty of Union (1707), 17; *see also*
   Scotland
Truro, diocese of, 103, 125

Unionism, 97, 99–100; *see also*
   Northern Ireland
United States of America, 28, 44,
   64, 67, 92, 94, 113, 116
urban priority area, 109–10, 151,
   153–4, 156, 176
Urban Theology Unit, 160
Urry, J., 202

Vigarello, G., 203
Vloet, A., 13, 27, 72
voting patterns, by denomination, 2,
   58, 62, 102, 104, 154–5, 160,
   171

Wales, 47, 88, 94–5, 96, 100;
   Roman Catholics in, 95
Walker, A., 37, 62
Waller, P., 104
Wallis, R., 7, 95, 96, 97, 203
Walter, A., 89, 92, 118, 120
Watkins, C., 116, 125, 137, 186
Weber, M., 106, 172, 198, 203
Welsby, P., 29, 33, 141, 145, 167–8
Wickham, E. R., 32
Wilson, B., 7, 37
Wiltshire, 101
Winter, M., 94, 112, 115–16, 125,
   137, 186
Worcester, R., 119
working class, 32–3, 34, 58, 104,
   106–7, 194
Worlock, D., 33, 70, 90–1, 104, 163

York, Archbishop of, *see* Habgood,
   J.